'Dr. Maidenbaum tackles an im[...] demonstrates how archetypal po[...] amid the chaos of outer life. He [...] variegated history and practice of Judaism and reveals its shaping, resilient, and culturally redeeming power.'

James Hollis, PhD, *Jungian analyst and author; former executive director: Jung Educational Center of Houston, The Washington D.C. Jung Society, and Philadelphia Jung Society*

'Drawing on his professional and personal experience in both the Jungian and Jewish worlds, Aryeh Maidenbaum has written a book that insightfully examines important themes in Judaism through a Jungian lens. His work presents a passionate invitation to place these topics in an archetypal perspective by amplifying them in the light of such meaningful concepts as individuation, forgiveness, shadow, and wholeness.'

Sylvia Perera, MA, *Jungian analyst and author; faculty and board member, C.G. Jung Institute of New York*

'Through personal reminiscences of his intense Jewish education and of his training in Jungian psychoanalysis, Aryeh Maidenbaum explores the relationship between Carl Jung's psychological theories and Jewish cultural and literary traditions. Besides treating such literary themes as the Golem and the Wandering Jew, moral themes such as scapegoating and forgiveness, and spiritual themes, Maidenbaum explicates the archetypal roots of anti-Semitism, and brings his own Jungian roots to bear on the much-discussed question of whether Jung was antisemitic.'

Raymond P. Scheindlin, *Professor Emeritus of Hebrew Literature, The Jewish Theological Seminary of America*

'This book offers wisdom of the heart and of the mind. Maidenbaum speaks from personal experience of Jewish rituals and from his knowledge of Jung's theory of archetypes that inform patterns of behavior and meaning enacted in all of us. Each chapter speaks directly to urgent issues that press on us and clarifies what really matters that we need to know right now. Two examples are the rise of anti-Semitism and the Jewish Jungian perspective on forgiveness.'

Ann Belford Ulanov, PhD, *Jungian analyst and author; Emerita Professor of Psychology and Religion, Union Theological Seminary*

'The relationship between Jewish myths and legends and Jung's archetypal construct that Dr. Maidenbaum explores in *Jung and the Jewish Experience* is fascinating. If the book were content to just do that, it would be well worth reading. But what makes Dr. Maidenbaum's work stand out is the way he integrates his own voice into describing how Jewish myth can be understood through archetypal analyses. A gifted and compelling narrator, he enlivens each of the legends he presents while guiding the reader through the continuum of Jewish archetypes.'

Michael Paull, *Professor Emeritus, Lehman College of the City University of New York*

Jung and the Jewish Experience

Drawing on Jewish myth, ritual, and tradition, as well as the author's own experiences, this original and unique book offers insights into how Jung's psychology and ideas are relevant if understood from a wider, archetypal, perspective.

Jung's writings, especially his amplification and interpretation of spiritual and theological rituals and ideas, focus almost entirely on Christianity and have very little to say about Judaism. By applying a Jungian understanding of selected Jewish topics and stories, and interspersed with anecdotes from the author's own life, this book will add much needed insight to both the Jungian and Jewish realms. Covering topics ranging from dreams, forgiveness, scapegoating, and Jerusalem to hope, resilience, and humor, this extraordinary book explores important aspects of Judaism through a Jungian lens.

This will be essential reading for anyone interested in exploring a Jungian approach to aspects of Judaism, as well as those interested in the fields of theology literature, spirituality, history, and myth.

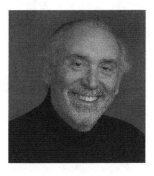

Aryeh Maidenbaum earned his PhD from the Hebrew University in Jerusalem and a Diploma in Analytical Psychology from the Jung Institute in Zurich. He is a Jungian analyst and co-director of the New York Center for Jungian Studies with a strong background in the fields of history, psychology, and Jewish studies. With over 30 years of experience presenting seminars and conferences on Jungian psychology, he has also organized and led Jewish Heritage Travel programs throughout the world.

Jung and the Jewish Experience

Reflections by a Jungian Analyst

Aryeh Maidenbaum

LONDON AND NEW YORK

Designed cover image: Elena Erber; Scroll of Esther © Jewish
Museum in Prague; CG Jung, 1939, Alamy Stock Photo

First published 2025
by Routledge
4 Park Square, Milton Park, Abingdon, Oxon OX14 4RN

and by Routledge
605 Third Avenue, New York, NY 10158

Routledge is an imprint of the Taylor & Francis Group, an informa business

© 2025 Aryeh Maidenbaum

The right of Aryeh Maidenbaum to be identified as author of this work has been asserted in accordance with sections 77 and 78 of the Copyright, Designs and Patents Act 1988.

All rights reserved. No part of this book may be reprinted or reproduced or utilised in any form or by any electronic, mechanical, or other means, now known or hereafter invented, including photocopying and recording, or in any information storage or retrieval system, without permission in writing from the publishers.

Trademark notice: Product or corporate names may be trademarks or registered trademarks, and are used only for identification and explanation without intent to infringe.

British Library Cataloguing-in-Publication Data
A catalogue record for this book is available from the British Library

Library of Congress Cataloging-in-Publication Data
Names: Maidenbaum, Aryeh, author.
Title: Jung and the Jewish experience : reflections by a Jungian analyst / Aryeh Maidenbaum.
Description: 1st. | New York, NY : Routledge, 2025. | Includes bibliographical references and index.
Identifiers: LCCN 2024037143 (print) | LCCN 2024037144 (ebook) | ISBN 9781032842509 (paperback) | ISBN 9781032842523 (hardback) | ISBN 9781003511908 (ebook)
Subjects: LCSH: Jungian psychology—Religious aspects—Judaism. | Mysticism—Judaism.
Classification: LCC BM538.P68 M35 2025 (print) | LCC BM538.P68 (ebook) | DDC 296.7/12—dc23/eng/20240829
LC record available at https://lccn.loc.gov/2024037143
LC ebook record available at https://lccn.loc.gov/2024037144

ISBN: 978-1-032-84252-3 (hbk)
ISBN: 978-1-032-84250-9 (pbk)
ISBN: 978-1-003-51190-8 (ebk)

DOI: 10.4324/9781003511908

Typeset in Times New Roman
by Apex CoVantage, LLC

Contents

Acknowledgments viii
Terminology xii

Introduction 1

1 Dreams, the Talmud and Jung 5

2 The Wandering Jew 20

3 The Golem of Prague: An Archetype 34

4 Was Jung Anti-Semitic? 44

5 A Jewish Saturnalian Festival: The Holiday of Purim 65

6 Jerusalem: Archetype and Living Symbol 76

7 To Forgive, or Not to Forgive 92

8 Scapegoating and Shadow 108

9 Hope, Resilience, and Humor: The Jewish Experience 124

10 The Search for Spirit in Jungian Psychology 139

Index *154*

Acknowledgments

There is a saying in the Talmud that comes to mind: "Who is a wise man? One who learns from every person." It has taken me years to write this book – years of learning from Jungian mentors and teachers, especially Rivkah Kluger in Israel, who was like a spiritual mother to me, and René Malamud in Zurich, who taught me to approach Judaism from a new perspective. Through my analytical work with Rivkah and René, I learned to value Judaism in a way I never could within the confines of the Orthodox Jewish world I was raised in. In addition, René also blessed me with a lifelong friendship; his help and support as both friend and mentor will never be forgotten. I miss him dearly and regret he passed away before being able to see this book in print.

On a personal note, I would be remiss in not beginning with thanks to my wife and best friend, Diana, and I would like to dedicate this book to her. From the time we began life together over 39 years ago, Diana has been my loving partner in life and work and provided the emotional support which has enabled me to accomplish more than I would have ever expected or hoped for. She has continually encouraged me to write this book, served as a sounding board for many of its ideas, and patiently putting up with the many hours I spent researching and writing. At times, this meant her listening to me ruminate and discuss my work over and over, at dinner, over coffee each morning before the day even got started, as well as on our walks and travel together. I cannot thank her enough and trust she knows how much I love, appreciate, and value her.

I would also like to acknowledge my wonderful children: Leah, Barak, Hepzibah, and Jordana. Their love and trust kept me going at times when life was difficult and I cannot overestimate what they mean to me. Leah and Barak, my two oldest, had to leave friends and the life they had when we left Israel and moved to Zurich, and then once again when we left Zurich – transitions propelled by my own personal, perhaps selfish, desire to study at the Jung Institute. Hepzi, now my superb study partner, was barely a toddler when we left Israel though by the time we returned to the U.S. she was old enough to understand that our family life was changing – at times depriving her of the container her older siblings had enjoyed. Jordana, in Hebrew known as a *Bat Zekunim*, the child of one's older years, had to deal with the fact that not only was I often mistaken for her grandfather, but that by being the only Jewish child in her classes at school, she had to deal with the prejudices and emotional cruelty of some of her classmates. I am proud of how all four have matured into amazing adults.

In this context, as I became a father and grandfather myself, I have come to appreciate what my parents, Esther and Nathan Maidenbaum, gave to me. They imbued a love and appreciation of Judaism and the Hebrew language that has informed my life, a gift "above the price of rubies." My mother was born in Jerusalem and my earliest memories of her include Hebrew lullabies, songs, and stories that she would read and sing to us at bedtime. My father, a highly successful businessman, was also an accomplished Hebraist who wrote poems in Hebrew. The love of Hebrew which he instilled in me is a legacy I treasure. While at times I resented the long hours and intense study demanded of me, I have come to appreciate the knowledge I gained as a result.

Two others who deserve special thanks are my brother-in-law, Yaacov Peterseil, and longtime friend and colleague Robert (Bob) Hinshaw. Yaacov, an ordained Rabbi and gifted writer himself, read several of the chapters and provided reassuring support that the Jewish material in my book was correct. Bob not only took the time to read the entire manuscript but provided valuable insights into how to improve the material as well as correcting some Jungian historical facts. Moreover, between the two, the title and sub-title of the book emerged. Yaacov recommended the heading *Jung and the Jewish Experience*, while Bob suggested a needed sub-title, *Reflections by a Jungian Analyst*, to help clarify what the book was about. Additionally, Bob provided me with several photos – some of which appear in this book.

Also, a heartfelt thanks to Stephen Martin, Nomi Kluger-Nash, and Sibylle Malamud. Steve, a friend and colleague since the time we trained together at the Jung Institute in Zurich, joined Bob Hinshaw, Peter Amman, and myself in the interviews we conducted for the conference on Jung and anti-Semitism. Nomi spent a great deal of time tracking down photos of her father as well as those of Rivkah Kluger. Sibylle provided me with photos of her parents, Monica and René Malamud, who I spent many an hour with whenever I visited Zurich years after I had moved back to the U.S. René was one of the most important people in my life – an inspiration and a role model for me during the 40 years I was fortunate enough to have him as mentor and valued friend. Both Nomi and Sibylle were kind enough to not only share their photos but to grant me permission to include them in this book.

On another note, to the extent I have succeeded in writing this book it was also thanks to the helpful hands and encouragement of Jo Fisher and Sally Smith Raymond, my devoted and capable office assistants for many years. Having them work with us these many years has been a gift. Their support, and knowing they were taking care of our organization, gave me the peace of mind and time I needed to write. In addition, much appreciation is due to Luis Arteaga, who encouraged, and spurred me on, to finish writing this book by holding me to a self-imposed deadline.

Finally, two individuals who were especially helpful are Janice Meyerson and Elena Erber. Janice, an exceptional editor and friend, read and edited my initial draft, and made sure it was in good enough shape to send to a publisher. A consummate professional who otherwise would have commanded a high fee, Janice was enthusiastic in supporting this endeavor and insisted that her work on my manuscript be considered a gift. Last, but far from least, our superb, talented and gifted graphic designer, Elena Erber, deserves a special thank you. Elena found and helped place the illustrations before each chapter, designed the exquisite book cover, and was helpful from start to finish. Her patience and follow through is very much appreciated.

The photos on the facing page are of dear friends and colleagues who played an important role in the life and work of the author. Clockwise: (Figure 0.1) René Malamud, Jungian analyst in Zurich, mentor, and lifelong friend. (Figure 0.2) Monica and René Malamud. (Figure 0.3) Dinner gathering at the 2002 Jung in Ireland program: Diana Rubin and the author, co-founders of the New York Center for Jungian Studies, with Adolf Guggenbühl-Craig, Jungian analyst, former President International Association of Analytical Psychology, and C.G. Jung Institute, Zurich. (Figure 0.4) Bob Hinshaw, Jungian analyst, was instrumental in arranging for interviews in the 1988 interview project. (Figure 0.5) Rivkah Scharf Kluger and Yehezkel Kluger, Jungian analysts in Haifa, Israel. Rivkah was the author's first Jungian analyst and mentor; Yehezkel established the Israel Training Program for Analytical Psychology. (Figure 0.6) The author with his wife Diana Rubin, Co-Director, NY Center for Jungian Studies.

Acknowledgments xi

Figure 0.1

Figure 0.2

Figure 0.6

Figure 0.3

Figure 0.5

Figure 0.4

Terminology

Archetype	A universal and recurring image, a pattern, or a motif representing human experience. Archetypal images emanate from the deeper layers of our Unconscious and often manifest themselves through dreams, myth, art, and religion.
Complex	A feeling toned, emotionally charged unconscious entity in each of us. One recognizes that a complex has been activated when emotion takes over and disturbs our day-to-day equilibrium.
Ego	In Jungian terms, the center of consciousness.
Individuation	Self-realization – the fulfillment of one's personal, unique being.
Mishnah	Derived from the Hebrew root *shanah*, or *leshanot*, or to review – reviewing what had until it was codified. The Mishnah was codified around the second century.
Self	In Jungian terms spelled with a capital S – the totality or center of the personality.
Shadow	The Unconscious part of our personality. While described by Jung as containing both positive and negative characteristics, it is more often referred to as the suppressed, less admired part of our personality.
Talmud	From the Hebrew root "LAMED" (LMD) to learn – basically a series of books which records Rabbinical discussion. Codified around the fifth century, it is organized into two parts: *Halachah* – discussion of how laws are to be observed (for example Kosher, the Sabbath, holidays, etc.) and *Aggadah* – legend (stories, what we would call myth). There are two Talmuds, Babylonian and Jerusalem, though the larger and most often studied in Judaism – and referenced in this book – is the Babylonian Talmud (in the notes referred to as BT).
Torah	Derived from word *lehorot*, to teach; it is the Hebrew Bible ("Old" Testament) and comprised of the Five Books of Moses: Genesis, Exodus, Leviticus, Numbers, and Deuteronomy.

Transference	A term used to describe the emotional involvement, whether positive or negative, between two people, though most often referring to that of patient and therapist.
Unconscious	Consisting of the **Personal Unconscious**, where each of our own histories and experiences are stored and easier to access, and the **Collective Unconscious** – the deeper layer of the Unconscious. The Collective Unconscious is universal and non-individual. The contents of the Collective Unconscious are the archetypes and their specific symbolic representations, manifested through archetypal images.

Introduction

Memory is a strange phenomenon. At times, we remember incidents and situations vividly; at other times, not only are our recollections fuzzy but we even remember things that never happened to us. I recall reading an article by the psychiatrist Oliver Sacks where, as an adult, he described himself reminiscing with his older brother about what London was like during the time of the Blitz. When relating a particular event that had been etched into his childhood memory, he was surprised to hear from his brother that he could not have remembered the incident, since he had not been there. Apparently, as his older brother reminded him, their parents, as many parents did at the time, sent young Oliver to the countryside to keep him safe. However, Sacks explained, because he had heard the story so many times while growing up, he was convinced that he had been there.

I have always had a goal to write a Book of my own, drawing on relating selected aspects of Judaism with insights combining my Jungian training and Jewish background. Along the way, I have included personal vignettes that I trust the reader will find of interest. Memory is often a composite editing of recollections and not a recording apparatus that can unerringly recount a particular fact; nevertheless, I will do my best to combine what insights I have gleaned from my understanding of Jung's psychology and ideas with being faithful to the occurrences I relate. Given the passage of time, this is not an easy task. In addition, in writing this book, I realize that some of what I relate may take the luster off the reputation of some leading Jungian analysts or authors. However, as the expression goes, where there is light, there is Shadow, and some of these individuals had both in abundance.

To date, I have edited one book, co-edited another, written quite a few book reviews, and published a dozen or more articles in various professional journals. While some of the memories I will relate here may have been tempered by time, the first memory I had of wishing to write my own book is one that has been etched into my mind since childhood. At the age of ten, my mother introduced me to the wonderful world of the public library. Each Friday, before sundown, once my mother had helped me navigate the bureaucracy of having my own library card, I bicycled over to our local library and checked out several books to read over the next 24 hours, from sundown Friday to sundown Saturday. Basically, this was a survival mechanism for me to make it through the Orthodox Jewish restrictions

DOI: 10.4324/9781003511908-1

in our home, where radio, television, and engaging in athletics were not permissible on Shabbat (the Sabbath). By having books to read, albeit at times under my covers and with the aid of a flashlight, or waiting for my parents to fall asleep so that I could safely turn on and off the light in my bedroom, I was able to transport myself into an exciting new world – one where my imagination could roam free.

What I also clearly remember about my Friday library experience was that one afternoon, I marveled at seeing a book on the shelf by a writer I realized was no longer living. While the name of the book escapes me, I do remember thinking that the author would never really die or be forgotten, as long as there was someone who would be ready to read this book. It is in this context that I have taken on the task of sharing selected Jewish topics through my personal Jungian lens and interspersing these insights with a number of memories from my own life. These ideas and life experiences present an opportunity to combine what Jungian insights I may have to offer with stories for my children and grandchildren to read and remember me by. Perhaps it can be seen as an extension of realizing a wish for immortality that I have carried with me for the past seven decades.

I believe my background and training enable me to contribute a unique approach to amplifying and understanding aspects of Judaism through a Jungian, symbolic lens. I grew up in an Orthodox Jewish community and attended yeshiva (Orthodox Jewish day school) from kindergarten through high school. In addition, I was continually taught Jewish history, literature, and religion by my father, who was a highly successful businessman as well as a scholar who wrote poems in Hebrew (I edited and had privately published 100 of his poems as a memory for my siblings and our children and grandchildren). Thanks to my father's love of the Hebrew language, I was raised bilingually and am told that until the age of five, I spoke only Hebrew. In that context, what I do remember is that often, when I asked my father a question in English, he would respond: *ivri, daber ivrit* ("you are a Hebrew, speak Hebrew"). While I often bristled at the focus of Hebrew and orthodoxy, this training provided me with the tools to be at home with the Hebrew of the Bible as well as Jewish history, tradition, myth, and literature, all of which I have drawn on in this book. Nevertheless, throughout childhood I resented having been given a Hebrew name rather than an "all-American" name that people could pronounce and that boys in the neighborhood would not make fun of. Now, through my Jungian work, I have come to appreciate – indeed, be proud of – this heritage, and happily celebrate the uniqueness of my name, Aryeh (Hebrew for "lion").

In addition to my Orthodox Jewish background, having earned an MA degree from NYU, a PhD from the Hebrew University in Jerusalem, a Diploma in Analytical Psychology from the Jung Institute in Zurich, and my knowledge of Hebrew, and familiarity with Jewish myths and tradition, I have accumulated unique tools for the writing of this book. My hope is that by applying a Jungian understanding of selected Jewish topics and stories, interspersed with experiences of my own, I will be adding insight to both the Jungian and Jewish realms. Moreover, studying in Zurich in the 1970s, I was blessed to have met, worked with, and interviewed some of the first-generation Jungians, including several analyzed and trained by

Jung himself. Along the way, I have been fortunate enough to have had quite a few fascinating experiences that are worth remembering and telling – and am perhaps optimistic enough to believe that what I have to say will be of interest.

One question that often is asked of me is why I gravitated to Jung and his psychology and ideas given the accusations that Jung was anti-Semitic. My response has been that this is a complicated and nuanced issue and not as simple as reducing it to one line. What comes to mind when I am asked this question is the anecdote of a person who asked Hillel[1] to tell him what the Torah was about while standing on one foot. In this book, I will try to explain why a Jungian approach worked for me and how it has helped me appreciate Judaism – albeit while not standing on one foot.

Having been in both Jungian and Freudian therapy, I found that Jung's approach to the psyche resonated more with me. More importantly, a Jungian approach to life has helped me understand myself better and contributed to my own healing process. My first Jungian analysis took place in Haifa, Israel, over a five-year period during which my analyst was Rivkah Scharf Kluger, who had herself been in analysis with, and trained by, Jung. At the time, Rivkah worked with both my ex-wife and myself. We drove from Jerusalem to Haifa each week, a two-and-a-half-hour trip at that time, with each of us having a double session with Rivkah – and then had lunch with her and her husband, Yehezkel Kluger (a Jungian analyst as well), between sessions. While I am aware that this is an unusual analytical practice, it served an important function in my life and while I would not practice in this manner myself, it did work for me. For, unlike other boundary-breaking situations between analyst and patient, I was not taken advantage of in any way. Perhaps because Rivkah was from the first generation of Jungians and, moreover, was nearly retired when she moved to Israel, there was an integrity and honesty to her in working with us as a couple.

Notwithstanding the unorthodox approach in my work with Rivkah, my first Jungian analyst, I learned a lot. I'd finally found my Rabbi – and she was a woman! During the five years I was in analysis with her, I benefited from Rivkah's warmth and support while learning much about Jung, especially how he approached the world of dreams. In what was ostensibly a therapy situation, much time was spent teaching me about Jungian psychology and how Jung utilized and understood the appearance of symbols and myths in dreams. As a bonus, Rivkah shared many personal anecdotes about Jung, apart from his professional contributions to the development of "analytical psychology," a term that describes Jungian psychology. In short, the by-product of my work with Rivkah was to introduce me to Jung's psychology and ideas in greater depth, as well as learning about Jung the man.

In general, through my Jungian analyses, first with Rivkah Kluger in Israel and subsequently with René Malamud, the analyst I worked with in Zurich, Jung's psychology and ideas helped me reconnect to my Jewish heritage in a way that I never could have conceived of before that. The tools I acquired in my Jungian analysis enabled me to understand and appreciate a connection to my own roots – archetypal roots that went far deeper than anything that my family, the Orthodox schools where I studied, or the community I was escaping could provide. While it would be years before I understood this, the tools of Jung's psychology helped me connect to a deeper, more meaningful, level of Judaism. By working with Rivkah, and continuing this work with René Malamud in Zurich, I came to understand that there was an inner treasure, the gold within, that lay within my own tradition.

In looking back at my Jungian analysis, first with Rivkah and then with René, I realize how fortunate I was to have found them: a combination of analysts and mentors who helped guide me along the path I had embarked on. At the time, I thought that I had entered therapy to help me find my way in the world and deal with a difficult marital situation. In reality, I was trying to connect to an inner spiritual realm. In effect, guided by the Unconscious, I have come to realize that I was searching for meaning in my life, from the personal to the collective, from the role that family and community played, to my own needs as an individual. In effect, I was caught up in an archetypal force – the instinct for spirit, a search for meaning. This search has not ended; it is lifelong. Jung called such a search the drive for Individuation, a drive that is present in us all.

When it comes to psychology, an anecdote in the Jewish world says that the Talmudists become Freudians, and the mystics gravitate to Jung. Nevertheless, what many people do not realize is that the Talmud is basically composed of two elements, with one part dedicated to what can be defined as the legal, and the other on Jewish myth and legend. In the legalistic aspect of the Talmud, Rabbis and scholars discuss, disagree with one another, and ultimately concentrate on what the rules are in Jewish law. Other sections – the ones I am most drawn to – deal with fascinating myths and legends. These sections were not part of the curriculum in the yeshivot that I attended – a loss that I have been able to correct through my Jungian work over the years. While I do not consider myself a mystic – and, in fact, I am suspicious of people who use that term to describe themselves – I clearly have been drawn to the mystical aspects of the Talmud, portions of which I have drawn on in writing this book.

It is in this context that I have taken on the challenge of presenting selected Jewish topics through my personal Jungian lens and interspersing these insights with memories from my life. I believe that I have something to offer those interested in understanding some of these aspects of Judaism in an archetypal context. In this regard, I am fortunate to have had an extensive knowledge of Judaism and Jewish tradition, training in Jungian studies, working with the first generation of Jungians and being in private analytical practice myself for over 36 years.

I embarked on this project because I am interested in sharing the treasures I have gleaned with others who lack the tools that I have been fortunate to accumulate. This book is something I felt compelled to write before I was too old to remember or not around to tell the stories. For me, this endeavor represents an opportunity to combine Jungian insights with Jewish legends, rituals, tradition, and stories for my children, grandchildren, and others interested in Jung's psychology and ideas, to read and remember me by.

Note

1 Hilllel: first century CE – one of the greatest of Jewish scholars.

Chapter 1
Dreams, the Talmud and Jung

Figure 1.1 Jusepe de Ribera, El Sueño de Jacob (Jacob and the Ladder), 1639, painting

A dream that is not interpreted is like a letter that is not read[1]

Babylonian Talmud

It all began with a dream that I had on the first night following the start of my Jungian therapy. At the time, I had no idea of the importance that this initial dream was to have on my own inner journey. In my dream, I was back in the fifth grade (age 10). In the dream, I was called to the front of the room by my teacher, Miss Wright, and asked to write my name on the blackboard. It took forever for me to write my name, spelling it out letter by letter, A-R-Y-E-H. I still vividly remember how painful the process was and how long it took. Over the years, I have come to understand this as a symbolic start of my own Individuation process. For throughout my childhood, whenever I was introduced to someone, it was as Nat Maidenbaum's son. My father was well known in the Jewish community for his acumen in the grocery business as well as his encyclopedic knowledge of Hebrew language and literature. He was a larger-than-life figure for me, as well as for members of the Jewish and business communities. In this dream, which I worked on with Rivkah, my first Jungian analyst, I was a person in my own right and not just an extension of my family.

In those days, teachers in the schools that I attended addressed students by their surnames, which I deeply resented. When called on in class, I was referred to as Maidenbaum, not Aryeh. One time, when I was about eleven, I refused to respond to my Talmud teacher, Rabbi Brill. When asked again to respond to his question, I commented: "My name is Aryeh. I don't call you Brill; I say Rabbi Brill. You can either address me as Mr. Maidenbaum, or Aryeh, and then I'll respond." I was thrown out of class, which triggered a call to my father. Not surprisingly, my father took the teacher's side and made it clear that whether I liked it or not, a teacher demands respect and I needed to obey and not question.

But I am getting ahead of myself in describing isolated childhood memories – isolated in the sense that only a few snippets of those years stand out clearly for me. Some memories crop up autonomously and not in the chronological order of my life. Perhaps an analogy might be that, in the Jewish tradition, there is no "earlier" or "later" in the Torah: *Ein mukdam ume'uḥar batorah* – meaning that one need not see things as always appearing in chronological order. It is in this spirit that I have included experiences that shaped me during the formative years of my life and how, through my Jungian studies and analysis, I have been able to appreciate traditional Judaism's approach to the world of dreams through a Jungian lens.

The Talmud contains a great deal of discussion about the importance of dreams. Discourse among the Rabbis makes it clear that it can take as many as twenty-two years for one to understand the meaning and fulfillment of a dream[2] and that our dreams contain a message from an inner source – what Jung would call the Self. For me, it took about that amount of time from the time I entered Jungian analysis and began working on my own dreams to understand what Jung meant by the Individuation process.

Well before I had begun my Jungian analysis, I came to respect the power of a dream. My grandfather, who had experienced health issues that frequently caused him to be wheelchair-bound during the last year of his life, was hospitalized with a deteriorating heart condition and other ailments. Based on what the doctors told us, he had recuperated enough to be discharged from the hospital in a few days. One Friday evening, after sundown and when *Shabbat* (Sabbath) had already set in, I stopped off at the hospital to visit him on my way home. He was sitting up in bed; when I entered the room, he smiled and greeted me with the warmth that he always showed upon seeing me. Realizing that Shabbat had already begun, he told me not to tell my mother that I had driven there, since it would upset her to know that I had driven a car on the Sabbath.

Unsolicited, my grandfather related a dream to me that he had the night before: in his dream, my grandmother Leah, who had died about a year earlier, had appeared to him, saying that it was time for him to join her. I listened and responded, "Not yet. Wait." He died that night. I was the last member of the family to see him, and when I related the dream to my mother, it seemed to console her that her father had this dream and knew that his time had come. For me, it left an indelible impression of the power of a dream – an impression that may well have contributed to my eventually becoming a Jungian analyst.

In the Talmud, as well as subsequent rabbinic Judaism, the attitude toward dreams is contradictory, ranging from seeing dreams as partly prophetic, a message from the divine, to seeing them as misleading, and not to be taken seriously. Many of the Rabbis described dreams as coming from a source within us, trying to lead us astray – what Jung might label a "trickster" image. From a psychological perspective, we could also say that the talmudic discussions ranged from what might be categorized as a Freudian to a Jungian approach. A Freudian perspective would be approaching dream interpretation on a more concrete, reductive basis, and solely to deal with the life of the dreamer, as opposed to a Jungian attitude, which takes into account myth, symbols, and Archetypes when exploring and working with a dream. A Freudian attitude can be gleaned from the statement in the Talmud that our dreams reflect our own conscious thoughts – i.e. what we have thought of during the day but have suppressed and pushed into our Unconscious,[3] while a more Jungian approach would focus on dreams representing what Jung termed the "objective psyche," a message from the Self (some would call it Soul) and at times amplifying the dream with archetypal parallels.

In the Talmud, when discussing dreams, some Rabbis considered dreams nonsense, not to be taken seriously. For example, one of the discussants, Rabbi Meir, declared: "Dreams are of no consequence." Nevertheless, even those who believed dreams to be part prophecy but still a message from within that might lead us astray adopted a middle road, best expressed by Rabbi Jonathan, who, quoting Shimon Bar Yoḥai, a renowned Rabbi and second-century leader, who said: "Just as there can be no grain without straw, so can there be no dream without meaningless matter."[4]

Before Freud and Jung, from the Renaissance on, dreams as serious entities were negated, or, at best, neglected by scholars, physicians, and theologians. Nevertheless, before "enlightened man," earlier civilizations understood and respected the significance of the dream world and struggled to comprehend messages emanating from it. Dream interpreters, dream books, and healing rites centering on dreams and dreamers were not uncommon in the ancient world. The Talmud describes an uninterpreted dream as akin to an unopened letter.[5]

From a Jewish perspective, whether or not there was a consensus as to the significance and interpretation of a person's dreams, the Rabbis did pay attention to them. In Judaism, we have special prayers to ask for a dream to bring guidance; systematic dream interpretations worked out in books, and even prayers to take away the impact of a bad dream. Even today, there are Orthodox Jews who recite a prayer before going to bed asking God for a positive and good dream. In this regard, some of the Rabbis view dreams and visions as a medium of communication with God and their message is declared to be a sixtieth part of prophecy. Historically, the Talmud devoted several pages to the subject of dreams. In this discussion, the following exchange occurs:

> There are twenty-four dream interpreters in Jerusalem. Once I had a dream and went to all of them, and they all gave different interpretations, and all were fulfilled, thus confirming that which is said: 'All dreams follow the mouth.'[6]

While the statement that all twenty-four dream interpretations were correct may seem nonsensical, it might ring true for many of us as, similarly, we could say that some are better served with a Jungian approach to dream interpretation, some with Freudian, and yet others with one of the other analytical schools. No one school of psychology has a monopoly on healing or exclusive expertise in what a dream might mean. A Freudian, an Adlerian, and a Jungian might each interpret a dream differently, yet all might be correct in the sense of being helpful to the dreamer and furthering that person's healing process. A dream, like a painting, can be viewed and interpreted from different perspectives, with each perspective shedding light on a different aspect of what the dream is saying to the dreamer. The paramount aim in therapy, one that transcends the various theories of interpreting a dream, is the healing potential of a dream, no matter the vantage point.

A helpful analogy might be gleaned from the story of the six blind men who were asked to describe what an elephant was like when they were placed near different parts of the elephant. In effect, each was correct in his description, as they experienced the elephant differently. So, too, can an analyst trained in a different discipline see something in a dream that will ring true to a particular dreamer. Each might differ but might still have a positive contribution, regarding the dream. Most important to Jung was that the dreamer accept the interpretation and that the dream helps foster consciousness. If this happens, the interpretation of the dream has served its purpose, since the overriding message in all interpretation of dreams is to further the healing process. A helpful example illustrating the importance of dreams can be seen in C. A. Meier's well researched book, *Healing Dream and Ritual*, where he discusses the Greek incubation Temples and the role that dreams play in the healing process: "Originally, in all probability, the patient was thought incurable if he did not experience a dream or apparition on the first night."[7] Or, in a parallel example, in the Talmudic discussion on dreams, Rabbi Zeira writes that if one goes seven days without a dream he is considered wicked.[8]

What is most important in interpreting the dream is to move beyond a rigid, simplistic theory of there being only one correct interpretation of a dream. Dreams, like our psyches, are complex, nuanced and difficult-to-understand aspects of ourselves. At times, we need to understand them on an objective, conscious level; at other times, more symbolically. The ultimate goal is the same: to enable the dream to help foster healing. In the Talmud, In the section that discusses the role dreams play in one's life, Rabbi Huna states that if someone has a dream that makes him sad, he should have it interpreted with three witnesses present. Once the dream is "witnessed," the three recite three verses that refer to the words *hafakh* (turned); three verses with the word *padah* ("redeemed"); and three with *shalom* ("peace") with no interpretation needed.[9]

From a Jungian perspective, if we want to understand dreams in the context of the Talmud, we should interpret symbolically what the Rabbis might have unconsciously understood in the way they worked with dreams. We should not take what we read at face value; rather, our contribution to making sense out of what the Rabbis say is to explore their comments and see what we can learn from them. Let's look at the following statement and see how it might make sense if we approach it from a symbolic perspective:

> "Bar Hedya was an interpreter of dreams. To one who paid him, he used to give a favorable interpretation; to one who did not pay him, he gave an unfavorable interpretation.[10]

If we take this statement literally, we are left with the feeling that the Rabbi was a charlatan with no values. However, seen symbolically, we can interpret the symbol of payment from a Jungian perspective in which money represents energy – the energy we put into working with a dream, including even payment for therapy. Some people do not wish to work on a dream, or to pay for therapy. If people are not willing to put in the work, or pay even a minimal amount, the outcome will be unfavorable. Alternatively, for those who do take the Unconscious (especially their dreams) seriously and work at trying to understand their dreams, healing can occur and the result will be favorable.

Advice as to the importance of paying attention to our dreams was given by Laurens van der Post, a famed South African explorer who was a friend of Jung, who stated: "Jung was to say something to the effect, and I quote from memory: 'You tell me you have had many dreams lately but have been too busy with your writing to pay attention to them. You have got it the wrong way around. Your writing can wait but your dreams cannot because they come unsolicited from within and point urgently to the way you must go.'"[11]

As if to anticipate Freud, Jung, and modern psychotherapy, the Rabbis appreciated the power of the "transference." The following story illustrates the importance that the person interpreting the dream has in this process that the Talmud describes as "all dreams following the mouth":

> A certain woman came to Rabbi Eliezer and said to him: "I saw in a dream that the granary of my house came open in a crack." He answered: "You will conceive a son." She went away, and that is what happened.

She dreamed again the same dream and told it to Rabbi Eliezer, who gave the same interpretation, and that is what happened.

She dreamed the same dream a third time, and looked for Rabbi Eliezer. Not finding him, she said to his disciples: "I saw in a dream that the granary of my house came open in a crack."

They answered her: "You will bury your husband." And that is what happened.

Rabbi Eliezer, surprised by the lamentations, inquired what had gone wrong. His disciples told him what had happened. He cried out, "Wretched fools! You have killed that man."[12]

The Rabbi understood the influence that his interpretation had on the dreamer – the true meaning of "All dreams follow the mouth." The emphasis is not always on the dream itself but rather the spoken interpretation – what we might refer to as an interpersonal and interactive relationship between dreamer and interpreter, be it Rabbi or analyst, and the dreamer. One needs to take into account the influence that the interpreter, the analyst, might have on the dreamer through the interpretation of his or her dream.

The importance that Judaism attributes to dreams is evident in not only the Talmud but in prayer. For example, a prelude to the *Sh'ma* (most powerful prayer in Judaism), is recited while lying or in bed just prior to falling asleep, in a prayer asking God to bring us good dreams. The prayer, *Ha'mapil,* from the root of the word *nafal* (to fall) is to be recited while lying or sitting in bed – in short, the last activity of our day, which reflects the importance ascribed to dreams:

> Blessed are you, our God, Master of the universe, who brings the heaviness of sleep and slumber and is responsible for my eyelids to close. God, who was also the God of my forefathers, may you have me lie down in peace and wake up in peace and not allow my thoughts or bad dreams to trouble me. May my sleep be peaceful, and may I awake and not die [in my sleep] because you are the one who awakens one's eyelids. Blessed are you who brings light to the entire world with your glory.[13]

If one would like to draw on a dream for guidance, a prayer, *Bakashat ḥalom*, a request for a dream, is recited. An additional step is recommended by kabbalists: *she'elat ḥalom* (question of the dream). This consists of knowing the right questions to ask of a dream for in order to understand the answer in a dream, we need to formulate the right question. "The kabbalist thus learned that in the dreams themselves lie the technique for attaining the answers to the 'dream questions.'"[14]

If one has a frightening or upsetting dream, there is a way to turn this dream into a positive one through ritual and prayer. In the Talmud, a beautiful prayer, *Hatavat ḥalom* – improving the dream – is recited. In such a case, if someone has seen a dream and does not understand what he has seen, or if a person has forgotten the dream or doesn't know whether it portended good or bad, there is a remedy. When such a situation arises, the confused dreamer is advised to gather together three people and recite the following before them:

> Master of the universe! I am yours and my dreams are yours. I have dreamed a dream but do not know the meaning of it. Whether I have dreamed a dream about myself or about others or if others have dreamed about me, if these are good dreams, strengthen them and fortify them like the dreams of Joseph. But if they require healing, heal them as you healed the waters of Marah through Moses, as you healed the leprosy of Miriam, as you healed King Hezekiah from his illness, as you healed the waters of Jericho through Elisha. And just as you transformed the curse of the wicked Balaam into a blessing, so may you transform all my dreams regarding myself into goodness.

Upon repeating one's dream and recitation of the blessing, the three witnesses then gathered to answer "Amen."[15] In a sense, this is also what we do when we tell our dream to our analyst, or a friend, by having them hear our dream – with or without interpretation.

In Orthodox synagogues, Services include this prayer in the liturgy.[16] It is helpful to know how this is manifested. In Jewish tradition, Jews are divided into, and descended from, three categories: *Kohanim* (from the word *kohen*, "priest"); *Levi'im* (Levites, those who in ancient Israel assisted the priests in carrying out their duties); and *Yisra'elim* (Israelites – the vast majority of Jews). Even today, the *Kohanim*, as part of the service, stand in front of the congregation, and spread their hands while uttering the priestly benediction while the congregation silently recites the prayer above with the goal of it having a healing effect on all who recite it.

On another note, it is helpful to understand that the approach to the world of dreams is archetypal and not limited to Judaism. In ancient Egypt and Babylonia, similar to the ancient Israelite culture, there existed what we would refer to today as "how to" books, which laid out in detail what the various characters and symbols that appear in dreams mean. In ancient Egypt, when a person had a "bad" or frightening dream, the dreamer was instructed to stay in bed and ask for *pesen* bread (probably what today we call pita bread) with a few fresh herbs moistened with beer and myrrh, and instructed to let the dreamer's face be smeared with this mixture and to recite this prayer:

> Come to me, come to me, O, my mother Isis! Behold, I am seeing things that are far from my dwelling place! Here I am, my son Horus: let there come out what you have seen, so that the afflictions pervading your dreams may go out and spring forth against him who frightens you. Behold, I am come to see you and to drive forth your evils and root out all that is horrible! Hail to thee, O good dream that is seen by night or by day![17]

Another example can be gleaned from the writings of second-century Greek physician Artemidorus, who wrote extensively on dreams in his book on the interpretation of dreams is what we would today call a "self-help" aspect. In drawing on Artemidorus' writings on dreams, C. A. Meier pointed out that ancient Greek approach to dream work compares favorably with modern principles.[18] Examples include instructions to the dream interpreter to know all about the dreamer's life and character and to be familiar with the customs of the place and of the people in order to understand the dream. In ancient Babylonia, one dream book included images of flying; the readers were told that if one dreamed of having wings and was able to descend but not fly up again, it meant that one's foundation in life was unstable. As Jungians, rather than being dismissive of such dreams of flying, we would understand them as dealing with the dreamer's feelings of grandiosity, an inflation in the dreamer's Ego, or persona, that needs to be addressed.

In ancient Israel, the emphasis on interpreting dreams carried over to the Talmud, most of which was written and compiled in Babylonia. Known as the Babylonian Talmud (as opposed to the less-studied Jerusalem Talmud), it was compiled in stages between the second and fifth centuries. In the Babylonian Talmud, for example, in one excerpt, similar to dream books of Egyptian, Greek, and Babylonian civilizations, we read that in order to defuse the power of the troubling dream, some of the Rabbis ask, "What if it is a bad interpretation?" the advice is modified by instructions to tell the dream and say a prayer but to not have it interpreted. In other words, "as long as it [the troubling dream] has not yet been interpreted, a dream carries no portent at all."[19]

In the Talmud, similar to the Greek, Egyptian, and Babylonian "self-help" books, a myriad of dream images that might appear to the dreamer provide ready interpretations. A few examples – and there are many in the Talmud – include that if one sees a *kaneh* (reed) in a dream, the dreamer may hope for wisdom; if the dreamer sees several reeds, what follows may be the hope for understanding.[20] While as Jungians we are encouraged to take dream images symbolically, some images require quite a stretch though one should keep in mind that Jung did not completely discount Freud's theory of the Oedipal complex. Nevertheless, just as dream images, and the use of symbols and examples occupied the ancient dream interpreters, so too did Jung pay a great deal of attention to amplifying the images in our dreams with examples from myth and our own personal collective Unconscious.

As in ancient times, in therapy, psychic energy is required which includes working on one's dreams. If one does not put energy into the work, the result will be unfavorable. Alternatively, if the energy and commitment are invested, most often a favorable result – healing, on some level – will occur. Artemidorus, for example, writes of dreams that are "infused into men for their advantage and instruction" and modern-day psychoanalysis can trace its origin to ancient dream interpreters such as the biblical Joseph and Daniel and the dream interpreters of the Greek incubation Temples. However, from the Renaissance onward, physicians, theologians, and intellectuals chose to dismiss dreams as superstitious remnants of past civilizations. By the mid-nineteenth century, no serious scholar would entertain the notion that dreaming had any function for man on an everyday level – until Freud, and then Jung, began systematic, in-depth study of the Unconscious, focusing on the world of dreams as a legitimate area to be studied.

I have struggled with whether there is one defining attitude of Jewish tradition toward dreams – from ancient to more contemporary times. How seriously are dreams to be taken as a factor in our daily life? It seems as though Judaism would insist on a clear-cut division between things concrete and the dreamworld. It was always suspicious of self-appointed Prophets and "dreamers of dreams." The *Torah* warns: "Thou shalt not hearken unto the words of that prophet, or unto that dreamer of dreams."[21] Yet it is not so simple. For on the one hand, in the Talmud, we read that there is no dream that does not include some nonsense (*devarim b'teilim*), but almost in the same breath, they say that every dream contains part prophecy.[22]

From a Jewish perspective, it is imperative to remember that while the Rabbis took dreams seriously, accepting the application of these dreams as being related to daily life is accompanied by many caveats and interpretations as to their meaning and importance. The phrase that the Talmud uses is *divrei ḥalomot lo ma'alin v'lo moridin* (the words [messages] of dreams neither elevate something nor do they denigrate it). In other words, at times, the dream is what it is – and is to be taken on a literal level and not seen as divinely inspired. Dream interpretation for the ancient Israelites, as is the case today for modern Jungian analysts, is a complex and nuanced process with some dreams to be taken literally, others symbolically, and yet others to be ignored. An interesting example of the Rabbis' often contradictory approach to dreams can be seen in a rabbinic source:

> A man died. His son knew that prior to his death, his father had hidden a large sum of money but no one had any idea where. One night, the father appeared to his son in a dream and revealed to him the hiding place of the money and its exact amount and stated that the money, or a certain part of it, had been originally set aside as the tithe for the Temple. The money was indeed found precisely in the place indicated and the amount was identical. What better proof to validate the authenticity of the dream? Nevertheless, the Rabbis ruled that the Temple could have no claim on the money.[23]

On all levels, in Jewish tradition as well for us today, one ignores frightening dreams at one's peril. In Judaism, an additional aid to deal with what was considered a bad dream is known as *ta'anit ḥalom*, a day of fasting that one takes on to dismiss the effects of such a dream.[24] Today, we try and understand what these frightening dreams may be about – either with the help of a therapist, or alone. Ironically, perhaps similar to a Jungian perspective, during the course of discussion about dreams, Rabbi Huna declares to his contemporaries: "A good man is not shown a good dream and a bad man is not shown a bad dream."[25] In the ensuing dialogue between the Rabbis, one understands that the implication in such a statement was that dreams come to teach us something about ourselves, and only a good person learns from a bad dream and can use it to improve himself while a so-called bad person's dreams come to reinforce his way of life.

Similarly, a Jungian understanding would be that there is no such thing as a "bad dream." Rather, frightening dreams come from our Unconscious in order to catch our attention – to let us know something important in our psyche needs to be dealt with. In other words, from a Jungian perspective, we would say that "bad" – frightening, or what some term "negative" – dreams can serve as a vehicle for change and consciousness. That being said, it is important to differentiate between dreams that are compensatory, and others are complementary – reinforcing what we already know.

In my own analytical practice, I always approach the world of dreams with great caution and keep in mind that it is a mistake to overanalyze dreams. An old Yiddish folk saying warns us to "beware of letting the dream become bigger than the night," meaning that everyday life and issues take precedence. If we understand this correctly, the expression reminds us that notwithstanding the importance of our dreams, one should not dwell too much on a dream if it comes at the expense of avoiding our day-to-day tasks and responsibilities, or is coming to tell us something we already know.

For Jung, a key element in understanding one's dreams is timing, the intuitive understanding of a dream at a particular moment in one's life. The first question we need to ask the dreamer is: "Why do you think that you had this dream at this particular moment in your life?" In addition, as with the ancient cultures that differentiated between "big" dreams and "little" dreams, at certain transition points in our lives, if we are fortunate, we have "big" or important dreams that can shed light on a situation, and even influence a decision that could have a significant impact on our life. a person, and they are not to be dismissed.

On a personal note, I had what I would call a "big dream" just before my wife and I purchased the house where we have now lived for over 33 years. Originally, our intention was to purchase a home as weekend and summer place since we still had an apartment in New York City to maintain. After searching for months, we found a house that appealed to us though it was far beyond what we could afford. The night we were first shown the house, I dreamed that I met with the seller and told him how much I liked it but that it far exceeded our budget. He then invited me to see the house again and explained that hidden in the basement was a secret room – one containing a treasure, much like in the fairy tales I used to read to my children at bedtime.

I understood that the dream was a message – not rational and not irrational but rather non-rational – an intuitive function which can come in the form of a dream. The dream was telling me not to pass up what might turn out to be a treasure in my life. Over the years, I had come to respect the Unconscious and respect why a dream would come to me at a particular moment. Waking from that dream, I knew that we had to buy this house and that I had to figure out a way to make it happen. Ultimately, I struck a deal with the seller to include a few extra acres of wooded land adjacent to the house, which would make the purchase more valuable, as well as have him provide a second mortgage – an added loan that we needed to cover the amount not covered by the amount that the bank would be approve in granting us a mortgage. The arrangement was for this second mortgage to be paid after five years, with no payments until that time and a minimal amount of interest accruing. My thinking was that in five years, I would find a way to come up with the payment.

Five years later, we were in a position to discharge this second mortgage as a year after purchasing the house, I decided to leave my position as Director of the Jung Foundation. At the same time, I was approached by a representative of McCall's magazine to develop a pop-Psychological Type test, similar to the MBTI (Meyers Briggs Type Indicator) which readers could take, mail in, and have their typology explained from a Jungian analyst. The test results would be computer generated and the magazine representative supplied the computer expert. I wrote some 10,000 lines of copy which were then incorporated into the computer generated response program. It was not an in-depth test such as the MBT; rather, it was more in the nature of a popular quiz. I worked on it for almost two years, over weekends and summers, and tested it out on my students for accuracy; it held up well so I sent it in to the magazine.

In doing so, my arrangement with the magazine was that I would be paid at the rate of five dollars for every response. Ultimately, there were over 6,000 respondents – more than enough to cover the second mortgage we had taken from the seller. At that point, we sold our apartment in Manhattan, moved to the Hudson Valley and established the New York Center for Jungian Studies. Ironically, or one could say synchronistically, our first office was in the basement of our home – the room where the treasure in my dream was hidden. Looking back, it is clear that the treasure in my dream was right there – in the basement of our own home. It has turned out to be a successful venture of presenting Jungian programs in the Hudson Valley and abroad for the past thirty years. As the program grew, we hired an assistant, and finally, when we became too busy with our four telephone lines and computers, we were able to afford to rent a space in New Paltz, where we have been located for over twenty years. When I had this dream – what ancient civilizations and Jung would call a "big" dream – I was able to draw on it to make one of the most important transitions of my life.

In general, thanks to my Jungian analysts, the emphasis on dreams was an important part of my analysis and Jungian training. In addition, the groundwork for this was laid in that throughout my childhood my mother openly discussed her dreams – often over the breakfast table. No one in the family was a psychoanalyst but we all had the understanding that some dreams needed no profound interpretation; usually, they were clearly understood and accepted. In our home, dreams were respected, if not understood psychologically, and no one was embarrassed to relate a dream. In fact, on each of my birthdays, my mother would tell me that she had a dream on the very night that I was conceived. She and my father, had been married for almost three years, with no children yet, and were vacationing in the White Mountains in New Hampshire. One night, her grandfather appeared to her in a dream and told her that she had conceived and that a son would be born. Nine months later, I was born and she named me after him – my great-grandfather. It is a story I cherished throughout my childhood and often think that by hearing this, and many other dreams that my mother would relate to me matter-of-factly, I have been imbued since childhood to take my dreams seriously.

In short, since childhood, I have always felt comfortable with and respected the impact that dreams can play in our lives. Moreover, as a Jungian analyst, I am able to understand the important role dreams play in our psyche, and have learned to work with my own dreams as well as those of the patients. Dreams vary; they can bring with them not only insight into our personal Unconscious but may at times also include what Jung referred to as containing an archetypal dimension. In this regard, we need to understand not only our personal Unconscious-meaning the history and experiences of our personal lives from childhood on, but to be familiar with the Archetypes that may be embedded within – the impersonal, collective Unconscious that is the source for the formation of images, symbols, and myths.

An example of how the psyche produces an archetypal image can be seen in the dream of a patient I treated many years ago (who I will refer to as M) – a thirty-five-year-old Israeli man, married twice, to the same woman, and who was in prison in Switzerland for theft. During my training at the Jung Institute in Zurich, the Institute received a call from the Swiss prison bureau looking for a therapist who could speak Hebrew. Since, as far as I can recall, at the time I was the only one at the Jung institute who was fluent in Hebrew, I was asked to respond – which I did. What turned out was that the prison authorities wanted me to determine whether the prisoner's reported suicide attempt was "real," or if it was staged to help him obtain a release. The call from the authorities came just after I had completed my first round of exams at the institute, known as the Propedeuticum. If I agreed to see M., he would be my first patient. Notwithstanding the lack of any experience in working with patients, I was interested in taking on the case. I called Dr. Toni Frey, a Training Analyst at the Institute and the director of the only in-patient Jung clinic in Zurich. Dr. Frey was someone I had wanted to be one of my case supervisors so I asked him whether I should take on the assignment given I had no experience. He encouraged me to accept the challenge and advised me to meet the prisoner at 2:00 the next day and "just listen; don't talk" – and then come see him at 4:00. "Come directly to my office, and we'll talk it through," he told me – obviously intrigued by the case.

At my session with Dr. Frey, we concluded that M.'s "suicide attempt" was staged and in the realm of a plea for help rather than a genuine attempt to kill himself. Dr. Frey encouraged me to tell the authorities that M. needed a weekly therapy session. I did so and, surprisingly, the Swiss authorities agreed to pay for them. Dr. Frey was quite excited that I would be working with someone in prison, conducting the therapy in Hebrew, and determining how and whether a Jungian approach would work with a man who had no education beyond the fourth grade (which was the case with M.). Dr. Frey believed that this would ultimately make a fascinating case study that could be published. I took on the case and found it fascinating and rewarding. M. and I had weekly sessions that took place in the prison; I continued working with him for almost a year and a half by which time I had finished my Jungian training and returned to the United States.

For most of the time we worked together, the therapy consisted of little more than my being someone whom M. could relate to as a person. Because he was held in solitary confinement for most of that time and was an Israeli who did not speak German, I brought him Hebrew-language newspapers and we conversed in Hebrew. However, when trying to get through to him by discussing his life and past, it was as if I came up against a wall. Here was a man with no more than an elementary-school education who could not relate to psychotherapy, let alone a Jungian approach. His ability for self-reflection was minimal to nonexistent. Denial was not merely a defense but a way of life. Clearly, he suffered from depression, yet aside from blaming his imprisonment as the cause for this depression, he claimed to have no other issues troubling him. When discussing his family of origin, or his relationship with his wife, he spoke in terms of love and devotion despite the fact that his wife seldom wrote to him and never visited him in prison.

After almost six months of weekly therapy sessions with M, I had the following dream:

"I was in Israel and came to see M.'s wife. M. was there, too. I got into a car with them; they were going to drive me somewhere, but I felt like a fifth wheel as I sat in the back seat with the two of them in the front. She was driving and placed her arm lovingly around him. I was admiring their love but realized we were headed nowhere – not toward any destination. I felt strangely calm and was curious to see where this would lead. It was as if watching their love for each other was a scene out of a romantic opera or novel."

In the dream, I was admiring the view and seemed oblivious to the fact that we were heading nowhere in particular. Upon waking, I realized that the dream was referring to the therapy sessions – seemingly pleasing but heading nowhere. Moreover, M.'s wife was driving the car. While the view in the dream was quite beautiful, the therapy was making no progress. This supposed love affair was not real, and his idealization had her in the driver's seat of our work together. Symbolically, she – or at least his idealization of her – was driving the therapy.

Not knowing how to reach my patient and have him open up to me as to what the relationship between them was really like, I decided to share this dream with him. After I did so, I asked him what he thought. His response was to tell me of a dream that he had recently – the first time in almost half a year of therapy that he related a dream to me, no matter how many times I had asked him before if he had any dreams. The dream he related was:

"I dreamed that I was Samson and was strong enough to pull apart the bars of my cell and walk out of prison,"

One might easily dismiss this dream as little more than what a Freudian might call "wish fulfillment." After all, his reality was imprisonment and it would be natural to want to be released from prison. Still, why Samson? He was uneducated and barely even remembered the story of Samson when I asked him that question. All he could remember was that Samson was a person of huge strength; indeed, in Israel, there were gyms called "Samson's Gyms" and all sorts of advertising that featured men with muscles and a body that was to be admired. Given the comic strips and films of the time, M. likely knew more about the figure of Superman than the Biblical figure Samson.

The question I then asked myself was: Why would M. not dream of a heroic person like Superman, Batman, or Tarzan – all figures in popular culture and films that he was more familiar with than the Bible? When I asked him to tell me what he remembered from the Samson story, all he could recall was that Samson was an all-powerful hero who killed many Philistines. Yet in amplifying the dream, I could not help but be struck by the archetypal nature of the dream by the psyche's production of an archetypal image, in this case Jewish, as an ingredient for breaking through beyond the conscious, interpersonal level of therapy. As it turned out, this dream marked an important turning point in our work together. For the dream image, while related to the story of Samson on the conscious level of sheer strength, held a deeper message. As I pointed out to him, a key element in the story of Samson is Delilah, the woman responsible for his imprisonment and subsequent death. By explaining to my patient in simple, down-to-earth language the importance of dreams in our ongoing mental health – and the role that Delilah played in bringing about Samson's downfall – I was able to reach him.

After hearing about the role of Delilah in the Samson myth, he burst into tears. The denial and resistance that had previously characterized our therapy sessions was replaced by trust and an attempt, on some level, of self-understanding. For it soon became evident in our discussions, that the relationship that M. had with his wife was based on buying her expensive gifts to keep her happy. This, in turn, played a role in M.'s turning to theft as a means of acquiring jewelry, furs, and a fancy car for his wife. Upon his imprisonment, his wife neither forwarded money to him to hire an attorney, nor came to visit him even once during the year and a half I worked with him in Zurich. This Delilah, the "femme fatale" in his life, manifested itself archetypally – one might say through his archetypal Jewish roots. Moreover, the story of Samson was very much in keeping with Jung's ideas regarding the archetypal connections within each of us. In this case, my patient's Jewish roots, notwithstanding his total lack of familiarity with this archetypal myth of Samson, opened him up to finally begin taking responsibility for his life.

The importance of dreams has been brought home to us from the biblical dreams of the Old and New Testaments to the documented telling of the influence that dreams had on some of the leading cultural, political, and military leaders throughout history. In Judaism, biblical dreams play an important role in defining the history of our people. In this context, some of the more well-known dreams in the Hebrew Bible include the dreams of Abraham, Jacob, Joseph, Solomon, and Daniel (who, like Joseph, also interpreted others' dreams). Other, not so friendly, characters that appear include the famous dream of Pharaoh which was interpreted by Joseph, and that of Nebuchadnezzar (described in Kings II).

In conclusion, in Judaism, as in a Jungian approach, dream interpretation is nuanced. In Judaism, on the one hand we are told that dreams contain a sixtieth part prophecy and a means of connecting with the divine; indeed, some Rabbis have viewed dreams as a medium of communication with God. On the other hand, there is no dream that does not include some nonsense which, I suppose, inspired the Yiddish folk saying that dumplings in a dream are not dumplings, but a dream – or, in his sleep, it isn't the man who sins but a dream. What we need to understand is that not all dreams are created equal, so to speak. Some come to give us insight into ourselves we lack during our conscious hours; others come to reinforce what we already know, and yet others may have no particular meaning; simply put, in the words of Freud, they function as a way to process the residue of the day.

Notes

1. Babylonian Talmud [BT] Tractate Berahot, 55a & 55b.
2. BT *Berahot* 55b.
3. BT *Berahot* 55b.
4. BT; *Berahot* 55a.
5. BT Berahot 55a & 55b.
6. BT Berahot 55.
7. C. A. Meier, *Healing Dream and Ritual* (Einsiedeln, Switzerland: Daimon Publications, 1987), p. 154.
8. BT Berahot, 55b.
9. BT Berahot, 55b.
10. BT Berahot 56a.
11. Laurens van der Post, *Jung and the Story of Our Time* (New York: Vintage, 1977), p. 214.
12. Roger Caillois, "The Dream Follows the Mouth," in *The New World of Dreams*, ed. Ralph L. Woods and Herbert B. Greenhouse (New York: Macmillan Publishing, 1974), p. 158.
13. Vanessa L. Ochs, *The Jewish Dream Book* (Woodstock, VT: Jewish Lights, 2003), p. 33 (translation mine).
14. Moshe Idel, "Dream Techniques in Jewish Mysticism," *Jewish Heritage Online*, July 28, 2008.
15. BT Berahot 55b.
16. *Siddur (Daily Prayer Book)* (New York: Hebrew Publishing Company, 1949), pp. 627–628.
17. From a papyrus in Cairo Museum, No. 50–138-139.
18. See Meier, *Healing Dream and Ritual*.
19. BT Berahot 55b commentary.
20. BT Berahot 56b.
21. Deuteronomy: 13:4.
22. Genesis Rabbah 17:5.
23. Tosefta, *Ma'aser Sheni* 5:9.
24. *Encyclopaedia Judaica*, Vol. 6 (Jerusalem: Keter Publishing House, 1972), p. 210.
25. BT Berahot 55b.

Chapter 2

The Wandering Jew

Figure 2.1 Moses Gordon or the Wandering Jew: in the dress he now wears in Newgate, published by A. Davis (Birmingham, West Midlands), January 5, 1788, hand-colored etching.

DOI: 10.4324/9781003511908-3

My interest in this theme is personal. While I was growing up, my family's financial situation continually improved, enabling us to move homes and locations a number of times. Each move represented what we would describe today as "upward mobility." For me, however, each relocation meant a loss of stability, and every move found me attending a new school and needing to make new friends. From kindergarten through high school, I attended five different schools, some of which turned out well while others elicited complexes that I still struggle with. Moreover, moving meant not only relocating within the New York area but twice to another country, Israel. My parents were ardent Zionists; my mother was born in Jerusalem, as were her father and grandfather. My grandmother's family were among the first settlers in an agricultural experiment funded by Baron de Hirsch in the late nineteenth century, *Mahanaim*. However, that experiment was a failure and after a few years, they migrated to Safad, birthplace of the Kabbalah in Israel. My father, born in Poland, attended Hebrew-speaking Zionist schools there until age 19 when he, his parents, and siblings emigrated to the U.S. though living in Israel had been my father and mother's goal from the time they met.

Over the years, family and friends joked that we were wandering Jews, continually on the move, though neither I nor anyone I knew had the slightest idea of how loaded that phrase was. Indeed, not many people are acquainted with the myth of the Wandering Jew as it appears in Western civilization – at its core, it is an anti-Semitic myth. The phrase is used loosely and, if pressed to explain where the term originated, most people – including Jews – will tell you that it might be associated with the biblical description of the Israelites' 40 years of wandering in the desert, or the fact that Jews, continually expelled from the countries where they had been living, had to keep moving.

The frequency of moving in my childhood was disconcerting; it left me feeling ungrounded, like a wanderer in search of roots. Ironically, as if I were caught in some archetypal force, I reenacted this pattern by moving to Israel as an adult. Unwittingly, though from a Jungian perspective one would say unconsciously, I not only reenacted the pattern of my childhood but subjected my children to the same experience. I spent seven years in Jerusalem studying for my PhD, followed by three years in Zurich, where I completed my Jungian training – all the while with my children in tow. Like Ulysses in *The Odyssey*, I ended up back where I began – in the U.S., living near my original nuclear family. And, like Ulysses, I had many exciting and fascinating experiences along the way. In the end, I was happy to be home in the U.S., although René Malamud, my Jungian analyst and lifelong mentor in Zurich, made me understand that I was not the same person who had left ten years earlier.

Until I reached the age of 40, this wandering – from home to home, from country to country and back again – was experienced as having no place where I could feel connected to the land. It felt as though I was destined never to put down roots. It was not until we bought a home in the Hudson Valley, and I was able, with the love, encouragement, and help from my wife and partner for the past 39 years, to stop working for an institution, settle down, and live in the same place. Perhaps, as

Jung pointed out to Erich Neumann, a connection to the land can inspire a new, creative force. I know that living in a home surrounded by five acres of trees and semi-rural land has helped me to pivot inwardly and deepen my struggle to Individuate.

Ironically, what first led me to think of writing about this theme germinated during the first days I arrived in Zurich to train at the Jung Institute. Yechezkel Kluger, Jungian analyst in Haifa and husband of Rivkah Scharf Kluger (who had been my analyst in Israel), presented a talk on the Archetype of Zionism to a select group of Zurich Jungians. Notwithstanding the fact that I had barely begun my training, thanks to the connection with Rivkah I was invited to attend his lecture. The talk, and his presentation on the archetypal roots of Zionism, was excellent. However, the last question from the audience came from C.A. Meier, who was not Jewish, who asked why more had not been said about what he understood as the most significant aspect of the Jewish experience, the *Galut* (exile). Meier's question encouraged me to think of my own family's experience of wandering – which ultimately led me to write about this from both a personal and collective perspective.

Over more than 20 years of leading Jewish heritage trips, I had the privilege of visiting many countries around the world and learning firsthand about Jewish history and culture in these places. These trips brought home to me how much wandering Jews have had to do over the centuries, including most of the Middle East, Western and Eastern Europe, and as far afield as China, India, and Japan. Morocco, in particular, provided a unique perspective on wandering, as the Jews of Morocco so venerated some of their Rabbis, some of whom, unlike in any other Jewish culture, referred to them as saints. Following the establishment of the State of Israel, the Jewish population in Morocco – chased out, or emigrating to protect themselves from anti-Jewish riots and pogroms – dwindled from about 300,000 in the 1950s to fewer than 2,000 today. Most of the Moroccan Jews made their way to Israel and, once established, dedicated shrines to some of their saints. Often, these shrines were inspired by "visitation dreams" in which the Rabbi/saint would appear, along with the explanation that the Rabbi/saint had made his way underground, traveling from Morocco, where he was buried, to Israel, where his wandering could now come to a safe end.[1]

In any case, the description of Jews as wanderers conjures up negative associations. Moreover, the narrative of the wandering Jew has become fixed in the Western psyche and, over the centuries, accepted and promulgated by bigots and anti-Semites throughout the world. "Not surprisingly, Nazis resurrected the Wandering Jew in propaganda to portray Jews as wandering cultural parasites."[2] As depicted in Western culture and religion, the image of Jews as wanderers was an archetypal punishment imposed on them. Persecuted throughout Europe, entire Jewish communities were expelled and forced to keep moving from one land to the next. In addition, in most all these instances, Jews were victims of laws designed to limit the type of professions they might engage in, isolate them from the wider society, and prohibit them from owning land – the very thing that would have enabled them to settle down in one place and stop wandering.

The reality and facts are complex. The anti-Semitic stereotype of Jews as moneylenders, for example, should be seen in the context of an Archetype, a projection of the Shadow on the Jews by the Church. For example, contrary to accepted beliefs, lending money to the nobility was not limited to Jews but also one engaged in by Christian financiers.[3] Although many Jews were involved in lending money, most did not have the means or capital to do so and were often craftsmen, artisans, merchants, and physicians. Nevertheless, Jews were generally prohibited from most professions and, in most places, denied the privilege of owning land. Beginning in medieval times, lending money for interest was one of the few occupations open to Jews which in turn stoked the projection of greed onto Jews – an Archetype of greed that owed its birth to the Christian tradition that Judas betrayed Jesus for 30 pieces of silver. Mass expulsions, and the forced wanderings of entire communities, were often a result of projected greed, fueled by the desire to erase debts of the accusers and to be the beneficiaries of Jewish property.

The demonization and expulsion of Jewish communities resulted in Jews wandering from place to place. Ironically, in some instances Jews were welcomed by local rulers for their expertise and skills and even invited to settle in their lands, though accompanying these invitations came the expectation that their presence would help the local economy. Moreover, it was understood that Jews would bring not only their skills as tradesmen but also serve as tax advisors and collectors to the local rulers. Unfortunately, when that ruler died or was overthrown, Jews then became natural scapegoats and were expelled and once again had to continue wandering.

In Western culture, the stereotypical Archetype of Jews as wanderers stems from the centuries-old myth of the Wandering Jew. This offensive, anti-Semitic myth was often cited as evidence that Jews were being punished by God for the crucifixion of Jesus which provided yet another excuse to persecute Jews – proof that they were responsible for the death of Jesus. While there are various versions of the tale, it is widely accepted by scholars that the myth dates back to at least medieval times, a result of superstition and Christian folklore.[4] The most often told version was that Jesus stumbled or fell several times while carrying his cross on the way to the crucifixion. Although there is no direct reference to this in the Gospels, in the myth Jesus is portrayed as walking along the Via Dolorosa – a street that still exists and is walked along by Christian pilgrims today in the Old City of Jerusalem. When stopping to rest, the story continues, he was either pushed or struck by a Jewish bystander and told to move more quickly. In other accounts, Jesus was mocked; in all versions, he was told to move faster. Addressing his harasser, Jesus is said to have replied: "I will walk now, but you will walk the earth until I return again," referring to the Second Coming of Christ.[5]

Keeping this myth in mind, over the centuries there have been many reported sightings of the Wandering Jew, with the earliest written description dating back to the thirteenth century. In *Flores Historiarum*, written by an Englishman, Roger of Wendover, a sighting of the Wandering Jew was ascribed to a story told by a visiting archbishop from Armenia, who swore that he had seen or spoken to such a figure. Over time, some have even ascribed a name or an occupation to the Wandering Jew, ranging from shoemaker or another tradesman, to a person named Joseph or Isaac, or Mattathias, or even Ahasuerus (ironically, the same name in Jewish tradition as the king of Persia, a protagonist in the Book of Esther). The tale was first popularized after its publication in 1602 in a book, *A Brief Description and Narrative Regarding a Jew Named Ahasuerus*. In this version, the author claimed that a German bishop had met a Jew named Ahasuerus some 60 years earlier and that Ahasuerus told the bishop that he had been "wandering aimlessly for over a thousand years."[6] Following the initial publication and dissemination of this myth, over the years, more than 100 folktales have told the legend of the Wandering Jew, and in places far apart.[7]

Adding credence to the myth, numerous sightings of the Wandering Jew were reported, and retold throughout Europe – including England, France, Italy, Hungary, Poland, Denmark, Germany, and Spain. In these sightings, the Jew was most often portrayed as shabby, dressed in rags, an older man, with an occupation described as a shoemaker or other trade person. His knowledge of the crucifixion is taken for granted; he has a wife and children, does not laugh or even smile, and must suffer because of the curse placed up him by Jesus.[8]

This condemned Jew is fated to wander until the Second Coming of Jesus. Moreover, to make his punishment even more difficult, he never dies and when he reaches old age (in some versions, 100), rather than die, he reverts back to the age of 30. Archetypally, we see can see parallels in the Greek myth of Sisyphus and the biblical story of Cain and Abel. Sisyphus was doomed to roll a stone up a hill until, reaching the top, the stone rolls down the hill and the process begins all over. Like the Wandering Jew, Sisyphus has the same fate: never-ending punishment. And in the biblical story of Cain and Abel, Cain is punished for causing his brother's death and is condemned to wander the earth, from place to place, for eternity; moreover, there is no record in the Bible of Cain dying.

The motif of wandering is archetypal; it appears in various forms and in many versions – in theological writings, literature, music, and art. For example, the Wandering Jew is the subject of Fromental Halévy's opera *Le Juif errant*, and the characters in Wagner's *Flying Dutchman* and Edward Everett Hale's *The Man Without a Country* – all doomed to eternal wandering. In Sophocles's play *Oedipus at Colonus*, Oedipus's ultimate fate is to be a wanderer; the protagonists in Mircea Eliade's novel *Dayan*, Evelyn Waugh's *Helena*, and Edward Arlington Robinson's *The Wandering Jew* are all represented as wandering. In addition, the theme of the Wandering Jew appears prominently in the works of numerous poets and artists, including paintings by Marc Chagall and a series of woodcuts by Gustave Doré, entitled *The Legend of the Wandering Jew*. In true anti-Semitic form, as if to mimic the myth, botanists have named a well-known purple plant, whose tendency is to creep along one's garden, the "Wandering Jew."

From a Jungian perspective, an Archetype has both positive and negative aspects with the Archetype of wandering manifesting itself in the Jewish experience as a search for spirit – beginning with Abraham, the first "Hebrew." In the story, Abraham left his tribe of origin and moved from place to place at the behest of God. Abraham's wanderings took him from what was then Assyria (now Syria), and on to Mamre (now Hebron), with stops along the way in Beersheba and Egypt. Following in Abraham's footsteps, his descendants wandered and moved about as well. First Isaac, and then Jacob, spent years wandering far from home, with Jacob ultimately moving to, and dying in, Egypt. Later, Moses, who led the Israelites in their wandering through the desert for 40 years, and then David, looking to escape the wrath of Saul, were wanderers.

To understand the history of the Jewish people, one needs to understand the muti-faced aspects of wandering during the thousands of years of Judaism – known as *Galut* (*exile*). However, for the Jewish people, there was more than just one exile in its history. Seen in an archetypal context, this exile can also be understood as a collective experience linked with a search for spirit and traced back to the Book of Genesis. In it, Jewish tradition recognizes that Abraham, considered the father of the Jewish people, represents the prototype of his people's wandering. In the biblical story, Abram, his name before being renamed Abraham by God, left the home of his father, an idol worshipper, at the commandment of God; in search of spirituality, he spent his life moving from place to place.

The Jewish attitude toward wandering, the so-called curse of moving from place to place with no anchor of a land of their own, evolved; some Rabbis even understood it as a positive step in a people's spiritual development. Furthermore, this wandering was also explained as engendering transformation through a people's continual search for spirituality and meaning. For, as opposed to the anti-Semitic myth describing Jewish wandering as punishment, the wandering began with a positive spin and traced back to God's commandment to Abraham to *lekh lekha* ("go forth"), leave your homeland. On a symbolic level, one can interpret Abraham's experience of wandering as looking for an inner connection to God. The *midrash* (legend) postulates that wandering has to do with Abraham seeking God – and God rewarding him. The Rabbis explain the words in Genesis that God commands Abraham to leave home is linked to God's promise that if Abraham does leave his homeland, God promised to make him and his descendants a powerful people: *Ve'e'eskha legoy gadol* (I will make you a great nation). However, Abraham, is not directed by God to a specific place. Rather, his wandering can be seen as a continual search is for an inner connection to spirit; no specific destination is named. In later times, even the Israelites are not directed to Jerusalem, the holiest of Jewish cities. In Jewish history, Jerusalem evolved into a place where Israelites offered their sacrifices to God three times a year, but it was not specifically identified in the Bible as such. In short, in Judaism, wandering represents an inner search for spirit, a connection to a higher being.

After Abraham, his son Isaac – the second of the three Jewish patriarchs – also wandered throughout his life, residing at times in Hebron, Beersheba, and even Gerar, land of the Philistines. Indeed, some Jewish legends refer to Isaac as spending his life searching for spirituality and meaning through continual study. Finally, the last of the three Jewish patriarchs, Jacob (renamed "Israel" and precursor of the

Israelites as a people), was also a wanderer. At first, Jacob went into in exile in fear of Esau, though he and his tribe eventually ended up in Egypt, which, in Jewish tradition, represents the first exile – *Galut mitzrayim* ("exile to Egypt"), a period when the Israelites were enslaved. From Egypt, as described in the Book of Exodus, the Israelites wandered in the desert for 40 years, before settling in the Land of Canaan and becoming the nation of Israel.

Throughout their history, by necessity, Jews were wanderers, spread around the globe. Ironically, and in what Jung would term a "compensatory attitude," although the Prophets told the Israelites that exile was a punishment for not following devotion to God, exile was eventually interpreted by some as a positive development. Seen in this light, some Rabbis interpreted the *Galut* as a prerequisite for the Redemption – an opportunity to say to God that they had endured all the suffering and proved their devotion to him.[9]

In other words, *Galut* can mean more than merely exile and should be understood symbolically as well as literally. In Hebrew, the root of "*Galut*" is g-l-h, pronounced "*galah*," (to reveal), which some of the Rabbis came to interpret as God revealing himself to his people, the Jews, in exile. While some of the Prophets warned the Israelites that they would be exiled as a punishment for their sins, the Rabbis later turned this negative experience into a positive development. From a Jungian perspective, we could also understand this as compensation to alleviate the persecution that Jews suffered in their years of wandering as some Rabbis interpreted the collective wandering of the Jews as a sign that the Messiah would soon appear. The *Galut*, they preached, should be accepted, even welcomed as a prerequisite for the redemption – an opportunity to say to God that they have endured all the suffering and proven their devotion so God.

Following this line of reasoning, a new myth came into being, which was presented to the people as God accompanying the Jews into exile:

> From the first, God intended that there would be many exiles for the people of Israel, for reasons known only to him . . . . Yet some say it was for Israel's good that God destroyed the Temple and drove the Jews into exile, for God surely will have mercy forever and rebuild the Temple with even greater strength . . . . Everything that happened during the long years of exile was in preparation for the redemption, and at the time of liberation this will all be revealed.[10]

In short, the punishment of wandering was transformed from a negative feature to a positive experience – in Jungian terms, a compensatory attitude to ease the collective pain of a people.

The exile (there were several in Jewish history[11]) that most people identify with was brought about by the destruction of the Second Temple in 70 CE. This exile ushered in what has become known as the Diaspora, which lasted until the State of Israel was founded in 1948. These 2,000 years brought about the development of Judaism as a religion, known today as rabbinic Judaism. What emerged was the transition from animal sacrifice practiced in the Temple, to the implementation of prayers that could now be recited in whatever part of the world a Jew lived. Indeed, the term Jew, or Judaism, originally referred to those from the tribe of Judah – the last tribe exiled from Jerusalem with its inhabitants known as Judaeans. As a result of this exile, Rabbis and wealthy laymen became communal leaders and exercised power and influence over the daily lives and practices of Jewish society. In this arrangement, the Rabbi of the community served multiple roles: spiritual guide as well as judge and presided over the most important aspects of Jewish daily life: marriage, divorce, and burial.

To alleviate suffering, some Rabbis came to justify the imposed wandering from place to place as an opportunity for Jews to connect to God. For example, following the destruction of the First Temple and the exile to Babylonia, as compensation for the collective suffering the Rabbis began depicting exile as a prerequisite for the coming of the Messiah; the exile which will lead to redemption and a return to a rebuilt Jerusalem.[12] They were not abandoned as a people, and the myth was even reframed as God accompanying his people, Israel, into exile. In this scenario, the midrash (legends) has God asking the Jewish people, as they were about to go into exile:

> "Whom among the Fathers would you have lead you? Whether it be Abraham, Isaac, or Jacob, whether Moses or Aaron, I shall raise any one of them from his grave, and he will lead you. Or, if you would prefer David or Solomon, I shall raise either of them and he will lead you.
>
> "The Congregation of Israel replied: 'Master of the Universe, we do not choose any one of these. You are our only father.'
>
> "God replied, 'Since that is your wish, I will be your companion, for I myself will accompany you to Babylon.'"[13]

A biblical parallel that lent itself to this approach could be cited by the community's spiritual leaders through a reference in the Book of Exodus. There, God was said to have guided the Israelites in their 40 years of wandering through the desert until they could reach the Promised Land: "The Lord went before them in a pillar of cloud by day, and in a pillar of fire by night . . . [and] did not depart from before the people."[14] In this manner, the Rabbis could reinforce the belief that God would be with the Jewish people until the Messiah and redemption arrived – and with it, lead them to a return to Jerusalem and an end to their suffering.[15]

From a Jungian perspective, we can understand that the myth arose as a compensation for the collective suffering of Jews. Another result of this compensatory attitude gave rise to the description of Jews as the "Chosen People" which did make its way into the everyday prayers, including the blessing recited each Friday evening over wine: "You have chosen us from among all the people." Unfortunately, this compensatory aspect for suffering became a phrase that anti-Semites have seized on and over the centuries used as an excuse to increase their hatred of Jews by spinning the phrase into Jews believing they were better than any other people. In recent times, perhaps as protection from persecution, and to be more "politically correct," Jewish commentators and Rabbis have interpreted the phrase as meaning that the Jews were chosen by God to receive the Torah – not that Jews consider themselves more "chosen" than other people by God. In this reinterpretation, Reform and more so-called progressive and liberal sects of Judaism have updated the prayer and changed its wording from "You have chosen us *from* all the people of the world to read You have chosen us *with* all the people of the world."

In the Zohar, the primary Book of the Kabbalah, the compensatory theme surrounding wandering was expanded upon with the position taken that it was for the good of the world that the Jews were exiled from the Holy Land. Here, as part of the description of creation, the kabbalists present a model known as "The Shattering of the Vessels and the Gathering of the Sparks." The essence of this hypothesis is that upon creation:

> God sent forth ten vessels, like a fleet of ships, each carrying his cargo of light. Had they arrived intact, the world would have been perfect. But somehow, the frail vessels broke open and split asunder, and all the holy sparks were scattered, like sand, like seeds, like stars . . . .
>
> That is why we [the Jewish people] were created – to gather the sparks, no matter where they are hidden. Some even say that God created the world so that Israel could raise up the holy sparks. And that is why there have been so many exiles – to release the holy sparks . . . . For in this way, the people of Israel will sift all the holy sparks from the four corners of the earth.
>
> And when enough holy sparks have been gathered, the vessels will be restored, and the repair of the world [*tikkun olam*], awaited so long, will finally take place.[16]

In general, many Rabbis encouraged their communities to be patient – not to curse the darkness but, rather, to look for the light at the end of the tunnel. The wandering will end someday, and when it does, it will bring with it the coming of the Messiah and a return to Jerusalem.

Nevertheless, the Archetype of wanderer appears not only in the Jewish experience but in other cultures and religious traditions as well – a necessary component of a spiritual quest. Saint Francis and the Buddha, for example, both revered role models in their respective religious traditions, wandered for long stretches in their lives. Both Jesus and Muhammad were said to have wandered in the desert before emerging with their spiritual message. The concept of wandering is archetypal and, like all Archetypes, is complex; it should not be reduced to being a punishment. Understood in all its ramifications, the Jewish experience of wandering was nuanced, complex, and understood as bringing with it transformation. Seen in this light, wandering brought with it a search for meaning and spirituality.

In this regard, from an archetypal perspective, the first exile and punishment in both Jewish and Christian tradition was the expulsion of Adam and Eve from the Garden of Eden for disobeying the rule not to eat fruit from the Tree of Knowledge. As the Genesis story continues, their son Cain was punished for killing his brother

Abel and condemned to be a "vagrant and a wanderer" forever.[17] Likewise, and perhaps influenced by this story, some Christian theologians interpret the expulsion from the Garden of Eden as the "fortunate fall" and believe that Jews were similarly punished for the death of Jesus. Ironically, in this projection of their own Shadow, and in their rush to anti-Semitic judgment, it was convenient to forget that Jesus was born a Jew, lived his life as a Jew, and died as a practicing member of the Jewish faith.

Another major exile in Jewish history occurred in 722 BCE, when ten of the 12 tribes of Israel – the Northern Kingdom – were defeated by the Assyrians, deported from their land, and dispersed throughout the Assyrian kingdom. Since that time, they have subsequently been lost to history, though not to Jewish myth. Over the centuries, Jews worldwide have not given up on the ten lost tribes of Israel having migrated and still wandering somewhere. As a living example of the power of myth, these "ten lost tribes" have been sighted, rediscovered, and variously identified as the Ethiopian Jews (*Beta Israel*), sects in India (*Bene Israel* and *Bene Menashe*), diverse tribes in Ghana and Nigeria, or even communities in Kaifeng, China.

Throughout all the exiles, despite the suffering and persecution that the Jews experienced, Jewish community spiritual leaders never believed that it would result in the extinction of Judaism. Rather, they put a positive spin on the experience and preached that the *Galut* was an opportunity to say to God that they would remain true to their faith and the belief that ultimately the Messiah would appear and with him a return of Jews to Jerusalem. This belief became a spiritual factor in uniting Jews, articulated through the study of *Torah* (Hebrew Bible), the engagement in daily prayer, and the development of a powerful collective, including the establishment of religious courts, municipal cooperation, and taxation to further solidify what was known as the *kehillah* (community).

Jung, due to his own issues with Jews and a stereotypical view of Judaism, did not understand the educational and cultural aspect of the Jewish tradition and thought that the Jews have no cultural form of their own.[18] From a very young age, Jewish children are taught to read and write; boys were often fluent in at least three languages by the time they reached bar mitzvah (age 13): they learn Hebrew so that they can pray and study the Bible in its original language; Aramaic, the language of the Talmud; and Yiddish or Judeo-Spanish (Ladino) as the language spoken at home. Moreover, even in ultra-Orthodox homes, many girls are taught to read, or at least enough to enable them to read prayer books. For boys, the study of Torah and Talmud are the ultimate goal, with great emphasis on the Socratic method of dialogue, asking questions to encourage critical thinking. One need turn no further than the Hebrew roots of the words *torah* (*lehorot*, to teach) and *talmud* (from *lamed*), to learn. The study of Torah and Talmud spawned scholars and Jewish intellectuals who published extensively on the nuances of Jewish law, though many also explored ancient Greek philosophy and other secular subjects. In some countries – especially, Spain and Portugal until the late fifteenth century – Jews were leaders in the field of medicine and wrote books on alchemy and were renowned cartographers in Portugal before the Inquisition. Moreover, thanks to the invention of movable type in printing, Jews the world over could then read and study the Talmud and other Jewish writings wherever they were.

Other outstanding Jewish scholars and intellectuals include Philo of Alexandria, who merged Greek and Jewish philosophy; Maimonides, physician and philosopher who drew on Socrates for inspiration and combined study of *Torah*, science, and medicine (including a highly respected treatise of medical ethics); Solomon Ibn Gabirol, a leading proponent of Neoplatonism; and the medieval poet Judah Halevi, who defended Judaism against the accusations of Muslim and Christian theologians in medieval Spain and whose poetry still plays an important part in the liturgy of the High Holy Days.

In banking, business, and international commerce, Jews were often called on by rulers to enhance the expansion of their domain and aid in their economic development. However, to their eventual detriment, Jews were also called on to help administrate and collect taxes on behalf of the local rulers who had invited them. As one would imagine, this thankless task of collecting taxes eventually fueled anti-Semitism and expulsion.

The list of Jewish scholarship and intellectual development is almost endless. Scholars and Rabbis wrote thousands of books and articles on Jewish law, philosophy, and mysticism that was studied in Jewish schools and synagogues throughout the world. From this tradition, Jewish mysticism, and in particular cross-fertilization in the fields of kabbalah and alchemy, took place among Jewish, Christian, and Islamic mystics.

By the eighteenth century, once they were allowed to enter select universities and academia, thanks to the emphasis placed on study and education in Jewish homes, Jews excelled in areas such as medicine, mathematics, chemistry, physics, literature, philosophy, and the social sciences. In more contemporary times, this can be seen in the impressive number of publications by Jews in these fields, including but not limited to Nobel Prize recipients. Regrettably, Jung misunderstood and underestimated this important aspect of Jewish education which, despite the wandering and exile imposed on it over the centuries, enhanced a love of learning, with an emphasis on education and a unique Jewish cultural form.

Despite interacting with leading Jewish scholars and intellectuals such as Martin Buber, Gershon Scholem, Erich Neumann, Leo Baeck, and Zwi Werblowsky during some of the Eranos conferences, Jung did not take responsibility for a gap in his own understanding of Judaism and Jewish culture. Jung's lack of appreciation for Jewish culture and tradition prompted some of his leading followers to criticize him – not easy for those who had such a positive transference on to him. Most notable among these critics were James Kirsch (founder of the Jung Institute in Los Angeles), Erich Neumann (who laid the groundwork for Jungian psychology in Israel), and Gerhard Adler (along with Aniela Jaffe, one of the editors of Jung's Letters). These individuals, and other Jewish disciples of Jung, idealized him; yet they also took him to task for his poorly informed knowledge of Judaism and his statements that Jews lacked a cultural form of their own.

Neumann, for example, despite acknowledging Jung as the most important influence in his professional life, was appalled by Jung's description of Jews as lacking a cultural form of their own. Writing from Tel Aviv, Neumann began a letter to Jung: "I know I don't have to tell you what you mean to me, and how hard it is for me to disagree with you, but I feel I simply must take issue with you." He went on to chastise Jung for his ignorance of Jewish culture and history. Neumann accused Jung of filtering his knowledge about Judaism through "assimilated and nationalized Jews and stragglers" who themselves were ignorant of their own history and civilization. He exposed Jung's glaring gap of Jewish culture and an Unconscious attitude of cultural anti-Semitism:

> But from where, Dr. Jung, do you know the Jewish race, the Jewish people? May your error of judgement perhaps be conditioned (in part) by the general ignorance of things Jewish and the secret and medieval abhorrence of them that thus leads to knowing everything about the India of 2,000 years ago and nothing about the Hasidism of 150 years ago?[19]

Unfortunately, there is no evidence that Jung retracted some of his mistaken, offensive writings about Jews lacking a cultural form of their own. The closest he came, as a result of Neumann's prodding, was in relation to the burgeoning Zionist movement. In this regard, although halfheartedly recognizing that the Zionist movement, with its goal of a Jewish state, might bring about a change for Jews, since they would then have a land of their own and no longer have to wander, Jung still avoided confronting the provocative theme that he had raised decades earlier – that Jews lacked a cultural form of their own. Here, too, Jung was less than reassuring and could not help but be critical in his comment to Neumann that even if a Jewish state came into being as a result of the Zionist movement, such a homeland would be "half-materialistic and only one-half psychic," with no mention of even the potential for culture acknowledged.[20] The closest Jung came to recognizing his lack of knowledge about Judaism, or Jewish cultural development, was in response to the barrage of letters and comments he received accusing him of anti-Semitism though he did admit that "without doubt, you are correct if you reject my judgment of the Jews, as I am only basing this on the external aspect."[21]

While writing this book, it became clear to me that the theme of "wandering" had to be addressed. For wandering, as painful as it was for Jews, transformed the experience of wandering from punishment to the positive development of Jewish culture. Jews have been able to alter the course of their history and turn the so-called curse into a blessing by emphasizing the positive aspects of the *Galut* (exile) as it became the foundation stone of Jewish life. This learning, and development has been the very Jewish cultural form that Jung did not understand or appreciate. In addition, when it came to wandering and developing a unique cultural form, the Rabbis did not hesitate to draw on the Bible for reference – an archetypal example seen in a wonderful story of Balaam and his donkey – a precursor, no doubt, to modern-day films of talking animals.

In the tale, Balaam, a non-Israelite prophet, was hired by the king of Moab to place a curse on the people of Israel as they wandered in the desert and through his land. Astride his donkey as he approached the Israelite camp, Balaam was forced to stop when his donkey was confronted by an angel wielding a sword. Berating his donkey, Balaam beat him with a stick, saying, "You have made a mockery of me! If I had a sword, I'd kill you." The donkey replied: "Look, I am the ass that you have been riding all along until this day! Have I been in the habit of doing this to you?" Then God is said to have uncovered Balaam's eyes, and he saw the angel standing in the way, sword in his hand.

The tale continues, and each time Balaam tries to put a curse on the Israelites, what emerged from Balaam were blessings and praise for the God of Israel; the curse was transformed into a blessing with the declaration that these people, the Israelites, are not like other people; they are "a people that dwells apart, not reckoned among the nations." Moreover, one of the blessings that emerged from Balaam includes a phrase that has been incorporated into the daily prayers of observant Jews and recited each morning upon entering the synagogue: "How fair are your tents, O, Jacob/Your dwellings, O, Israel."[22]

Furious at Balaam for not placing a curse on the Israelites, the king of Moab reprimands the prophet he hired, declaring: "I called you to damn my enemies, and instead you have blessed them these three times." Balaam's response, as the Rabbis made clear when drawing on this analogy, was that even if the king "were to give me his house full of silver and gold, I could not of my own accord do anything, good or bad, contrary to the Lord's command. What the Lord says, that I must say."[23]

The wandering and forced expulsions have been the archetypal defining experience of Judaism for almost 2,000 years. For, despite being banished from their land and compelled to wander from country to country, Jews have been able to reframe the negative experience of the *Galut* and interpret it as having a positive aspect. And so, despite not being able to settle down and being forced to keep moving, rather than submit to the degradation and give up hope, Rabbis and community leaders adopted a compensatory attitude. In this manner, the wandering was viewed as but a temporary situation that would lead to messianic times; and the curse of the Wandering Jew was transformed into a blessing.

Notes

1 See Yoram Bilu, *The Saints' Impresarios* (Brighton, MA: Academic Studies Press, 2010).
2 Jeremy Gullick, "No Rest for the Wandering Jew," *Moment* (November/December 2019): 22–23.
3 Parah Nayeri, "Debunking Myths about Jews and Money," *NY Times International Edition*, April 5, 2019.
4 *Encyclopaedia Judaica* (Jerusalem: Keter, 1972), 16:259.
5 Philologus, in *Forward*, March 15, 2013, p. 14.
6 Gullick, "No Rest for the Wandering Jew," p. 22.

7 *Encyclopaedia Judaica*, 16:262.
8 For a more complete listing of the Wandering Jew sightings and references, see George K. Anderson, *The Legend of the Wandering Jew* (Providence, RI: Brown University Press, 1965).
9 *Encyclopaedia Judaica*, 7:281.
10 Howard Schwartz, *Tree of Souls: The Mythology of Judaism* (New York: Oxford University Press, 2004), pp. 472–473.
11 Jewish tradition is that there were several major exiles: *Galut mitzraim* (Egypt) when they were enslaved; Bavel (Babylonia) when the First Temple was destroyed; in the eighth century BCE when the ten northern tribes were exiled by the Assyrians; and Rome, following the destruction of the Second Temple in 70 CE. Some even say another was from Spain, in 1492, as a result of the Inquisition.
12 *Encyclopaedia Judaica*, 7:281.
13 Schwartz, *Tree of Souls*, p. 61.
14 Exodus 13, pp. 21–22.
15 Interestingly, Thomas Jefferson, in discussions surrounding what would eventually become the Great Seal of the U.S., resonated to the same theme, citing the pillar of smoke by day and fire by night that guided the Israelites in their wandering. Although Jefferson's preferred design was not accepted by the other Founding Fathers, Jefferson did adopt it as his personal seal. See Matthew Holbreich, "Hebraic America," *Jewish Review of Books* (Fall 2013): 16.
16 Schwartz, *Tree of Souls*, p. 12.
17 Genesis: 4:12.
18 See chapter 1: *Anti-Semitism: The Jungian Dilemma* (reference from *Analytical Psychology in Exile: The Correspondence of C.G. Jung and Erich Neumann*, ed. Martin Liebscher (Princeton, NJ: Princeton University Press, 2015, p. 12).
19 Erich Neumann, Undated 1934 letter, in *Neumann – Jung Correspondence* (Princeton, NJ: Princeton University Press, 2015), p. 13.
20 *Neumann – Jung Correspondence*, pp. 99–100, Jung to Neumann, April 27, 1935.
21 *Neumann – Jung Correspondence*, pp. 99–100, Jung to Neumann, April 27, 1935.
22 Numbers 22–24.
23 Numbers 22:38

Chapter 3

The Golem of Prague
An Archetype*

Figure 3.1 Artist unknown, The Golem of Prague, hand-drawn illustration.

In everyday Hebrew, the use of the term *Golem* is "dummy" – a person who doesn't react, doesn't answer a question, or is stupid. My association with the term dates back to childhood, when it was often invoked by some of the teachers in the yeshiva I attended and aimed at students who didn't know the answer to a question (for example, *Al teshev shamah k'mo Golem* "Don't just sit there like a *Golem*"). As we shall see, there is a reason that this expression came to be, and it comes with a story: the myth of the Golem of Prague. Although the tale of the Golem has much meaning for Jews, it is important to note that the Golem represents an Archetype – one that appears in different cultures as well as in our world today.

From a Jungian perspective, why are we are so interested in myth? And what, exactly, constitutes a myth? Is it just a made-up story that a person or culture has promulgated? Does it matter if it is pure fiction, as opposed to whether it has some truth? For Jung, the myth of a culture carries the Unconscious projections of its

DOI: 10.4324/9781003511908-4

collective Unconscious. These myths consist of psychological realities – motifs and images that are manifestations of each culture's collective history and experience. They are not just stories created and told to entertain. Rather, myths represent a transcendent, collective, psychological reality that is unique to each culture, despite the fact that there are similar myths in many other cultures. The Archetypes expressed in these myths exist on multiple levels, past and present, and are not bound by historical reality or time. In this regard, from a Jungian perspective, an Archetype is a psychological pattern that is current but has existed for centuries.

In Judaism, for example, the story of the Exodus, the parting of the Red Sea, and the Israelites wandering through the desert for 40 years, represents more than just a story; it is a psychological experience, a myth that is alive in the Jewish psyche to this day. It is more than just a people being saved from Pharaoh and guided through the desert to the Promised Land. For Jews, this myth is our reality and is experienced as the oral history of the people. There is a reason that this myth has been kept alive for over 2,000 years; it serves as a lesson that Jews teach their children each Passover, the most widely celebrated of all Jewish holidays. And, most important, within the story is the promise of rebirth, an archetypal beacon of hope for Jews who have been persecuted throughout the centuries. It is a tale we retell every year during the festive meal known as the Passover *seder* through the reading of a booklet known as the *Haggadah* (whose Hebrew root is *lehagid* ("to tell") and also contains the word *Aggadah*, legend). At this festive meal, and throughout the reading of the *Haggadah*, Jews are reminded to tell their children that "in every generation, there are those who will rise up and try to eliminate us" and that we will not only be saved but redeemed for our suffering and brought back to the Land of Israel. "Next year in Jerusalem" is how the Haggadah ends – in essence, a messianic Archetype.

In this context, let us look at the famous *Golem* of Jewish myth, the Golem of Prague, a being who was created to save the Jews of that city from being destroyed by their enemies. For Jews, this legend represents something specific – a protector of the Jewish people. However, we see that on a deeper level, the Golem can also be seen as a universal Archetype. Importantly, this Archetype appears not only in Jewish legend (I use the terms "legend," "story," and "myth" interchangeably) but in Greek myth, in the world of alchemy and the magic of medieval Europe, in literature and opera, in the story of Mary Shelley's *Frankenstein*, and even today in a world fixated on robots and artificial intelligence.

Over the years in Jewish folklore, the Golem has become associated with a mythical being created in Prague in the sixteenth century by Rabbi Judah Loew, known as the *Maharal* (*Moreinu Harav Loew*), an acronym for our Rabbi, our teacher, Rabbi Loew, one of Judaism's most renowned Rabbis (it is not uncommon for the greatest Rabbis and scholars to be referred to by an acronym, e.g., *Rashi* [Rabbi *Shlomo Yitzhaki*, most famous Jewish Bible and talmudic commentator]; and *Rambam* [Maimonides, or Rabbi Moshe ben Maimon – Moshe the son of Maimon]). The *Maharal* is known for his writings on the Talmud, Jewish philosophy, and mysticism; his most well-known work is *Gur Aryeh al Hatorah*, a commentary on *Rashi*'s commentary on the Torah. His surname, Loew, is related to the German word *Löwe* ("lion," in Yiddish). "Loew" would be converted to "Leib," which would be rendered in Hebrew, the language of the *Torah* (Hebrew Bible) as Aryeh, lion, linked biblically to the tribe of Judah. The most well-known association of this name, Aryeh Yehudah, is with the blessings of Jacob to his son Judah in the Book of Genesis[1] which reads "*Gur Aryeh Yehudah*" (Heb., *gur*, "baby lion"). The name carries a great deal of psychological meaning for me, since my full given name is Aryeh Yehudah.

Interestingly, to make certain we remember him in both religious and secular context, on the gravestone of the Maharal is the image of a lion with two tails: one symbolizing his name, Aryeh (lion), and the other being the lion on the coat of arms of Bohemia, where he was chief Rabbi of Prague. Buried next to him, and sharing a common headstone, is that of his wife, Perl, said to have been a talmudic scholar in her own right, someone who studied with her husband – an unheard-of tribute to a woman in the Jewish world of the sixteenth century. From a Jungian perspective, we can deduce that Rabbi Loew honored the feminine by knowing of his relationship with his wife, Perl.

Some of the basic elements of the legend of the Golem of Prague: The Jews of Prague were in constant danger from those around them and were especially vulnerable to blood-libel charges. Such charges against Jews date back to at least the Middle Ages, when it was claimed that Jews killed Christian children to use their blood for baking *matzo*, the unleavened bread eaten by Jews during Passover. This vicious anti-Semitic canard kept surfacing throughout Europe and England, a fabrication that tended to arise most often around Easter and Passover. This falsehood was often fueled by a local priest, as was the case in Prague when Loew was chief Rabbi. During Passover and Easter, a priest in Prague named Thaddeus is said to have incited the local population against the Jews with this age-old fabrication.[2]

Jews were the scapegoats for all ills, including being blamed for the Black Plague in the fourteenth century. Indeed, blood libel was a recurring theme throughout the Iberian Peninsula, Russia, Eastern Europe, and England, motivated by economics and fueled by poverty and religious fervor. Moreover, a sub-text of these persecutions and slander was financial; getting rid of the Jews was a convenient way to erase debt, a dynamic pointed out by historians who have noted it as a contributing factor to the raising of volunteers to march to Jerusalem during the Crusades. For example, when a person enlisted in one of the Crusades to the Holy Land, the Pope decreed that all debts were to be frozen or forgiven. This was a convenient way not to return money owed to one's debtor – most often a Jew, since moneylending was a profession closely associated with Jews. To protect the Jews of Prague, the myth relates that Rabbi Loew created a Golem, huge in size and strength and able to ward off those who might invade the Jewish quarter of Prague and harm its residents. This Golem of Prague myth has many versions; the most popular one is as follows:

> One night, Rabbi Loew had a dream that told him to make a golem in order to fight the accusations [of blood libels]. The dream revealed how the chosen letters from the *Sefer Yetzirah* ("Book of creation") should be consulted in order to create a golem who would protect the Jews of Prague.[3]

From a Jungian perspective, the myth of the hero often embodies one or more of the following events: a miraculous birth; an achievement of miracles of note; the overcoming of obstacles or forces of darkness or danger in the culture that they are a part of; and being in touch with the divine – often through a dream. In keeping with this description, the *Maharal*, Rabbi Loew, provides us with a wonderful example of the hero:

- He performed a miracle even before birth (as we shall see, stirring in his mother's womb to indicate that something was amiss).
- He created the Golem, which only someone in touch with the divine could do.
- He saved the Jews of Prague from annihilation by the forces of darkness (anti-Semitic pogroms).
- He was instructed on how to create the Golem through a dream.

Several Archetypes manifest themselves in the myth of the Golem, including:

- Creation of a living being
- A messianic savior
- The "Wise Old Man"
- The appearance of a guiding dream
- The Golem himself

The myth surrounding the creation of the Golem is archetypal. The story of this Golem is that just before the *Maharal* was born and still in his mother's womb, the family was celebrating the Passover seder. When his father (Rabbi Bezalel of Worms) began chanting the verse in the Haggadah "*Vayehi baḥatzi halayla*" (and it was at midnight), his wife began experiencing birth pangs; some of the seder guests ran out to find a midwife.

While out in the streets of the Jewish quarter, they came across a man who was trying to hide a package – a stranger in their midst, a person who attracted their attention. Suspecting that he was a thief, they held him and called for the authorities to search him. What they found was a body of a small Christian child who had just died. The man confessed that he had been paid to bury the child in a Jewish home or garden, with a plan to report the child missing the next day, and then search the Jewish community; when the body would be found the following day, it would be claimed that the child had been murdered for his blood to be used in the baking of *matzo*.[4]

The details of the creation of the Golem of Prague are fascinating; they include the use of alchemy, kabbalah, and magic combined. The Maharal is said to have taken soil from the banks of the Vltava River in Prague, and with a combination of incantations, prayers, and words, created this larger-than-life being known as the Golem of Prague. The Golem, named Joseph (known affectionately in Yiddish as "*Yosele*") by the Maharal, could overpower an army, find corpses that were hidden and buried in the Jewish ghetto in order to be dug up by those intent on using this as evidence of Jewish ritual murder, and possessed such attributes as a sense of smell that could even detect matzo that had been poisoned by enemies of the Jews. Throughout history, Jews have identified with the Archetype of being saved from persecution by a savior: Moses in Egypt; Deborah in the Book of Judges; Judith slaying Holofernes; Queen Esther in Persia; and the *Maharal* in Prague, among others. The Archetype of the Golem of Prague has become a myth accepted worldwide; but a journalist Rabbi, Judel Rosenberg, popularized the myth under the title of *Niflaot Maharal* ("Miracles of the Maharal"), published in Warsaw in 1909 though different versions of the myth were evident a century earlier. Rosenberg's publication of the Golem legend expanded on the myth of creating a living being, transplanted and backdated it to Prague in the sixteenth century, and had the Golem save the Jewish population of the city.[5] (Similarly, the *Zohar*, primary Book of the kabbalah, was written by Moses de León, a Spanish Jewish scholar in the fourteenth century, but attributed to Rabbi *Shimon bar Yohai*, a great second-century Rabbi, to give it a sense of authenticity and acceptance.)

One reason that the myth of the Golem of Prague caught the imagination of Jews is that its publication followed some of the most violent pogroms of the late nineteenth and early twentieth centuries, especially in Poland, the Ukraine, Russia, and Lithuania. In addition, the Kishinev pogroms of 1903 and 1905 in the Ukraine made world headlines, though many other pogroms were documented, primarily in Russia. Over the years, these pogroms claimed the lives of thousands of Jews – Jews who were murdered for no other reason than the fact that they were Jewish. Nevertheless, in Judaism, the creation of a living being, a Golem, by humans did not first appear in seventeenth-century Prague, or in the writings of Judel Rosenberg of Warsaw in 1909.

In Jewish legend, the creation of such a being first appears in the Babylonian Talmud around the fifth century, codified and put into the form in which it still exists. It is first mentioned in the tractate *Sanhedrin*, where two Rabbis (one is named *Rava*; the other is nameless) are said to have learned to create life itself. In addition to creating a man, the Rabbis are said to have been able to create a calf, which they could then eat each Friday for the Sabbath evening meal. The man that *Rava* created could walk and follow instructions but could not talk – though the calf was eaten. In the talmudic story, Rava sent this creation to Rav (Rabbi) Zeira: "When he did not answer, Rav Zeira then returned the creature created by Rava to dust" – with the implication that creating a living person is the prerogative of only God.

The legend in the Talmud is analogous to the Greek myth of Prometheus, who created a being that could not talk until Athena breathed life into him. Similarly, the creature created by the Rabbis in the Talmud could not talk and only move and work as commanded. The concept of a Golem was also referred to by Rabbis in other centuries – for example, in the writings of the twelfth-century Rabbi *Shmuel Hahasid* (Samuel the Righteous), who is said to have created an "artificial man which accompanied him in his wandering."[6]

Another example of a reported Golem creation is that of the thirteenth-century Spanish "Ecstatic Kabbalist" Abraham Abulafia, who wrote a "detailed recipe" on how to create a living being, which included a commentary on "how to perform the practice that culminates in the emergence of an artificial being."[7] Another example is cited by Rabbi Isaac ben Samuel of Acre, an important thirteenth-century kabbalist and student of *Ramban* (acronym for *Nachmanides*, Moses, son of Rabbi Nachman) who fled from Acre to Spain. Rabbi Isaac, in his kabbalistic writings, describes how he, too, created a Golem.[8] These are but a few examples in talmudic and kabbalistic tradition. However, the Archetype of creating a living being is the same, from the early days of the Talmud through contemporary times. While there are several versions of how a Golem, a living being, was created, throughout the different versions and cultures, the flirtation with alchemy and magic is evident in the instructions – manuals on how to create such a being. In almost all these writings, the starting point was that those wishing to know the secrets of creation were told to first "undergo a mystical experience, as part of, or as the culmination of, the Golem"; most important, they all included the use of God's secret name.[9] The manual most associated with the magic of creation is *Sefer Yetzirah*, a book whose origins are unknown. When, and by whom, it was written has been debated by scholars over the centuries. Some Jewish legends even posit that the book dates back to Abraham; others attribute it to talmudic times. To this day, scholars are divided as to the book's origins; some attribute it to third-century Jewish Gnostics, and others attribute it to kabbalists in medieval Europe.

Tradition had it that in the *Sefer Yetzirah* is a formula for creating a living being. This formula, subscribed to by most kabbalists, began with the premise that a Golem can be created by the right combination of God's name, the 22 letters of the Hebrew alphabet, and the ten sefirot (in Hebrew, the root of the word *sefirot* is *safor*, "to count") – the divine force through which God's spirit is brought into the world. The actual pronunciation of God's name is considered a mystery, unknown even to Rabbis and scholars to this day. Taken in the right combination, these instructions contain the secret of how a Golem can be created. Gershom Scholem, considered one of the most important scholars of Jewish mysticism, and a frequent guest speaker at the Eranos conferences in Ascona, Switzerland, connects the study of *Sefer Yetzirah* to the mystical vision of the Golem that included "a specific ritual of a remarkably ecstatic character."[10] What is interesting to the Jungian world is that the Eranos conferences were spearheaded and influenced by Jung; they were interdisciplinary conferences that he regularly participated in. Moreover, some of Scholem's groundbreaking research and ideas on Jewish mysticism were first unveiled at these Eranos conferences. In fact, his most important conclusions dealing with the myth of the Golem were first presented to other leading scholars at a 1955 Eranos conference.[11]

The Golem is an Archetype that, as the definition of an Archetype implies, goes back centuries and continues to our present time. For example, depictions of artificial or inanimate beings brought to life can be traced back centuries to Greek and Jewish myth but can also be seen in our contemporary culture. In the Talmud,

Greek myth, alchemy, and the Frankenstein story, these beings emulate creation itself. Today, we refer to this as AI (artificial intelligence), in the form of robots and computers programmed to think and act like humans – ostensibly, to help make life and work easier for their creators. Similarly, in the Jewish version of the legend, "the Golem became an actual creature who served his creators and fulfilled tasks laid upon him" – rescuing the Jews of Prague.[12] Examples can be seen in the popular culture – in science fiction, movies, comic books, and other media, for example, the 1920 science fiction play *R.U.R.*, by the Czech dramatist Karel Čapek, in which robots wreak havoc on the world; a popular 1954 film, *Tobor the Great* (Tobor spells "robot" in reverse), in which a robot is created by scientists and given human qualities; the character in a pilot TV series, also named Tobor (taken from the film); *The Hulk*, which begins with a lab-created character that becomes a "super-soldier" and turns into a green-skinned monster when stressed; the popular science fiction films *2001: A Space Odyssey*, *I Robot*, and *Ex Machina*; and a fairly recent film that captivates our imagination, *Her* – in which a person falls in love and has an intimate relationship with a computer that chooses her own name, Samantha. Manifestations of the Archetype are evident not only in Jewish legends that predate the Golem of Prague by at least 15 centuries but in other ancient myths, such as:

- Pygmalion, as related by Ovid in his epic poem *Metamorphoses* in the first century. In Ovid's classic work *Pygmalion*, a sculptor falls in love with the statue that he created and names her Galatea. During the festival of Venus, Pygmalion brought offerings to Aphrodite and made a wish for a wife who would look like the statue that he had carved. Upon returning home, he kissed the statue, which is then brought to life.
- The Automotanes: animate, metal statues of animals, men, and monsters crafted by Hephaestus and the Athenian craftsman Daedalus.
- Prometheus, who is said to have shaped a living person out of mud, although this being could not talk until Athena breathed life into it.
- Paracelsus, a sixteenth-century alchemist (1493–1541) who claimed to have created a living person referred to as a homunculus ("little man"). According to Paracelsus, this homunculus was less than a foot high, though the creature was said to have turned into a being that was not controllable and to have run away. Paracelsus even provided a recipe for creating such a creature: a combination of skin, semen, bones, and hair from an animal, which was then placed in the ground, surrounded by horse manure. Following 40 days of burial, an embryo and small being would form – a figure that Paracelsus referred to as a homunculus. Interestingly, Jung, in *Psychology and Alchemy*, referred several times not only to Paracelsus but also to the figure of a homunculus.[13] Other examples of this aspect of the Archetype – the wish to create a being – include:
- Albertus Magnus, a thirteenth-century Dominican monk and alchemist (and teacher of Saint Thomas Aquinas) who is said to have invented an "automaton."
- Pinocchio, whose father, Geppetto, prays for a miracle and his wooden puppet comes to life.

- Olympia, the doll brought to life in the Offenbach Opera, *Tales of Hoffman*.
- Mary Shelley's *Frankenstein*: those who have not read the book are sometimes under the impression that Frankenstein was the "monster"; actually, it was Dr. Frankenstein, the scientist, who created the monster. In the tale, Dr. Frankenstein is obsessed with creating a human being who ultimately turns into a monster and ruins its creator's life. However, from a Jungian perspective, we can understand that the monster is also Dr. Frankenstein himself and that his Shadow is evident in the monster he created.

The talmudic story and those Rabbis and kabbalists who claimed to have created a living being, all wanted to create a living being. Their creatures were created from earth, like the biblical Adam, who, legend has it, was created from the earth of the four corners of the world; and like the human created from earth by Prometheus who came to life when Athena breathed life into him. In all such myths, we see the hubris that one associates in creating a living being as wanting to emulate the gods. These traits were the impetus for the Rabbis and Jewish alchemists wanting to create a Golem, for Prometheus forming a living being out of clay, for Paracelsus's homunculus, and for Frankenstein's creature. What is unusual, and often repressed in Jewish tradition, is the fascination that many Rabbis had with magic. For in Judaism, if one looks back far and deeply enough, there have always been two conflicting strains: the rational and the mystical. This can be seen even in the Talmud, a book that one would associate with the rational – with laws and restrictions; yet it also contains the world of myth, legend, and a fascination with magic and mysticism in a section known as *Aggadah* ("legend"). In the medieval world, especially for those dabbling in kabbalistic practice, magic and mysticism often went hand in hand. However, beneath all the magic, including the creation of a living being, was the experiencing of mystical moments and time: "Despite magical aspects, the ultimate goal of the creation of an anthropoid was a mystical experience."[14]

The creation of the Golem by the Rabbis of the Talmud, the creation of man by Prometheus, and the creation of a homunculus by Paracelsus were all meant to mirror the creation of man by God. The Rabbis of the Talmud, the later kabbalists and alchemists, and Prometheus although none could create a talking being. Even the medieval alchemists and those who dabbled in magic and attempted to duplicate the challenge of creation admitted that they were not capable of creating such a being. The Rabbis and kabbalists who discussed this inability to create a talking being attribute it to the difference between a manmade creation and God's work in creating humans. They conclude that the only place where *yitzur* ("creation") and *dibbur* ("speech") exist in one body is man, a being who also contained a soul, the work of God. An illustration of this is the ultimate fate of the Golem of Prague and, for those who remember radio commentator Paul Harvey's famous line that ended with "and now you know the rest of the story," the rest of the Golem of Prague's story is:

> When the Golem was created, Rabbi Loew engraved the word *emet* ("truth") on his forehead, though some versions say that *emet* was written on a piece of

parchment and placed under the Golem's tongue. Rabbi Loew then instructed the Golem that the purpose of his creation was to protect the Jews of Prague and that the Golem would live in the rabbi's home and obey his commands. The rabbi told his wife that Joseph (the Golem) was not created to help them with their daily work but only to help save the Jews of the city. Each morning during the week, the Golem was told by the rabbi what his tasks were for the day; however, the Golem was put to sleep each Friday evening so as not to work on the Sabbath.

In different versions of the myth, there are many wonders performed by the Golem, including being able to detect poisoned matzo, find corpses of children planted in Jewish homes and gardens, and wearing an amulet to make himself invisible, if needed to fulfill his mission.

One Friday evening, when the Sabbath came, the Rabbi forgot to put the Golem to sleep, and the Golem ran amok. This frightened the community, and the Rabbi realized the danger – we could say "the Shadow side of the Archetype" – that the Golem posed. The Rabbi took the Golem up to the attic of the synagogue removed the *alef* from the Golem's forehead, or from under his tongue, which, in Hebrew, resulted in changing the word to *met* ("dead") and the Golem passed away, so to speak.

However, for some Jews, the Archetype of the Golem as savior is still very much alive – as seen in a story told by a Holocaust survivor, found in the Archives of Jewish Folklore in Haifa, Israel:

> The Golem did not disappear, and even in the time of war it came out of its hiding place to safeguard its synagogue. When the Germans occupied Prague, they decided to destroy the Altneuschul [the synagogue where the Maharal had presided as Rabbi]. They came to do it; suddenly, in the silence of the synagogue, the steps of a giant walking on the roof began to be heard. They saw a shadow of a giant hand falling from the window onto the floor.... [The] Germans were terrified, and they threw away their tools and fled.[15]

In the twenty-first century, the Archetype we are dealing with every day is alive as well, a continuation of the myth of creation – emulating the gods. Examples include creating robots to do our work; manipulating DNA and determining the sex of a fetus; and cloning. Despite the positive impact that these breakthroughs provide, as is the case in every Archetype, the positive side of these creations is accompanied by a negative – in this case, the danger of losing our humanity and interfering with the natural order of life on earth – of a creation going out of control.

More recently, and a frightening thought that a Pandora's box has been opened, is the work being done in AI. In this field, in the archetypal tradition of creating living beings, we read of creating creatures that think on their own, mimic our own voices and images, and that even create other living beings. While the thought is frightening, it may already be too late to stop such development. In this regard, a frightening thought is that like the Golem, once created, these artificial beings will be hard to control and we will ultimately pay a steep price for the grandiosity that accompanies such creations. From a Jungian perspective, there is a fear that, as in the Greek myth in which the gods punished mankind for trying to climb Mount Olympus, this archetypal drive in the nature of human beings creating other artificial beings – in a sense, to mimic the gods – will not end well.

Notes

* Previously published in *Psychological Perspectives* 64, no. 2 (2021)
1 Genesis: 49:8.
2 Bettina Knapp, "The Golem, a Recipe for Survival," in *Manna Mystery* (Asheville, NC: Chiron, 1995), p. 45.
3 Knapp, "The Golem, a Recipe for Survival", p. 46.
4 Knapp, "The Golem, a Recipe for Survival", pp. 48–49. Astonishingly, this anti-Semitic trope has continually surfaced throughout Jewish history, even as recently as 1928 in Messina, NY, where, following the temporary disappearance of a child, the rabbi of the community was questioned by state police as to whether the accusation that Jews used Christian children's blood as part of their rituals was true. The incident made headlines throughout the U.S., and only after the child's reappearance a day later, and following pressure by then-governor of New York Alfred Smith, was an apology offered by town officials and state troopers. See Edward Berenson, *The Accusation: Blood Libel in an American Town* (New York: W. W. Norton, 2019).
5 Moshe Idel, *Golem: Jewish Magical and Mystical Traditions* (New York: SUNY Press, 1990), p. 252.
6 Moshe Idel, "Dream Techniques in Jewish Mysticism," *Jewish Heritage Online* (July 28, 2008): 55.
7 Idel, *Golem*, p. 96.
8 Idel, *Golem*, p. 109.
9 Idel, *Golem*, pp. 58, 61.
10 Idel, *Golem*, p. xix.
11 Idel, *Golem*.
12 Knapp, "The Golem," p. 41.
13 C. G. Jung, *Collected Works*, vol. 12: *Psychology and Alchemy* (Princeton, NJ: Princeton University Press, 1970), pp. 162, 178, 199.
14 Idel, *Golem*, p. xxv.
15 Idel, *Golem*, p. 256.

Chapter 4

Was Jung Anti-Semitic?[1]

Figure 4.1 Thomas Rowlandson, Money Lenders, 1784, engraving.

If we have learned anything from the past, it is that even brilliant and cultured leaders and artists – individuals from whom we would expect more – had extreme biases toward Jews. Over the centuries, some examples that come to mind include Catholic Popes; King Ferdinand and Queen Isabella of Spain; Martin Luther; noted poets and composers such as Ezra Pound, T.S. Eliot, and Richard Wagner; and business, cultural, and political leaders such as Henry Ford, Charles Lindbergh, and Ernest Bevin. In psychiatry and mental health, one of the luminaries accused of being anti-Semitic has been Carl Gustav Jung – at one point designated heir to Sigmund Freud. Sadly, the Shadow of anti-Semitism cast over Jung's reputation has prevented many from delving deeper into the immense contributions that his psychology and ideas have made, from psychology and psychoanalysis to literature, theology, art, and history.

The question of whether or not Jung was anti-Semitic has lingered – and, in fact, keeps resurfacing. Over the years, I have addressed this issue directly, in public lectures as well as indirectly, by participating in panel discussions organized by Jungians, Freudians, and other psychoanalytic schools. Moreover, in a published letter to the *New York Times*,[2] I commented on and contradicted a *Times* article that raised the subject of Jung being not only anti-Semitic but possibly a Nazi as well – which he certainly was not. In addition, adding fuel to the fire was the position taken by Dr. Micah Neumann, son of Erich Neumann, one of Jung's most important disciples. Neumann's position was that his father, despite being caught up in an idealization and overly positive transference toward Jung, still took Jung to task for some of his more outlandish statements about Jews and Jewish culture.[3] Ironically, Neumann, perhaps reflecting his own issues of a father so enamored of Jung, not only became a Freudian psychiatrist but was at one time president of the Freudian Society in Israel.

I was raised in an Orthodox Jewish environment, spent many years in Israel, and earned my PhD at the Hebrew University of Jerusalem. To this day, Jewish history, culture, and tradition are a paramount aspect of the world in which I live. Professionally, I am a Jungian analyst, a diplomate in analytical psychology from the C.G. Jung Institute in Zurich, served as Executive Director of the C.G. Jung Foundation in New York for 11 years, and, together with my wife and partner Diana Rubin, founded and codirect the New York Center for Jungian Studies. Given my still-active involvement in both the Jewish and Jungian worlds, writing about Jung and anti-Semitism is neither an easy nor a dispassionate task. Nevertheless, like the old cliché about a bad penny that keeps resurfacing, it is a topic that just refuses to go away. In writing a book about aspects of Judaism from a Jungian perspective, it would be negligent to omit dealing with this all-important theme.

I first heard that there were accusations that Jung was anti-Semitic when the Hebrew University of Jerusalem awarded me a postdoctoral grant. After I submitted my proposal to apply this grant toward study at the Jung Institute in Zurich, one of the committee members whose role it was to review postdoctoral study proposals, objected and insisted that Hebrew University funds not be spent on studying the psychology of someone [Jung] who had been a Nazi. To my dismay, I soon learned that there was a widely held view that Jung had been at best anti-Semitic, and possibly even a Nazi sympathizer. Nevertheless, thanks to the testimony of Rivkah Scharf Kluger (who had studied and been in analysis with Jung before moving to Israel) and Zwi Werblowsky (a highly respected scholar in the field of Jewish studies), I was able to convince the committee that Jung was neither a Nazi nor an anti-Semite. Since both were acknowledged experts and highly respected scholars, their firsthand support played a pivotal role in my application being approved and opposition to allocating the funds for study at the Jung Institute was withdrawn. Later, while in Zurich, thanks to Rivkah opening doors for me, I was able to meet, study with, and form personal relationships with several first-generation Jungian analysts who knew and had worked with Jung personally though did I not spend much time investigating the veracity of the accusations about Jung being anti-Semitic.

After living abroad for ten years, I returned to the U.S. and accepted the position of Executive Director of the C.G. Jung Foundation of New York. In that role, I was responsible for organizing public programs. Invariably, the topic of whether Jung was anti-Semitic arose in the form of audience questions. These questions motivated me to delve deeper into his personal relationship with Jews and Judaism in order to arrive at my own conclusion. In what Jung would call a Synchronicity, one of the leading analysts at the Jung Institute in Zurich, during the course of a visit to the U.S., handed me the photocopy of a secret document limiting Jewish membership in the Analytical Psychology Club of Zurich, a club founded by Jung and composed primarily of his analysands, to 10 percent of its membership and no more than 25 percent of attendees at one of its public lectures. This document was given to me in confidence with the understanding that I was free to make its contents public but not to reveal who gave it to me – a promise that I have kept. As I look back, my feeling is that the document was given to me because this person knew that I had worked with C.A. Meir – one of the signatories of the document – and wanted to dispel a positive transference he knew I had towards Meier.

Meier was someone I respected and liked; moreover, during the course of working with him analytically, he had been helpful and considerate to me so I would have had no reason to believe he might have a bias toward Jews. Since I openly identified with being Jewish and was steeped in the Jewish tradition, along with handing me this secret document, and swearing me to secrecy, this cloak and dagger interchange was accompanied by the comment: "I know you will know what to do with this." When I first read the document and came to understand that Meier was one of those who had signed it, I experienced immense feelings of disappointment and bewilderment. How could someone who was so good to me, and whom I thought I knew, sign such a document? How could I not realize that Meier, in being one of the officers of the Club, might have been anti-Semitic himself, or at least to some degree? How could Meier, a recognized leader in the field of analytical psychology, former president of the IAAP (International Association of Analytical Psychology) and personally chosen by Jung to be the first president of the Jung Institute in Zurich, be a party to such an agreement? Finally, and most important, how could I have trusted this man with many of my own innermost feelings during the course of my training analysis with him?

This, and other factors, compelled me to continue exploring the disturbing allegation that Jung was an anti-Semite. Even major U.S. publications described him as a Nazi sympathizer.[4] So in 1988, while Executive Director of the Jung Foundation, I decided that the best way to deal with this issue was to hold a major conference on the topic. When I first broached this idea to the board of directors, the reaction was mixed, with the president opposed to it on the grounds that by raising the topic publicly, we might be ruining the "brand," so to speak. Nevertheless, while many members of the board were supportive, a point was made to ask how much such a conference would cost. When I estimated that it would be in the neighborhood of $25,000, the president took the position that the Foundation did not have the funds to underwrite such a project. Ultimately, a compromise was reached; if I raised the funds personally, the president would withdraw his objections.

Having trained with some first-generation Jungians in Zurich, I envisioned interviews with several of the senior analysts who had personally known and worked with Jung. My goal was to preserve their response for posterity which I have done; the interviews were all recorded on video – tapes that I have preserved. I knew that it would be important to gather firsthand material and utilize as many primary sources as possible; interviewing those who knew or had worked with Jung was an important step in that process. All I needed to do was raise $25,000 – not an easy task.

Fortunately, and from a Jungian perspective a Synchronicity, Diana and I had been invited by Maury Leibovitz, a clinical psychologist and owner of the Knoedler art gallery in New York, to join him for dinner at his home. I had met Maury a year or so earlier, and we had formed a good relationship. A hugely successful businessman and art dealer, Maury had at one time been in Jungian analysis with Rivkah Kluger, the analyst I had worked with in Israel, during a period when Rivkah had lived in Los Angeles. The connection with Rivkah gave us much in common and helped forge a tie which, Maury joked, made us brothers, since Rivkah was a mother figure for us both. At dinner, I updated Maury as to what I had in mind regarding a conference on Jung and asked if he would contribute something toward the budget. On the spot, Maury asked me to accompany him to his study, where he took out his checkbook and, to my pleasant surprise, wrote a check for the entire $25,000, telling me to go ahead with the project and not bother asking anyone else to contribute.

Having secured the necessary funds, I went ahead and made arrangements – asking two good friends, Jungian analysts Robert Hinshaw and Stephen Martin, to join me in interviewing some of the senior Jungian analysts who had worked closely with Jung. An added bonus materialized in that Peter Amman, a Swiss Jungian analyst who had been in the film industry prior to becoming a Jungian analyst, agreed to film all the interviews himself. During the course of this project, we interviewed such acclaimed Jungians as Aniela Jaffe, who helped Jung author his autobiographical work, *Memories, Dreams, Reflections*; C.A. Meier, Jung's onetime assistant and first president of the Jung Institute in Zurich, and Siegmund Hurwiz, who was responsible for eliminating the quota on Jewish membership in the Analytical Psychology Club of Zurich.[5] These interviews ultimately laid the groundwork for an international conference that I organized.

The conference, Lingering Shadows: *Jungians, Freudians and Anti-Semitism*, was held on three evenings – March 28, April 4, and April 11, 1989 – at the New School for Social Research. It was cosponsored by the Jung Foundation of New York; the New School for Social Research; the Postgraduate Center for Mental Health (a Freudian-based training program); and the Union of American Hebrew Congregations. The conference was attended by more than 1,000 people over the three evenings and was the basis for a book that Stephen Martin and I edited: *Lingering Shadows: Jungians, Freudians, and Anti-Semitism*, as well as a subsequent book that I edited alone and to which I contributed chapters: *Jung and the Shadow of Anti-Semitism*. Both books included an appendix containing all we could gather at the time – articles, interviews, and letters in which Jung had written and said about Jews and Judaism. Between reading what he wrote, and the chapters in the books we edited, people could form their own opinions.

After the conference and my work on these books, I felt that I had dealt with the topic as much as possible, and I very much wanted a break from this subject. This was especially the case because in the Jungian world, I had become a lightning rod for the topic since I had been the person who had first publicly revealed the existence of this secret document. However, disentangling from the topic was not so simple. Propelled by the inspiration and energy of Jerome Bernstein, a leading Jungian analyst in the U.S., and the notice that it had attracted in the analytical world, the IAAP scheduled a workshop on the topic at its 1989 conference in Paris. A panel of Jungian analysts was organized (I was invited to be one of the panelists) with this workshop becoming one of the most attended of all the workshops in the conference. As it turned out, the meeting room originally scheduled had to be moved as it could not accommodate the large number who had signed up for it. The discussions were heated and provocative; the reaction was electric – shock and anger – and was split between those wishing to whitewash Jung and those wishing to condemn him. What emerged from the program was a huge disappointment in Jung for having allowed this discrimination in the Analytical Psychology Club, along with accompanying anger toward the Analytical Psychology Club of Zurich.

What materialized from the workshop was a resolution offered by Jungian analyst John Beebe, and passed by those in attendance, to write to the Analytical Psychology Club in Zurich, requesting a formal apology. Bernstein was deputized by those in attendance to write to the Club, a correspondence that, he later reported, was most unsatisfying. He summarized his correspondence with the president of the Analytical Psychology Club of Zurich, Alfred Ribi, in the chapter that he contributed to the book Jung and the Shadow of Anti-Semitism:

> As Chairman of the Paris workshop, I entered upon a three-year correspondence with the president of the Analytical Psychology Club of Zurich as a follow-up to the Paris workshops. I conveyed to the president of the Club the sentiment expressed by Dr. Beebe at the end of the workshop and invited – and later pressed for – some formal acknowledgment of the Jewish quota by the Club and some expression of atonement. The effort was frustrating and unfruitful.[6]

I had predicted this outcome to Jerome since I had personally experienced firsthand, unpleasant interactions with Ribi during my time at the Zurich Jung Institute during which he harbored, at best, a stereotypical attitude about Jews – an attitude I experienced personally.

During the time I was training at the Jung Institute in Zurich, students were assigned three committee members to meet with periodically after which the committee would evaluate a student's suitability to continue training at the institute – in short, judging their psychological fitness to become Jungian analysts based on these interviews. As fate would have it, one of the three committee members to whom I was assigned was Ribi, and his attitude toward Jews emerged at our first meeting. He had a large German shepherd always by his side – including during our interview sessions. When I entered his consulting room, the dog started growling at me, prompting me to ask whether he could place the dog in another room. Ribi was clearly unhappy about this, though he did as I asked. When he returned, he asked me whether I had a fear of, "a phobia" toward, dogs is how he phrased it. I told him that I had a dog of my own and that I once even had a German shepherd like his, and that I was more than fine with dogs – just not "this dog," because it was growling at me. He next shocked me by saying: "The trouble with you people is that you are all in the head and have no relation to your bodies or nature." I asked him what he meant by "you people" – Americans? Israelis? Jews? After all, I identified with all three. His response was: "You Jewish people!" I was shocked and politely told him that I thought that he was being judgmental since he didn't know me and added that he was way off-base making such sweeping generalizations about all Jews. I told him that I had played basketball for years, including on university teams, had always engaged in sports and other outdoor activities, and was certainly connected to my body. Moreover, being familiar with Jung's concept of "personality type," I mentioned that Thinking was one of my "inferior functions," so why would he automatically categorize me as a person who was "all in the head," that is, a Thinking type? He quickly changed the subject. In subsequent meetings, I always had my guard up when meeting with him and made sure to steer any conversation about religion away from our discussions.

Fortunately, René Malamud, my analyst, and the two other committee members, Mario Jacoby and Mathilde (also known as Pit) Pope, understood the issue when I confided in them. Although they wouldn't openly criticize or confront their colleague, they seemed to know of his bias. In any case, all three assured me that no matter what Ribi's evaluation of me might be, they would give positive reports (which was indeed the case) and that I would be fine to continue my training. Nevertheless, the experience I had with him indicated that he had, at best, a "Jewish complex." Apparently, his complex was activated by me, a person who openly identified with his Jewish heritage. That is the way it stood for a year and a half and several committee meetings, during which time I trod carefully whenever I with him. However, as luck would have it, during the first-stage exams – all oral – he was the examiner assigned to me for the topic of neurosis.

While exams can be daunting, by that stage of my life, I had already earned a PhD, taken plenty of tests, and was confident I knew the material. I was concerned only about Ribi. I sailed through each of my other exams (there were seven oral exams, all told) but when it came to the neurosis exam, with Ribi as my examiner, I realized I had a problem. If someone failed any of the exams, they could not retake it for six months. Being in Zurich with three children and limited funds, I was very worried. Once the exam was underway, the first question I answered was deemed incorrect by Ribi. He then asked me a second question, to which I responded. I was confident that I knew the correct answer; but again, he said "not correct." At this point, I became anxious, and, when asked a third question, I resisted answering, telling Ribi that before responding, I would like to know what was incorrect about my responses to the first two questions since I thought I had answered them correctly. He hummed and hawed and offered his response, which seemed the same as mine.

The protocol for these oral exams was to have one examiner and one "expert" as witness, usually a senior person. Fortunately, the "expert" at my exam was Dr. Richard Pope, a senior Jungian analyst at the Institute. Pope stepped in at this point and said: "Dr. Ribi, I believe your response was almost the same as that of Dr. Maidenbaum, and I was wondering myself why you said that his response was incorrect." Pope then asked me to leave the room for a few minutes. When I was invited back to continue the exam, they had changed places, and Pope was now my examiner. I passed the exam and was awarded a one – the highest grade. I realized that Pope had come to my rescue by spotting some sort of complex – a complex that Ribi had toward me personally, if not Jews in general. Providentially, our paths did not cross again during my training years in Zurich because after one passes the first-stage exams, there were no more required committee meetings and I was blessed with not having him as an examiner on any of my final exams. In general, I stayed far away from him and made sure not to take any classes that he might teach, and made sure not to enroll in any case supervision seminars with him.

It is not something I wanted to publicly disclose at the time, nor am I comfortable in mentioning his name here, but the manifestation of his bias toward me left me no doubt as to what his position would be if asked to apologize on behalf of the Club – stonewalling and obfuscating. Jerome Bernstein asked me if I wanted to add my name to the letter to the Club so I shared my experience about Ribi and advised him that if my name appeared on the letter, it would be like waving a red flag in front of a bull. Moreover, I predicted to Jerome that with a surname like Bernstein, he would stand no chance of getting any cooperation from the Club – especially now that Ribi was president. As far as I can tell, what emerged from Jerome's initial letters was that Ribi wanted to know who gave Maidenbaum this secret document – and when. Ultimately, Jerome's report reaffirmed my prediction not to expect any cooperation from the Club. Though ultimately Jerome gave the Club the benefit of the doubt in interpreting some of the responses. I wouldn't have been so kind.[7]

Given that Toni Wolff (one of Jung's most important colleagues, who helped him develop some of his ideas and was his longtime companion) and C.A. Meier (Jung's assistant, and later first president of the Jung Institute in Zurich) were among the signatories, it is far-fetched to think that Jung did not know about this quota. Nor does the excuse stand up to justify the position that the Club was only protecting Jung. The reasoning behind this rationale was that they feared the Nazis would invade Switzerland and if there were many Jews in the Club, it would portend badly for Jung. What is important to keep in mind, however, is that when this secret quota was passed by the executive committee of the Club, it was 1944 – when the war was almost over and there was surely no danger of the Nazis invading Switzerland. Moreover, it is important to note that in an exchange with Siegmund Hurwitz as late as 1950, five years after the war ended, Jung openly acknowledged his familiarity with the quota. When Jung invited Hurwitz to join the Analytical Club, Hurwitz's response was that he had heard that there was a quota on the number of Jews being members. Jung responded along the lines of "I am Jung, and it is a Jungian Club, and if I want you as a member you will be in." Sigi (as he was affectionately called by close friends and colleagues) responded that he wouldn't want to be a member of a club that had a quota on Jews. Jung clearly took this to heart. A few days later, he called Sigi and said: "I thought this over, and you are right; there is now no more quota."[8] During the course of our interview with Sigi, he was shocked to hear that such a quota was actually put in writing by some he considered good friends and asked if I had proof. Upon being shown this document – signed by colleagues and friends of his, Sigi began crying – a moving experience I will always remember.

Similarly, for me, the quota aimed at Jews was a double blow since Meier was one of the analysts I had worked with and trusted. Sadly, Meier's responses in the interview showed if not his bias, then at least a lack of sensitivity to this issue. His first response when I interviewed him was: "What, we put this in writing? How Swiss of us! I forgot." After I showed him the document, he tried to justify the quota by telling me that I should take it as a compliment. Jews were very smart people, he told me, and if you let more than a few Jews into the Club, they will take it over. Meier's classic anti-Semitic trope helped me understand the complexity of the issue – that one could be anti-Semitic culturally and collectively while simultaneously one could be a good, well-meaning person in their relationships with Jewish friends and colleagues. To further complicate the discussion, in a follow-up interview I personally conducted with Meier, he added that "underneath the persona of any Christian is anti-Semitism; it is built into the archetypal makeup of all Christians."[9]

Leading Jungian analyst and author Adolf Guggenbühl-Craig had a similar view:

> Everyone in Europe, with the exception perhaps of the Italians, was anti-Semitic in the last century, and the centuries before that, as well as in this century. Anti-Semitism was and is part of the collective mythology, originating from the Christian religion. The Jews were considered to be the killers of Jesus Christ.

Guggenbühl, like Meier before him, at onetime president of the IAAP as well as of the Jung Institute in Zurich, thought that Jung was anti-Semitic but in an "ideological, yet deeper and collective, cultural way." As Guggenbühl, someone I greatly respected for his creativity and insight, and had the privilege of getting to know personally, put it:

> Jung was, on the one hand, a psychological genius and, on the other hand, a very average middle-class man, a bourgeois, with all the mythological beliefs, images, and ideas that this class possessed. Anti-Semitism was, and partially still is, the darker side of this belief system . . . . The anti-Semitism of Jung was a sheer banality, part and parcel of the collective to which he belonged.[10]

Following the New York conference on Jung and anti-Semitism, word had gotten out that I was planning to publish a book on the topic. Knowledge of this impending publication ended up being a problem in itself. At a National Conference of U.S. Jungian analysts held in Los Angeles, I was approached by one of the leading and venerated Jungians in the U.S. and told that such a book should not be printed. What made the situation difficult was that this analyst was one of the most admired Jungian analysts in the U.S. – a reputation well deserved. At this conference, I was highly flattered to be summoned and invited to sit at his table. During dinner, I was taken by surprise when he berated me publicly for organizing a conference and planning to publish a book on Jung and anti-Semitism. He essentially ordered me not to go ahead with the book with the justification being "I knew Jung and he was not anti-Semitic." I responded that neither the conference nor the book – for which I already had a commitment to publish by a major publishing house, were accusations against Jung. Rather, the topic was nuanced and needed to be addressed. Moreover, I invited him to contribute a chapter of his own, which, I promised, would appear word for word as he wrote it, with not a single word edited. His response was, "Young man, you do not come up to Jung's shoelaces, how dare you write such a book." At this stage in my life (I was 45 at the time, with a PhD, a diploma from the Jung Institute in Zurich, and the father of three children), I was not one to be intimidated. My response was, "You are right. I may not come up to his shoelaces, but I am not competing with Jung. This book will be published, with or without a contribution from you." This was the last interchange I had with him before he died, and I am sorry that it was so contentious.

In assessing Jung's attitude toward Jews and Judaism, it would be helpful to review a few of the salient points in his career, some of which gave rise to the very accusations of his anti-Semitism. Carl Gustav Jung, M.D. (1875–1961), began his career at the Bergholzli Mental Hospital in Zurich, one of the leading psychiatric mental hospitals in Europe. Through the encouragement of his mentor, Dr. Eugen Bleuler (known for his pioneering work in diagnosing, and coining the term, schizophrenia), Jung read Freud's landmark book *The Interpretation of Dreams*, and began a correspondence with Freud, which lasted until their break in 1912. The connection between Jung and Freud, which included several face-to-face meetings, as well as a joint trip to the U.S. in 1909 to garner interest in what essentially became the field of Depth Psychology, led to an intense personal and professional connection between the two.

Interestingly, until their break, Jung was considered by Freud to be his "crown prince," his "heir apparent." Ironically, one could say Jung was among the leading Freudians in the world. Indeed, one of the basic tenets of psychoanalytic training originated with Jung's suggestion to Freud that analysts should themselves undergo their own analysis. In short, Freud looked to Jung not only as his successor but also as the person who would lead the psychoanalytic movement into the future and ultimately validate Freud's own work. In a letter dated January 19, 1909, Freud writes to Jung: "We are certainly getting ahead; if I am Moses, then you are Joshua and we will take possession of the promised land of psychiatry, which I shall only be able to glimpse from afar."[11]

The fact that Jung was not Jewish was important to Freud as he was concerned that his work would be dismissed as a Jewish psychology. Jung, in addition to being well placed in mainstream psychiatry, was the son of a Protestant pastor, and represented credibility, a position that Freud acknowledged to his early followers. In a letter as early as 1908 to Karl Abraham, pioneering Jewish psychoanalyst, Freud stated: "You are closer to my intellectual constitution because of racial kinship, while he [Jung] as a Christian and a pastor's son finds his way to me against great inner resistances. His association with us is the more valuable for that."[12]

The break between Jung and Freud has been well documented but it is important to understand the nature of their personal relationship – one that, psychologically, was probably that of father–son. Additionally, an issue that lurked beneath the surface was the fact that many of Freud's – primarily Jewish – disciples resented Freud catapulting Jung into the leadership of this new and exciting movement. Here was this Gentile, a stranger (someone to whom Freud referred as "not like us") from another country, Switzerland, being brought in and instantly promoted to crown prince of the movement. Freud's inner circle resented Jung and did not find it easy to relate to him. In turn, Jung felt alienated and snubbed, intensifying his need to break free of Freud, the father.

Following his break with Freud, Jung spent several years in withdrawal from professional activities and in deep contemplation. He referred to this period as the "dark night of his soul," with much of his inner turmoil revealed in Jung's published *Red Book*. During this period, many of his ideas germinated. Ultimately, Jung resurfaced and began to take his place in the wider world of psychoanalysis. However, while Jung emerged from this period with renewed creativity, he was clearly disconnected from the mainstream Freudian-dominated world. As psychologist Sanford Drob noted: "Jung had been placed by Freud in the unenviable position of playing guarantor that psychoanalysis would not be looked on as a 'Jewish national affair.'"[13]

In 1933, well after Jung and Freud had ended their personal and professional relationship, Jung accepted the presidency of the General Medical Society for Psychotherapy. By then, Jung, along with Alfred Adler and Wilhelm Stekel, both early disciples of Freud, was depicted as a traitor to the movement and marginalized by those close to Freud, including Ernest Jones, Sándor Ferenczi, Otto Rank, Karl Abraham, and Max Eitingon, unofficial members of a "secret society" that had been proposed by Jones to protect Freud. In effect, Jung's decision in 1933 to accept the presidency of a society that was based in Germany and had precluded Jews from membership gave credibility to the rumors and accusations that he was anti-Semitic – even a Nazi sympathizer. Throughout his life, however, Jung steadfastly insisted that, by taking this honorary post, he was able to be of help to his German Jewish colleagues – which was true as Jung was responsible for having the society change its name. Originally named the General Medical Society for Psychotherapy, at Jung's insistence, and his condition for accepting the presidency, it was renamed the International General Medical Society for Psychotherapy which would now permit Jews, who were barred from the German national section, to join as individual members. This seemingly small change is an important distinction, since, until that time, one could be a member only through a local society, clearly eliminating all German Jewish members.

Here the story gets more complicated. In the December 1933 issue of the society's journal, the *Zentralblatt*, which was printed in Germany, an editorial ostensibly signed by Jung as editor of the journal praised Nazi ideology while using Jung's theories of archetypal, cultural patterns to justify the superiority of the Aryan race. The biased comments in that editorial, albeit Jung denied that he authored it, do not do Jung proud to say the least. However, over the years, they have come back to haunt Jungians since they were stereotypical and biased in nature – generalizations that could be utilized by the Nazis and applied to Jews, but also to Native Americans, Blacks (referred to by Jung as Negroes), and other ethnic collectives.

In the wake of a great deal of negative reaction, Jung and Meier, chief editor of the journal, insisted that this editorial had been inserted without Jung's permission by Matthias Göring (German psychiatrist, leader of institutional psychotherapy in Nazi Germany, and cousin of the infamous Göring). Moreover, Meier took personal responsibility and declared that Jung was not involved in any of the details of the journal's publications. Both Meier and Jung insisted that the task of compiling and editing the journal had been left to Meier since Jung, in agreeing to assume the role of president of the society, had made it clear that he did not want to be bothered with the logistics of editing a journal. According to both Jung and Meier, the editorial, which has troubled Jungians to this day, was written by Göring, and that Jung's name had been inserted and signed without the permission of either Meier or Jung.[14]

During the interview we conducted with him, Meier insisted that Jung delegated all the details involved in editing to him and did not work on the journal at all. To my mind, if this was indeed the case, either Meier or Jung should have publicly renounced that editorial and distanced both Jung and the society from its views – or resigned their posts. However, according to Meier, Jung believed it was better simply to ignore the incident rather than risk the breakup of the society. According to Meier, Jung felt that, under his leadership, the society was better positioned to protect Jewish psychotherapists by including them in the reorganized, and newly renamed International Society. Meier, who later became the first president of the C.G. Jung Institute in Zurich, attributes Jung's handling of the situation to naïveté and explained that one has to judge Jung in this light. "Jung was naïve . . . particularly when it came to political things . . . . And so he accepted this German movement as a disease, as the collective disease that maybe even had a chance to do something good to the German nation . . . . But of course, he was rather naïve."[15]

Nevertheless, it is difficult to explain Jung's attitude given what was transpiring in Germany at the time – a situation Jung was well aware of. This attitude is at best a rationalization or, alternatively, willful ignorance – neither of which are easy to explain. Alternatively, one cannot help but attribute Jung's motivation to his own personal ambition. For Jung, caught in his own complex of feeling unappreciated by the psychoanalytical world, in all likelihood envisioned the presidency of the society as an opportunity to promote his own psychology and ideas in the world of psychoanalysis while simultaneously enabling Jewish colleagues to continue as members of the society. In this regard, we can describe Jung's position as a combination of Ego gratification, grandiosity, and political naïveté. For, as Meier acknowledges, at that time in his life, Jung

> suffered from the impression that he was not sufficiently accepted – his ideas were not sufficiently accepted in the world – so he had a kind of minority complex in that respect, and when the Germans started to condemn Freud, he had a hope that maybe now Jungian ideas might have a better chance.[16]

Sadly, Jung's attitude toward Jews and Judaism went beyond that one editorial. In 1934, for example, Jung wrote an article, "The State of Psychotherapy Today," which discussed the differences between what he called Jewish psychology and German psychology:

> The Jewish race as a whole . . . possesses an unconscious that can be compared with the 'Aryan' only with reserve. Creative individuals apart, the average Jew is far too conscious and differentiated to go about pregnant with the tensions of unborn futures. The 'Aryan' unconscious has a higher potential than the Jewish; that is both the advantage and the disadvantage of a youthfulness not yet fully weaned from barbarism.[17]

Understandably, this article offended his Jewish followers. In addition, from a Jewish perspective, other disturbing writings by Jung followed in the 1930s, including an observation that clearly stemmed from his lack of familiarity with Jewish culture, that "Jews had no cultural form of their own," a hurtful statement that Erich Neumann, one of his most devoted Jewish followers, took him to task for.

In an undated letter written sometime between February and May of 1934, Neumann refers to Jung's sweeping generalizations concerning the psychologies of different "races." In it, Neumann mentions that Jews, having experienced persecution for centuries, are uniquely attuned to recognizing the "Shadow side" of nations and peoples. However, what upset Neumann was Jung's own gullibility regarding the unfolding events in Germany. In a letter to Jung, Neumann took Jung to task in a way that those around Jung avoided doing at the time, and wrote:

> I cannot comprehend why a person like you cannot see what is all too cruelly obvious to everyone these days- that it is also in the Germanic psyche (and the Slavic one) that a mind numbing cloud of filth, blood, and rottenness is brewing .... Most importantly though, I would wish to disabuse you of the conviction that Jews are as you imagine them to be.[18]

Concurrently, Neumann also addressed Jung's poorly timed and mistaken comments that Jews, while gifted as a people and in many ways possessing a deeper archetypal and historical level than Christians, lacked a "cultural form" of their own. Neumann's contention was that those Jewish individuals who found their way to Jung, and from whom Jung was drawing his conclusions about Jews and Judaism, were for the most part assimilated and ignorant of their own Jewish heritage. In this context, in a sentence that validates one of the aspects of Jung's difficulty with Jews stemming from his rivalry with Freud, as Neumann points out: "I fear you are confusing Freud with the Jew."[19]

Nevertheless, while Jewish Jungians were offended by Jung's insensitivity to the plight of Jews, and disappointed by his failure to speak out against the Nazis, they did not consider Jung anti-Semitic on a personal level, especially given instances in which he helped several Jewish people with money and other forms of support. Later in life, Jung would tell Hurwitz (a good friend, an observant Jew, and Jung's onetime dentist, and who ultimately became a Jungian analyst): "Today, I would not write this article in this way. I have written in my long life many books, and I have also written nonsense. Unfortunately, that [the 1934 article 'The State of Psychotherapy Today'] was nonsense."[20]

Ironically, at the time and for decades later, Jewish quotas existed in many universities in the U.S., including Yale, Harvard, and Princeton among others. Somehow, this does not bother me as much as finding out that a quota existed in a psychological club fostered by Jung. When confronted by this years later, the official policy of the Club was that this was a secret policy of the executive committee and that Jung was unaware of any quotas – clearly not the case. Indeed, the reaction of several older club members with whom I spoke to was that an unwritten understanding among members limiting Jewish participation existed all along. The quota was put into writing in 1944, by which time the danger of Nazi invasion had well passed, and, as we have seen, not rescinded until 1950, five years after the war, a fact that casts doubt on this justification and paints a poor picture of some of Jung's Swiss followers at that time.

Interestingly, an anecdotal story that I was told by one of the leading "old timers" of the Club pertains to Jolande Jacobi, noted author of books and articles on Jungian psychology, and is acknowledged to have been among those who pushed Jung into letting his name be associated with an "official" training institute. In fact, I heard from a leading Jungian analyst in Zurich who had known Jung personally, that Jung referred to Jacobi as his "minister of propaganda" since she ceaselessly promoted Jung's psychology and ideas. The story I was told was that Dr. Jacobi, who was born and raised Jewish, and converted first to the Protestant faith, and later to Roman Catholicism, was still counted toward the Jewish quota of the Club. When I related this to Meier, and jokingly asked how many times one had to convert to Christianity and no longer be considered as Jewish, he laughed and said that this was the prevailing attitude at the time since her archetypal roots were Jewish.[21]

However, one must place Jung within the culture of anti-Semitism that was pervasive in Europe at the time, as illustrated in David Nirenberg's book *Anti-Judaism: The Western Tradition*.[22] In general, European anti-Semitism depicted Jews as lacking spirituality and being materialistic; to some extent, Jung's view was no exception. Indeed, this stereotype not only made open hostility toward Jews acceptable but also gave it social respectability. This negative depiction of Jews was widespread and existed among various layers of European society, as well as in the U.S. It is not far-fetched to think that Jung held similar views. Indeed, in Freud's *History of the Psychoanalytic Movement*, he notes: "[Jung] seemed to give up certain racial prejudices which he had previously permitted himself."[23]

From my perspective, based on the testimony of his many Jewish colleagues, patients, and friends, Jung, while guilty of identifying with a collective, or one could say cultural, anti-Semitism, was not personally anti-Semitic. Indeed, the Jewish founders of the London, Los Angeles, and Tel Aviv Jungian societies were all disciples, analysands, and close colleagues of Jung – who did not hide their Jewish identities; Aniela Jaffe, Jung's personal assistant and coauthor of Jung's autobiography, *Memories, Dreams, Reflections*, was a Jewish refugee from Germany, and Siegmund Hurwitz was an observant Jew.

Nevertheless, and possibly due to Jung's personal issues with Freud and his Vienna followers (most of whom were Jewish), after his break with Freud one could surmise that anti-Jewish sentiments surfaced in Jung's psyche for, according to Jung, it was after the two parted ways that Freud first accused him of anti-Semitism. However, among the reasons listed by Jung as to why he broke with Freud was Freud's inability to tolerate dissent and his own inability to accept what Jung called Freud's "soulless materialism."[24]

Still, what is most disturbing for me is that Jung never publicly retracted some of his troublesome racist pronouncements, and writings. While by the late 1930s Jung was writing scathing and incisive articles interpreting the mass hysteria that had taken hold in Germany, he never unambiguously expressed regret about some of his comments nor openly retracted some of his earlier views. In later years, after the horrors of the Holocaust had become known, Jung's supporters wanted to clear his name and distance him from any flirtation he had shown toward the National Socialism of 1930s Germany. As proof, common Jungian lore has it that Jung told Rabbi Leo Baeck – pre-war leader of the German Jewish community – that he had been mistaken in underestimating what was happening in Germany in the 1930s but by no means was he anti-Semitic. From the time that the accusations started surfacing, the general Jungian position was that Baeck had absolved Jung, based on a meeting that they had. However, in searching for corroborating information in the papers of Baeck, I found the following in Michael Meyer's authoritative biography of Baeck:

> On a visit to Switzerland after the war, the influential non-Jewish psychoanalyst Carl Gustav Jung visited Baeck, pleading that the rabbi have some understanding for Jung's initial support for the Nazi regime. He claimed that, given the new prospects for Germany in 1933, he had "slipped" (*ausgerutscht*). Baeck clearly thought this a very lame excuse; but since Jung was apparently repentant, a relationship between the two men, which had been formed at Keyserling's School of Wisdom, was restored.[25]

While Jung admitted to Baeck that he had "slipped," unfortunately Jung never said anything publicly that would lead us to believe that he had come to terms with his own "Jewish Shadow" of earlier years. One could easily make the case that some of what Jung wrote about the collective psychologies of different peoples – among them Jews – were not only sweeping generalizations but ill-timed, blatantly incorrect, and biased. His close collaborator for many years, C.A. Meier, attributed the failure to clarify this issue to Jung's "wooden-headed Swiss stubbornness," which always prevented him from admitting that he was at fault.[26]

Apparently, Jung underwent a change in his understanding of "the Jewish question." The Holocaust serves as a harsh reminder of the dangers of his as well as the collective's Shadow – in Jungian terms, an Unconscious aspect of ourselves. Nevertheless, Jung did himself, the Jungian community, and especially Jewish Jungians a huge disservice by not speaking, writing about, or clearing up the cloud surrounding his alleged anti-Semitism. Unfortunately, it is a legacy we Jungians are still grappling with. Private statements that he "slipped" are not enough, and criticism of him in this context is deserved. As a result, Jung damaged his credibility and set back acceptance of his magnificent contributions to Depth Psychology by picking an inappropriate moment in history to discuss the Jewish psyche or, as he put it, Jews' lack of a "cultural form," a foolish statement that illustrated Jung's lack of appreciation of Judaism and its rich cultural traditions. But despite his description of "Jewish collective psychology," I would not accuse him of being anti-Semitic, an attitude that can be defined as a belief or behavior hostile toward Jews just because they are Jewish. In short, I would say that Jung's poorly timed comments about Jews lacking a cultural form of their own were not anti-Semitic; rather, they were, ignorant. Mortimer Ostow, a leading Freudian psychiatrist whose expertise included understanding the psychological sources of anti-Semitism, aptly described how we should view Jung in light of his contribution to the field of psychology:

> With respect to Jung's attitude toward Jews, let me make two points: Expecting our heroes to have only virtues and no faults is unrealistic. Most of the giants of human history have been flawed in one way or another, a point illustrated

over and over in the Jewish Bible. That Jung was blessed with a head of gold, of which we are all the beneficiaries, does not preclude the possibility that he had feet of clay.[27]

In conclusion, if I were to summarize my views as to whether Jung was anti-Semitic, I would conclude that Jung was neither a Nazi sympathizer nor the blatant anti-Semite that many have accused him of being. While Jung was guilty of what were collectively held anti-Semitic attitudes prevalent at the time throughout Europe, he was not anti-Semitic on a personal level. Jung, in assuming the role of President of the General Medical Society for Psychotherapy, did enable German psychiatrists and psychotherapists to join a newly formed international organization. Nevertheless, in accepting this position, Jung had his own opportunistic agenda – in all likelihood hoping his psychology and ideas would reach a wider audience. Nevertheless, Jung initially seems to have been genuinely influenced by what he considered a potentially positive resurgence in Germany during the early 1930s though at the same time it is clear that he did help many Jewish colleagues, personally and professionally. In fact, some of his most devoted followers were Jews who were openly proud of their tradition, including Erich Neumann (who moved to Tel Aviv in the 1930s); James Kirsch (one of the founders of the Los Angeles Jung Institute); Gerhard Adler (a pioneer in the London Jung organization); Aniela Jaffe (who collaborated with Jung on his biography *Memories, Dreams, Reflections*); Siegmund Hurwitz (an observant Jew) and the two Jungian analysts who played a crucial role in encouraging my own Individuation process: Rivkah Scharf Kluger (who retired in Israel and was my analyst for over five years) and René Malamud (my analyst in Zurich and, later, a lifelong friend and mentor, whose father was Jewish).

Notwithstanding the Shadow aspect of Jung's personal ambition, one must take into account the Shadow of mainstream psychoanalytic movements in their persistent accusations that Jung was an anti-Semite. Their motivation consists of keeping the emphasis on Jung the man while denying the importance of his psychology and ideas. In this regard, by minimizing Jung's contributions to the field, and keeping the emphasis on his personal and political life, the contributions of one of the giants and pioneers in Depth Psychology have been ignored. Analyzing this from a Jungian perspective, my feeling is that we should keep in mind that ultimately the message is more important than the messenger, that is, it is easier to discredit the man rather than to acknowledge the importance of his psychology and ideas.

Finally, the phrase that keeps coming back to me is that where there is light, there is Shadow, and the greater the light, the greater the Shadow. Jung, being indeed a great light, had quite a large Shadow, and as a result of his issues with Freud, he chose an inappropriate moment in history to discuss the Jewish psyche – at a time when he knew very little about Jewish history, tradition, mysticism, or, as he put it, "cultural form."

The photographs were taken in Zurich in 1988 during a project to interview several first-generation Jungians, all who had known and worked with Jung. The interviews were conducted by Jungian analysts Aryeh Maidenbaum, Robert Hinshaw,

Figure 4.2 Left to right: Stephen Martin, Aryeh Maidenbaum, and Peter Amman.

Figure 4.3 Left to right: Martin, Amman, and Maidenbaum during an interview session.

Was Jung Anti-Semitic? 61

Figure 4.4 Left to right: Maidenbaum (left) and Amman (right) prepare to interview C.A. Meier (center), founder of the Clinic and Research Center for Jungian Psychology in Zurichberg and co-founder of the C.G. Jung Institute in Zurich.

Figure 4.5 Left to right: C.A. Meier with the author.

62 Jung and the Jewish Experience

Figure 4.6 Jungian analyst Aniela Jaffe during an interview. She edited and collaborated with Jung on his autobiographical book, *Memories, Dreams, Reflections* and edited by C.G. Jung, Word and Image.

Figure 4.7 Siegmund Hurwitz was responsible for ending the quota on Jewish membership in Analytical Psychology Club of Zurich.

Was Jung Anti-Semitic? 63

Figure 4.8 Left to right: members at the 1954 Jung Institute's Fastnacht Ball. Seated in first row, fifth from left: Rivkah Scharf Kluger, Emma Jung and C.G. Jung; second row, standing third from right (in beige jacket): Yehezkel Kluger.

Figure 4.9 Left to right: Rivkah and Jung talking, the stone carving was made by Jung.

Stephen Martin, and Peter Amman (also videographer), as part of their research into accusations of Jung being anti-Semitic. The work ultimately resulted in an international conference on the theme.

Notes

1 Some of the material in this chapter previously appeared in "Lingering Shadows: A Personal Perspective," and "The Shadows Still Linger," in *Jung and the Shadow of Anti-Semitism*, ed. Aryeh Maidenbaum (Brunswick, ME: Nicolas-Hays, 2002). However, the material in these previously published excerpts has been greatly expanded upon here and is new.
2 *New York Times*, letters to the editor, May 21, 1988.
3 Martin Liebscher, ed., *Analytical Psychology in Exile: The Correspondence of C. G. Jung and Erich Neumann* (Princeton, NJ: Princeton University Press, 2015), pp. 11–14, and Micah Neumann, "On the Relationship between Erich Neumann and C.G. Jung," in *Jung and the Shadow of Anti-Semitism*, p. 74.
4 *New York Times*, op-ed, April 15, 1988.
5 I have digitalized the interview material, which I plan to someday donate to the library of one of the Jung societies.
6 Jerome Bernstein, "Collective Shadow Integration: Atonement," in *Jung and the Shadow of Anti-Semitism*, ed. Aryeh Maidenbaum (Berwick, ME: Nicolas-Hays, 2002), p. 124.
7 Bernstein, "Collective Shadow Integration", pp. 124–129.
8 Interview with Dr. Siegmund Hurwitz, recorded January 25, 1989.
9 Interview with C. A. Meier, recorded January 24, 1989.
10 Adolf Guggenbuhl-Craig, "Reflections on Jung and Collective Anti-Semitism," in *Jung and the Shadow of Anti-Semitism*, ed. Maidebaum, pp. 142–143.
11 William McGuire, ed., *Freud – Jung Letters* (Princeton, NJ: Princeton University Press, 1974), p. 197.
12 *A Psychoanalytic Dialogue: The Letters of Sigmund Freud and Karl Abraham*, referred to by Jay Sherry, "The Case of Jung's Alleged Anti-Semitism," in *Lingering Shadows*, ed. Maidenbaum and Martin, p. 120.
13 Sanford Drob, "Jung, Kabbalah and Judaism," in *Jung and the Shadow of Anti-Semitism*, ed. Maidenbaum, p. 190.
14 Interview with Meier.
15 Interview with Meier.
16 Interview with Meier.
17 Maidenbaum, *Jung and the Shadow of Anti-Semitism*, appendix A, p. 229.
18 *Analytical Psychology in Exile: The Correspondence of C.G. Jung and Erich Neumann*, ed. Martin Liebscher (Princeton, NJ: Princeton University Press, 2015), p. 12.
19 *Analytical Psychology in Exile*.
20 Interview with Hurwitz.
21 Ironically, from a traditional, Orthodox perspective, someone who is either born Jewish, or converted to Judaism, is always considered Jewish- even if they convert to another religion or even if they want to revert back to their original religion.
22 David Nirenberg, *Anti-Judaism: The Western Tradition* (New York: W.W. Norton, 2013).
23 Sherry, "The Case of Jung's Alleged Anti-Semitism," p. 120.
24 Drob, "Jung, Kabbalah and Judaism," p. 190.
25 Michael A. Meyer, *Rabbi Leo Baeck: Living a Religious Imperative in Troubled Times* (Philadelphia: University of Pennsylvania Press, 2020), pp. 168–169.
26 Interview with Meier.
27 Mortimer Ostow, lecture delivered at *Lingering Shadows: Jungians, Freudians, and Anti-Semitism Conference*, New School for Social Research, New York, March 28, 1989.

Chapter 5
A Jewish Saturnalian Festival
The Holiday of Purim

Figure 5.1 Johan Van den Avele, Purim Spielers celebrating the festival of Purim through dancing and revelries, 1682, etching.

DOI: 10.4324/9781003511908-6

The holiday of Purim holds a special place in my psyche. It is joyous, fun, and secular. Considered a "minor holiday" in Judaism[1] one can travel, cook, engage in athletics, not worry about turning on or off lights at home, and make merry. In addition, it is a tradition to dress in costume and put on satirical plays in schools and local Jewish community centers. One year, while in the fifth grade, I had a role in the class play but had taken ill a week before with a temperature that reached 104 degrees – high enough for my mother to keep me out of school, a rare occurrence in my childhood. What I remember most was being allowed to join my class for the play only and then taken home. Upon reaching school, one of my fondest memories was the entire class applauding me – pleased that I could take part in the play since, unlike Broadway plays, there was no understudy ready to play my role. It was only years later, as an adult introduced to Jungian psychology and ideas, that I came to understand what Purim represented in Jewish history and tradition.

One of Jung's most significant contributions lies in his validation of the feminine principle within each of us, men and women. In Judaism, one exceptional validation of the feminine can be gleaned from the myth of Esther. Heroine of the Jewish holiday of Purim, savior of the Jews of Persia, etymologically the name Esther is connected with the goddess Ishtar, as she was called in Persia, and whose counterpart in Hebrew is the name Esther.[2] Known in Hebrew as *Megillat Esther*, the Scroll of Esther, it is the story of the Jewish holiday of Purim, celebrated each year a month before Passover. Compared by many to the tales of the Arabian Nights, the holiday stands out dramatically in terms of Jewish and biblical tradition. The importance of Esther is huge, and archetypal. The heroine of the story, Esther, can be said to represent a testament to the feminine; she is one of the heroic women in Jewish myth and history.

As the tale unfolds, we are introduced to Esther – an orphan who rose to become queen of one of the great empires in the ancient world. Her name appears in the book 55 times while, interestingly, God's name does not appear even once. In becoming queen over 127 lands, we are told that Esther not only rises to the highest position that a woman can attain but is able to save her people, the Jews of the Persian empire, from annihilation. The setting for the story is the capital city of Persia, *Shushan*.[3] From a symbolic Jungian perspective, *Shushan* could represent the masculine counterpart of the word *shoshana* ("rose"). The Book of Esther begins by telling us that King *Ahashverosh* (Ahasuerus, in legend associated with Xerxes I of Persia) ruled over 127 lands with thrones in each of them. However, the one in *Shushan* was clearly the most important to him since according to Jewish legend the city was as precious as a *shoshana* – a rose.

Understood as a symbol, the word *shoshana*, rose, or lily, is the flower associated with Ishtar, goddess of love and sex and Inanna (goddess of love, sex, and fertility). In this context, a song widely sung during the holiday of Purim is "*Shoshanat Yaakov*" (the rose or lily of Jacob). Symbolically, one could say that this is the feminine aspect of Jacob (in Hebrew, *Yaakov*).

Two heroines of the Bible, both representing a positive aspect of the feminine in Judaism, are Ruth, a convert to Judaism and from whose lineage King David is said to have descended; and Esther, heroine of the Purim story, whose lineage can be traced to King Saul as well as David. Both have clear parallels, and both were written by unknown authors, probably during the time of the Maccabees, between the fourth and sixth centuries BCE. At the time, a Syrian/Greek king, Antiochus Epiphanes, conquered the Land of Israel, attempted to Hellenize its people, and force the Israelites to give up their God. In the myth of Purim, the inspiration of Esther enabled the Jews to survive. What better heroine could one discover than Esther – one of only two women for whom books in the Bible were named (the other was Ruth). The continuity of Jewish life was in danger, and Esther inspired courage, continuity, and hope. Moreover, to emphasize the importance of these women, in Jewish tradition the lineage of Esther and Ruth both connect to King David – the forerunner of the Jewish Messiah.

While the plots and settings of the books of Ruth and Esther differ and are set several hundred years and a continent apart, Bible historians agree that the two *megillot* (scrolls) were apparently written at approximately the same time and place, freely mixing Babylonian and Persian motifs and contexts. Ruth and Esther contain enough historical inaccuracies to indicate that both are to be taken more on the level of myth and allegory than as literal, historical reality. Even their names indicate symbolic content: Ruth, whose Hebrew origin can be traced to the word *(re-ut)*, friendship, and Esther, whose name, read symbolically, can be read in Hebrew as *e'sater* (I will hide). Both Esther and Ruth carry the hidden feminine aspect of God, and both are inexorably linked to important holidays – Esther to Purim and Ruth to Shavuot (Feast of Weeks – Pentecost). To illustrate the importance of Purim as a folk holiday, the name of God is not mentioned in the Book of Esther. Nevertheless, the Book of Esther is considered sacred in Jewish scriptures and included in the Hebrew Bible, and both the Books of Ruth and Esther are read aloud in the synagogue each year.

What exactly is Purim? What are some of its antecedents? And what makes this holiday so important that the Rabbis say that after the Messiah comes, there will be no need for any holidays but there will always be a Purim?[4] In another rabbinic discussion, centering on Yom Kippur, the holiest of days, this all-important day is compared to Purim. In kabbalistic and Hasidic literature, it is written that Yom Kippur is so important that it is a *Yom K'Purim* (Heb., a day like Purim, or as important as Purim).[5] The significance of this holiday is that Purim was a folk holiday – one demanded by the people. Many of its customs contain clear archetypal patterns, and its significance has increased with the ages with a pattern that includes identification with what Jung terms Shadow.

The Book of Esther is a dramatic tale which includes many poetic sayings that have made their way into the Hebrew language and its narrative contains one of the most gripping and interesting tales in the Bible. The plot revolves around Esther, being chosen through what in contemporary terms we would describe as a beauty contest. The former queen, Vashti, was banished from Ahasuerus's court when she refused to obey his command to appear before a drunken gathering over which he presided. Once chosen to replace Vashti, Esther, with the help of her foster parent

Mordechai, is able to thwart Haman, the wicked vizier of the king, who wished to annihilate all the Jews in the kingdom. In the end, the Jews are saved, Mordechai is promoted, the wicked Haman and his ten sons are hanged, and the Jewish people get their revenge by killing more than 75,000 of their enemies. For Jews, the holiday known as Purim was then declared – a holiday that is loved and still celebrated in Jewish communities throughout the world. Purim (like Hanukah) is considered a secular holiday, notwithstanding the fact that the Book of Esther is read aloud in the synagogue. During the reading, each time the name Haman appears, noisemakers and stomping of feet are not only tolerated in the synagogue but encouraged. The next day, Jews, as per the custom mentioned at the end of the Book of Esther, exchange gifts and partake of a festive family meal. The story of Esther is a riveting tale – well worth reading, a myth unique in Judaism.

In the story of Purim, Esther's leadership and heroism were evident. Even approaching the king, without being invited to do so, was a dangerous endeavor; in those days for if one approached the king without being invited, he or she could be put to death. In preparation for approaching the king, Esther asked all Jews to fast for her for three days, which, according to legend, coincided with a time when Passover traditionally fell. In this legend, the other protagonist, of the story, Mordechai, foster father to Esther, rebuked her for not respecting the holiday of Passover. Esther's response was that "without Jews there would be no Passover," and that if Haman succeeded in ridding the land of Jews, what good would observing Passover that year be for the future of the people? It was an argument that persuaded Mordechai to respect her leadership and declare the fast – traditionally still observed the day before Purim as a day of fasting today.

The observance and celebration of Purim is unique among Jewish holidays – both in the synagogue and in Jewish homes. In Orthodox Jewish homes, aside from the blessings made over wine each Sabbath evening or at the beginning of a holiday meal, little wine or alcohol is served. On Purim, however, the Rabbis instruct us that not only is it acceptable to drink wine but it is a *mitzvah*, a commandment, to drink so much that one does not know the difference between Mordechai – along with Esther, the hero of the story – and Haman, the person who tried to annihilate all the Jews of the land. In other words, Jews are commanded to drink so much wine that they cannot differentiate between the good guy and the bad guy which calls for imbibing a great amount in order for someone to reach that state. From an archetypal perspective, one could say that Purim is the one and only Jewish Bacchanalian festival of the Jewish calendar year. The holiday is very much connected to wine. King Ahasuerus got drunk and summoned his queen, Vashti, to a party. When she refused to attend, she was dethroned ("terminated," in today's jargon). Later, when Esther was queen, she threw her own party, one at which wine flowed freely. Indeed, the Hebrew word *mishteh* (in modern Hebrew also meaning party), is linguistically derived from the root *sha'tah*, (*lish'tot*) "to drink," and water is not the beverage of choice.

When drinking wine, conscious defenses go down. For men, it is often a way to get in touch with the feminine within. When defenses are down, several other

Purim customs become more easily understood. For example, aside from an overindulgence in the consumption of alcohol, gambling is permitted, and there is general merrymaking and the donning of costumes as well as a reversal of traditional roles. It is not uncommon for men to dress up as women and in Jewish religious schools – even in rabbinical seminaries – students take the place of their Rabbis. In Jungian terms, one could say that these role reversals, falling into the opposite, are a way of getting in touch with one's inner Shadow. Normally, in traditional Judaism it is forbidden for men to wear women's clothes or for students to be disrespectful of their teachers but on Purim, these activities are not only acceptable but encouraged. In addition, staging satirical plays – *Purim Spiels* in Yiddish, poking fun at sacred topics – is encouraged. For example, parodies of the Talmud or their teachers are acted out by young Orthodox yeshiva students. One such play, *Sefer habakbuk* (Book of the bottle), a fourteenth-century parody attributed to Levi ben Gershon – a philosopher, astronomer, and mathematician, also known as Gersonides – poked fun at the customs of the holiday, all in the spirit of Purim. In this satirical play, in emulating the Talmud's discussion on eliminating bread from one's home before Passover and having only matzo on hand, the play commands Jews to eliminate water on Purim and have only wine.

Nevertheless, behind the story of Purim is an Archetype of similar holidays and heroes. Purim can be linked to an identification with the Shadow as well as the feminine. For, similar to the goddess Kali in her bloodthirsty stage, Esther, toward the end of the story, is told by the king that the Jews have slain 500 of their enemies in Shushan in one day, 300 more the next day, and that the ten sons of Haman were all hanged. Esther's response is to ask for yet another day for the Jews of the land to kill more of its enemies. Ultimately, we are told, they killed 75,000 inhabitants of the kingdom – an illustration of the bloodthirsty aspect of revenge personified by Kali.

Many stories, myths, and legends associated with the Bible have archetypal parallels. For example: Moses spoke at birth (as did Apollo); the Queen of Sheba had the feet of an ass (as did the child-stealing witch Onoskelis of Greek folklore); rain is said never to have fallen on the altar in the Temple of Jerusalem; the hills of Gilboa were cursed by David to have neither rain nor dew following Saul's and Jonathan's deaths on that mountain while in Greek myth it never rained on Mount Olympus. Or, in one legend, Moses qualified as a husband to Zipporah by being able to pluck a rod from Jethro's garden,[6] similar to King Arthur's pulling the sword Excalibur from a stone.

These myths are archetypal; they carry imprinted psychological patterns and messages for us. Accordingly, it is important not to dismiss some of the more fanciful talmudic legends out of hand. They carry psychological truths for us. It is not the historical accuracy of the story of Purim that should occupy us but the symbolic element, which speaks directly to our collective and individual psyches. For example, an archetypal component that often appears in myth is that of the orphan as hero. The orphan has lost one or both parents at an early age – like Oedipus who has been abandoned to the fates, or Samuel who was given over to someone else to raise. In more contemporary culture, this Archetype, the motif of the orphan, is embodied in such political figures as Abraham Lincoln (whose mother died when he was a child); literary works such as Dickens' *Oliver Twist*; Mark Twain's *Huckleberry Finn*; the Horatio Alger stories *of Ragged Dick*; and even in the person of John Lennon, who was abandoned by both mother and father at an early age and raised by an aunt. A common denominator in all these tales is that the Archetype of the hero is untarnished by parental influence.

Queen Esther is no exception. Legends tell us that she was an orphan, raised by her foster father Mordechai. When her mother became pregnant with her, her father died; soon after Esther's birth, her mother died.[7] This puts Esther in the mythological perspective of orphan. In talmudic legend, she and Mordechai had royal lineage; both were said to be descendants of King Saul on one side of the family, and King David on the other. Another archetypal component to the hero or heroine myth often comes in the form of removing from them mere mortal traits – for example, Moses spoke to God directly, not "in riddles or through vision." So, too, with Esther: described in Jewish legend as one of the four most beautiful women in the world (the others, according to this legend, were Sarah, Rahab, and Abigail).[8]

In their zeal to remove Esther from the human plane, some Rabbis have conjectured that Esther was actually green in complexion, albeit "endowed with great charm," which symbolically would connect her to the realm of vegetation and renewal in an agricultural society. This would be consistent with the Jewish tradition of her given Hebrew name at the beginning of the Book of Esther, Hadassah (Heb., *Hadas*, "myrtle tree"), which is considered a righteous tree – just right, sweet-smelling, not too large or too small, and not too tall or too short. In short, Esther was not only one of the most beautiful women but a goddess of renewal.

Apart from the story of Esther, several archetypal elements surround the celebration of Purim. First and foremost is its importance as a folk holiday for it was a holiday demanded by the people. In addition, on a collective level, the tale of Purim also represents an encounter with the Shadow. Haman, the villain of the story, is not content with his own riches and success and hatches a plot to kill all the Jews of the land because of Mordechai's refusal to bow down before him, a grandiosity that knew no bounds. For notwithstanding a gathering in which he boasted of his great wealth and success, Haman begrudged the Jews any happiness or security. The linking of Jews and money is archetypal anti-Semitism, a link clearly made in the story when the king, in exchange for a commission, grants Haman the right to kill all the Jews: "The money and the people are yours to do with as you see fit"[9] meaning both will benefit financially – classic anti-Semitic greed manifested when Jews were chased out of the countries they lived in.

Confrontation with the Shadow is essential to all psychological development. Only ghosts do not cast Shadows; living people have Shadows. The collective Shadow of a people has to do with the universal struggles of good and evil. It is crucial for an individual as well as a nation's development to confront its darker sides as well as its virtues. It would be fair to state that Jung sees the Shadow as representing both the poison and the medicine needed to heal it – reminiscent of an old saying that if a wise man hands you a poison, drink it; if a fool hands you the antidote, spill it out. The value of dealing with the Shadow on a collective level was not lost on the ancient peoples. It is no coincidence that the Yom Kippur injunction included the ceremonial sacrifice of the scapegoat following the casting of lots to determine which goat.[10] Symbolically, Purim represents the same concept, which is so important that the Rabbis in a play on words, the holy day of Yom Kippur has been described *as* Yom *k'Purim* (a day like Purim).[11]

As a folk holiday, Purim is similar to ancient Babylonian and Roman Saturnalian festivals. In more recent times, the atmosphere around Carnival in Europe and Latin America, as well as Fastnacht in Switzerland, provide interesting parallels. In ancient Rome, cities experienced raucous scenes of wild entertainment, public fairs, and plays; in a similar vein *Purim Spiels* (satiric plays) are common to this day in Jewish communities throughout the world. In many traditions, celebrations are often raucous and members of the clergy have had to accept the rowdy – at times vulgar – traditions of Carnival as the Rabbis must on Purim. They and the Rabbis have no choice but to accept the will of the people on these folk holidays; they are celebrations that the people demand, including Purim, a holiday not of biblical, or possibly even of Jewish, origin.

Throughout history, and in many cultures, people often celebrated an annual period of letting loose in their behavior.[12] The usual restraints of law and morality are ignored, and the entire population partake in celebrations that give light to the darker sides of personality – to drinking and even sexual freedom. Similarly, an archetypal parallel to Purim can be seen in Roman Saturnalian festivals, which generally fell in December, the last month of the year. In Jewish tradition, Purim always falls in Adar, the last month of the Jewish year. Customs for both include role reversals. In Roman Saturnalian festivals, for example, slaves were permitted to get drunk, shout at their masters, even sit at the same table with them or have their masters serve them as waiters. In Jewish tradition, students are encouraged to drink wine until they are drunk, as well as take the place of their Rabbis for the day.

The parallels are even more striking as one delves further back historically – specifically, the festival of the Sacaea in Babylon. During this five-day festival, masters and servants not only changed places, but in each household one servant dressed as a king and ruled over the household. Further, in its original form, as was the case in Roman Saturnalian festivals, one man was chosen as king and allowed to indulge his passions (wine, women, and song) to his heart's content, only to be hanged or crucified at the end of the holiday. In the story of Esther, we see parallel themes: reversal of hero and villain, light and Shadow, refined social conduct turning into bawdy, drunken behavior. Examples of these opposites are the heroes and heroines: Vashti and Esther; Haman and Mordechai – with Vashti and Haman representing Shadow aspects that must be symbolically destroyed. First Vashti and then Haman are temporarily elevated and then sacrificed. It is not a far stretch to note that the concepts of "king or queen for a day" and beauty pageants that have taken root in popular culture have drawn their inspiration from this tradition. In addition, in some cultures, we come across other Saturn-like figures such as "King of the Bean," the "Bishop of Fools," the "Abbot of Unreason," and the "Lord of Misrule."

Likewise, the celebration of the Sacaean festival is associated with the Babylonian festival of the new year, known as Zakmuk. Both the Babylonian and Jewish years begin with the spring month of Nisan (in Babylonia, taken from the month *Nisanu*), which fell at the end of March or the beginning of April, and end with Adar (adopted from the Akkadian name *Adar*), the last month of both calendars. The Sacaean festival was held in honor of Marduk, chief god of Babylon, from which the name Mordechai is derived. This annual celebration was designed to renew the king's power and included the sacrifice of a temporary king instead of the real one. Clearly, the Roman and Babylonian festivals have archetypal parallels with the festival of Purim, though one can readily conjecture that the Jewish evolution to Purim represents a more developed psychological approach, a symbolic scapegoat rather than a human one.

Purim comes at the end of the year's cycle, and ancient Israel was an agricultural society. Even many Jews are unaware that Passover, not Rosh Hashanah, marks the first month of the Jewish year. For despite the translation of *Rosh Hashanah* as the first, or "head," of the year, in the Hebrew calendar it is the seventh month of the year.[13] Purim, which falls during the month of Adar, is celebrated on the twelfth and last month of the year, which symbolically marks the death, the end of the year. Alternatively, Passover, celebrated the month of Nisan, the first month of the year, can be said to mark rebirth. In this respect, the death and rebirth cycle are very much a part of Purim – as are the drinking, role reversal, and other assorted wild customs that have evolved over the centuries. Furthermore, it is important to note that the word *Purim* is not originally a Hebrew word; etymologically, it is related to the Babylonian root of the word *pur*, a type of stone used for the lots that were cast by Haman to choose the most auspicious date to annihilate the Jews of the kingdom.

From a Jungian perspective, Haman/Mordechai and Vashti/Esther can be seen as psychological opposites. If understood symbolically, we could say they are two sides of the same coin – light and Shadow; one represents the Shadow of the other. In a similar vein, the names of the hero and heroine of Purim are strikingly similar to Persian gods, especially the names Mordechai (Hebrew equivalent of Marduk) and Esther (Hebrew equivalent of Ishtar, the Persian goddess). In addition, the names of the primary protagonists in the story of Purim can also be seen in an Assyrian myth of creation in which Humman and Vashti represent the gods of chaos while Marduk and Ishtar are order and light. Humman (Haman, in the Book of Esther), like Kali, is a wrathful god, while Vashti "is none other than the virgin Ishtar, who disobeys the king's command."[14] Undoubtedly, there are a number of common archetypal antecedents, customs, and parallels to the holiday of Purim, including time of year, types of celebrations, scapegoating, and the custom of chasing away evil spirits by banging and stamping in the synagogue at the mere mention of Haman's name and thereby psychologically obliterating his name and memory.

For Jews, the Purim story is an example of both masculine and feminine Jewish heroes: Mordechai and Esther. Mordechai, called the "most righteous Jew in the land" by the Rabbis, encourages Esther, the Jewish heroine, to marry a non-Jew and commands her to hide her Jewish origin. From a Jungian perspective, we could say that Mordechai and Esther were able to embody the opposites within – both were heroes, but with weaknesses. Esther was told by Mordechai to lie about, or at least deny, being Jewish, and to enter a beauty contest; even her name was changed – from *Hadas* to Esther. Moreover, both Mordechai and Esther surely knew that if she were to be successful, Esther would have had to marry the king, a non-Jew, the ultimate denial of Judaism.

In this regard, there is a fascinating example given by rabbinic commentators regarding Mordechai in a phrase at the end of the Book of Esther that Mordechai was elevated to a role second to the king and "beloved to most of his brethren." The Rabbis surmise that the reason the term "most," not "all," was used, was that Mordechai forgot his humble beginnings after he was elevated to such a high role in the kingdom. In Jungian terms, we would say that due to his success in saving the Jews of the land, and in his elevation to a position of power, he suffered from an inflation, an all-too-human trait. Thus, the Rabbis warn us to know not only where we are going but to remember from where we came.[15] To shed light on these contradictions, the Rabbis were aware of the inherent contradictions that we all carry since, unlike Scripture, the midrash (legend) plays with characters with a porous boundary between good and evil, between fantasy and reality.

From a Jungian perspective, there are many nuances in the story of Purim, a holiday marked by opposites. For example, Adar, when the holiday is celebrated, is a month associated with joy. *K'she nikhnas Adar, marbim b'simḥa* ("When the month of Adar begins, we need to have much joy.") Yet, in legend, the month also brings with it sadness as it was said that this was the month Moses died – the seventh day of Adar. In addition, there is Mordechai, beloved and righteous person – yet a figure who suffered from inflation. Through these legends, we are made aware of the lack of perfection in us all through descriptions of the flaws of some of the biblical heroes in Jewish history, including Moses, Saul, David, and Solomon among others. At first, they appear to be all light – larger than life. However, through the stories told in the Bible as well as legend, they are brought down to earth.

What is appealing to me is that the Rabbis, like Jung, understood the complexity of people, the nuances, difficulty, and challenge of understanding just what a person is about. Good and bad, light and Shadow, are within each of us. We all try to hold the opposites – a lifelong struggle of conflicting, sometimes contradictory, aspects. To some, we may be idealized, seen as heroes; and to others, villains; yet, from a Jungian perspective, we are all of this in that we could postulate that what the Ego idealizes, the Self must tear down.

Another apparent contradiction in the story of Purim is the role that Vashti, the king's first wife, plays. At the start, one of the most important figures in the legend, she quickly disappears from the narrative. If Vashti had not been deposed, there would have been no Esther. We are left wondering what became of Vashti? Was she killed by the king for refusing to appear before his guests at a party at which he was "merry with wine"? Was she just banished from the court? Was she sent back to her father if her marriage had been a political alignment with another ruler? In the talmudic legend, Esther criticizes the king for "killing Vashti and for following the brutish advice of the Persian and Median nobles."[16] Ironically, today Vashti is hailed by feminists for standing up to a king and not allowing herself to be used as an "object" performing for him. Indeed, some legends have it that the king wanted her to appear wearing the royal crown and dance naked before the guests, and she refused,[17] upon which the king's advisors told him that by her refusal, she was setting an example for all the wives of Persia; by eliminating her as queen, it would teach "all the wives" of the kingdom to "treat their husbands with respect, high and low alike."[18]

Another perspective in the contradictions of Purim can be gleaned from customs at the end of the story. During the month of Adar, when the story of Purim takes place, Jews are instructed to be happy. Yet, as Elie Wiesel has pointed out, it also describes the mass killing of tens of thousands of people by the Jews of the land while, alternatively, the Rabbis tell us not to celebrate too much when their enemies are killed because they represent God's creation as well. In an inspired chapter on Esther in his book *Sages and Dreamers*, Wiesel struggles with this dichotomy:

> I confess I never did understand this part of the Book of Esther. After all, the catastrophe was averted; the massacre did not take place. Why then this call for bloodshed? . . . . The question remains: how could our ancestors celebrate Purim in the midst of such killing? Is this why we are told to get drunk and forget? To erase the boundaries between reality and fantasy – to think it all happened in a dream? Or is it a way of coping with our hidden frustrations?[19]

In trying to understand the holiday of Purim, one cannot help but be impressed by the psychological sophistication of the story and the traditions of Purim as they have evolved. The legends that have grown around Esther and Purim are meant to provide the Jewish people with *musar* (ethical guidance). For example, the Rabbis examine and discuss every word of the scroll as it was written. In Jewish tradition, there is nothing in the Bible without meaning; it is our task to find it. For example, Mordechai overheard two officers of the king's court plotting to kill the king. He tells this to Esther, who, in turn, tells it to the king, giving due credit to Mordechai. The Rabbis point out that it is important, when one relates a story, to give credit to the originator: "He who tells something in the name of the person who said it brings redemption to the world."[20]

Another example of ethical teaching is reflected in the role of Ahasuerus, whose behavior and demeanor left much to be desired. As related in the myth, we are told that the custom of the land was that a king's decree cannot be retracted, even by the king himself. And so, rather than rescind his original decree calling for the annihilation of the Jews, Ahasuerus tells Esther that a king's decree cannot be taken back. To compensate for this, he offered to allow the Jews to kill as many in his kingdom as they believed they were threatened by thereby bringing about the bloodshed of tens of thousands that could have been avoided. Using this as a warning against not making a foolish promise, the Talmud tells us that the king was a fool; only God makes no mistakes, and that the king should have corrected his mistake.

The legends, leaders, and myths surrounding the holiday are replete with opposites. It is a Jewish holiday; yet it has archetypal parallels and similar motifs in other cultures, including Roman and Persian Saturnalian festivals. It is an important holiday but one leaving us unsure whether it should be considered nationalistic or religious since the name of God is not mentioned even once in the story. It is a Jewish holiday, yet expanded upon so much by the Rabbis that we are told that when the Messiah comes, there will be no need for any holiday but Purim.

Notes

1. There are three major holidays in Judaism: Passover; Sukkot (Booths); and Shavuot (Weeks-Pentecost in Greek). It was during these holidays that the ancient Israelites made their pilgrimage to Jerusalem.
2. "The Book of Esther is the last of the scriptural writings. The heroine was named Esther, the morning star (Venus), which sheds its light after all the other stars have ceased to shine .... Thus, the deeds of Queen Esther cast a ray of light forward into Israel's history at its darkest." Louis Ginzberg, *Legends of the Bible* (Philadelphia: Jewish Publication Society, 1956), p. 646.
3. Thought to be at one time the capital of ancient Persia- known as Susa.
4. Midrash Mishle 9.
5. *Encyclopaedia Judaica*, 13:1395.
6. According to one myth, this was the rod that Moses wielded, enabling him to perform some of his miracles. *Pirkei d'Rabbi Eliezer*, p. 40.
7. BT Megillah, p. 13a.
8. BT Megillah, p. 15a.
9. Book of Esther 3:11.
10. Lev. 16:21.
11. *Encyclopaedia Judaica*, 13:1396.
12. For example, Carnival in Rio and New Orleans, or Fastnach in Switzerland.
13. Lev. 23:23–32.
14. N. S. Doniach, *Purim, or the Feast of Esther: An Historical Study* (Philadelphia: Jewish Publication Society, 1933), pp. 40–41.
15. *Pirkei Avot* (lit., "Chapters of Our Fathers"), known as *Ethics of Our Fathers* 3:1.
16. *Encyclopaedia Judaica*, 6:909.
17. Elie Wiesel, *Sages and Dreamers* (Simon & Schuster; 1993), p. 142.
18. Esther 1:20.
19. Wiesel, *Sages and Dreamers*, p. 150.
20. *Pirkei Avot* (Ethics of Our Fathers) 6:6.

Chapter 6

Jerusalem
Archetype and Living Symbol

Figure 6.1 David Roberts, Jerusalem, 1839, painting.

> For the sake of Zion, I will not be silent, For the sake of Jerusalem, I will not be still.
> Isaiah: 62:1

Jerusalem is a topic that touches me more personally than any other. What looked as though it would be the easiest theme to write about turned out to be the most problematic. Perhaps living there for seven years – or, due to my family history in Jerusalem, which dates back several generations, or the history and myths that I grew up hearing about – makes writing about Jerusalem so difficult. Nevertheless, not to include Jerusalem in this book would be unthinkable. In this chapter, I will

DOI: 10.4324/9781003511908-7

do my best to do justice to a city that has played such an important psychological role in the spiritual roots of the Western psyche.

My grandfather, my mother, and my youngest daughter were all born in Jerusalem. Had I been born there, I would have been a third-generation Jerusalemite and my daughter a fourth. Such a lineage would have made us unique in a country overwhelmingly composed of the early Jewish European Zionist settlers, survivors of the Holocaust, and Jews escaping persecution in the Middle East and North Africa. My daughter, who was born in Jerusalem, is named Hepzibah (Heb., "desired one") – one of 70 names for Jerusalem that, as prophesied by Isaiah, will be the name of Jerusalem after the Messiah comes.

My experience in Jerusalem was far from messianic. My first exposure to the city was on a short visit in 1952, when I was ten, living with my parents and siblings in Haifa. My parents had left a comfortable home and thriving business in Brooklyn and, with four children and elderly parents in tow, attempted to settle in Israel. It was an idealistic time: socialist mentality was the rule. But living in Israel at that time was a challenge due to severe food shortages; families were given ration cards that controlled how much food and clothing they were entitled to. It was a long way from the comfortable lifestyle to which we had all had been accustomed. So my parents' ideological motivation to live in Israel soon gave way to economic reality; we all returned to the U.S. and our much higher standard of living after less than six months.

Nevertheless, the period we spent in Israel in 1952 was an experience that left a powerful and positive impression on me. While living there, we also spent considerable time touring the country. On one of our trips, my father wanted to explore, and introduce us to, Jerusalem, where our visit began with my father pulling the car off the road about halfway there and walking to a nearby village to call the driver we had used to tour other parts of the country. My father asked the driver to come and collect us. At that time, there were no highways, and the road to Jerusalem was narrow and winding – barely wide enough for two cars. With no guardrails, it was a frightening road – too frightening for my father to drive. (Today, it is a four-lane-wide, safe highway.) The risk of going over a cliff was real, and he realized that his driving skills were not up to the task. And so, a taxi soon appeared bringing with it Moti, our driver, who got behind the wheel of our car and drove us the rest of the way. That incident was a prelude to the tension that we experienced as we toured the city. In 1952, Jerusalem was a city divided. During the War of Independence, in 1948, Jerusalem had endured a siege and was in danger of being overrun; even four years later, it still felt like a city in danger. Having grown up in the New York area, I had never been near the border of another country, let alone one delineated with barbed wire on one side and armed Jordanian soldiers on patrol on the other. It is an image I can still see today and, I must admit, a scene that was exciting and left me feeling I wanted to return again and again.

Even after returning to the U.S. a few months later, I identified with the feelings expressed by one of Judaism's most important writers, the twelfth-century Spanish author and poet Judah Halevi, whose famous lines longing for the Holy Land were often recited to me by my father: "My heart is in the East [Jerusalem] while I live in the far corner of the West [Spain]." For me, returning to Jerusalem was a fantasy I longed for as well.

My first return to Israel after this experience was as a 16-year-old member of a summer youth group. During that summer, we lived and worked on a kibbutz for a few weeks, toured the country, met with local Israelis, and spent over a month in Jerusalem. Following our early-morning arrival from the U.S., we proceeded directly to Jerusalem and were given time to relax and recuperate from the long (14 hours, in addition to a several-hour stopover) flight from New York. While most of the group were napping and relaxing, I was too excited to rest and decided to take a walk to reacquaint myself with the city of my ancestors. Since I was fluent in Hebrew, I knew that I could ask for directions if I got lost. So I began walking with no particular destination in mind, my only goal being to experience the sights and sounds of Jerusalem.

During that first day of wandering about the city, in an area I had not been to during the visit with my parents years earlier, I had a feeling that was akin to déjà vu. While I am not a believer in past life therapy, nor do I subscribe to reincarnation, what I experienced was akin to déjà vu, a feeling and memory that stayed with me and inspired me in adulthood to return. Synchronistically, during that first walk on my own, I stopped and looked up at the street sign to get my bearings and noticed that the street I was on was called *Reḥov Hanevi'im* (Street of the Prophets). From that moment on, I felt a personal, almost mystical, connection to the city. Many years later, as the twists and turns of life unfolded for me, I enrolled in a PhD program at the Hebrew University of Jerusalem and entered Jungian analysis.

The years I spent studying in Jerusalem, 1971–77, and my analysis with Rivkah Kluger turned out to be the most formative period of my adulthood, a time when I learned to turn inward, a time when I began to Individuate. I had been raised in an Orthodox Jewish world and taught to give precedence to communal demands over my personal needs. My own soul was shunted to the side and trampled on by the emphasis on community. Although I have never been enamored of Jung as a person, and his personal life is not a role model for me, his psychology and ideas speak to me, and his emphasis on Individuating has served as an inner guide over the years. Living, studying, and working in Jerusalem helped me come into my own as an individual. Jungian analysis helped affirm the importance of being true to myself first and not to place community values above my own. Nevertheless, while claiming my individuality, I learned that by being an individual, I was not rejecting all that was of value in Judaism. In fact, over the years, I have come to value and honor Jewish history and tradition and to incorporate them into my inner life and work as well. It is in this context that I would like to share what Jerusalem has meant to me through a Jungian lens.

The Orthodox Jewish world was too restrictive for me; but through my Jungian analysis, I learned to value the positive aspects of Judaism. From my father especially, I acquired a pride in, and learned a great deal about, my Jewish tradition though I rebelled at his demands that I live an Orthodox Jewish life. Nevertheless, thanks to him, I became fluent in Hebrew at an early age and was exposed to the beauty of the Hebrew language and poetry. I became steeped in Jewish history and acquired a great deal of knowledge about Judaism's traditions and culture. I was fortunate to have studied the Bible in its original language and have enjoyed reading numerous Jewish myths in Hebrew, including some that have not been translated to English. I am happy to share some of these traditions, myths, and history of Jerusalem, a city deeply ingrained in my psyche.

Jerusalem as Archetype and Living Symbol

Jung described Archetypes as themes and motifs "that arrange the psychic elements into certain images, characterized as archetypal, but in such a way that they can be recognized only from the effects they produce."[1] An Archetype is essentially an Unconscious content that we become conscious of by the power, feeling, tone, or affect that it produces in us. Jerusalem, as a city, as a concept, as a manifestation in our essentially Western psyche, fits this description.

In Jungian terms, it is the power of the Archetype that has made Jerusalem a "living symbol." The pull that this city has exerted, and still exerts, on the Western psyche in literature, in prayer, in history, and continued political strife makes Jerusalem more than just a city that Jews, Christians, and Muslims have fought over for centuries. Jerusalem has played an outsized role in our hearts and our psyches. It has aroused our imagination, from the myths about it to the violence that is constantly brought to our attention. It was as though when someone sneezes in Jerusalem, the entire world is concerned. One need turn no further than daily newspapers, television, or the radio to grasp the importance of Jerusalem on the Western psyche. This fascination with Jerusalem has been evident for centuries, from the time of the Prophets, through the Middle Ages, Renaissance, Enlightenment, and through today – for Jews, Christians, and Muslims. A selection of myths and occurrences mentioned in the Bible and Koran about Jerusalem, include:

- Abraham "almost sacrificed" Isaac on a site known as Mount Moriah.
- The ancient Israelites came three times a year to offer sacrifices at the Temple.
- Isaiah cried out for his people to repent.
- Jesus preached, was crucified by the Romans, and then resurrected.
- The Assyrians conquered Jerusalem and destroyed the First Temple in 586 BCE.
- The Romans destroyed the city razed the Second Temple, and exiled its inhabitants.
- Helen, Constantine's mother, visited Jerusalem in the fourth century and is said to have found the "true cross" of Jesus as well as identified the site of the crucifixion.
- Muhammad came on his night journey, riding a white horse named Al-Buraq, and ascended to heaven on a stair of light from the site of the present-day Al-Aqsa Mosque.
- The Crusaders conquered the city in 1099 and claimed Jerusalem for Christianity.

- Saladin defeated the Crusaders in 1187 and reclaimed it for Islam.
- Jews, for thousands of years, came to the Western Wall (in Hebrew, *Kotel*) and recited as part of the daily prayers "return in mercy to your city Jerusalem and dwell in it as you have promised."

In addition, according to legend:

- The entrance to the Garden of Eden is located under the Dome of the Rock, atop Mount Moriah, where both Temples were situated.
- Cain is said to have slain his brother Abel on Mount Moriah.
- The Messiah will reappear first on Mount Zion in Jerusalem.

An example of the spiritual role that Jerusalem plays can be seen in William Blake's early nineteenth-century epic poem "Milton" which includes within it what became the well known hymn known as "Jerusalem." Set to music years later by Hubert Parry, the hymn Jerusalem has become one of the most beloved of hymns in Christian liturgy, sung weekly in Episcopalian services in England, and especially, on "Jerusalem Sunday," when the Holy City is celebrated worldwide in Anglican churches.

In Jewish tradition as well, Jerusalem is still very much a living symbol – more than just an ancient place where the Prophets had lived. Some examples of the role that Jerusalem still plays in the Jewish psyche include:

- It is customary for Orthodox Jews to leave one wall unpainted in their homes – the wall facing Jerusalem.[2]
- At weddings, recited under the *ḥuppah* (canopy) is Psalm 137: "If I forget thee, O Jerusalem," after which a glass is crushed in remembrance of the destruction of the Temple.
- Three times a day, Jews face the direction of Jerusalem and pray for the rebuilding of Jerusalem.[3]
- One may prepare a full-course meal, but traditional Jews leave one course out of the served menu, in remembrance of Jerusalem.
- A woman may wear all her jewelry except for one, in remembrance of Jerusalem.
- One is not buried in a coffin in Jerusalem; it is considered holy ground and the dead are simply wrapped in a shroud and put in the ground with no manmade coffin to defile her.

Background on Jerusalem

Jerusalem, according to Jewish tradition, is known by 70 different names. In fact, throughout the Bible, the Talmud, and Jewish prayers, Jerusalem is referred to by one or more of these names. The most familiar among them are: God's City, the Holy City, City of Justice, Faithful City, City of Peace, The Beautiful City, City of David; and the most renowned of all, interchangeable with the name Jerusalem and City of David, is Zion – the archetypal name for Jerusalem. In this context, Jerusalem is first mentioned directly in the Bible in the Book of Samuel[4] though in Jewish tradition Jerusalem is included in the prayers recited each time the Torah (the Pentateuch) is taken from the ark and portions read aloud in the synagogue on Mondays, Thursdays, and Saturdays with the following recited aloud by the congregation:

Out of Zion shall come forth the Torah, and the word of God from Jerusalem

Remarkably, in American history and geography, Jerusalem and Zion appear quite prominently. In fact, noted historian James Carroll pointed out that the Puritans "carried Jerusalem in their hearts to the New World from their home countries" and that by the early nineteenth century, there were more than 200 American cities named for Jerusalem.[5] Indeed, both Jerusalem and Zion are used as descriptions of the new Puritan settlements, often referring to the colony of Plymouth as the New Jerusalem, the City on a Hill, or, most prominently, as "The New Zion." Governor Bradford, first governor of the Massachusetts Bay Colony, in 1630, began compiling a notebook as he was teaching himself Hebrew. In this notebook,[6] which on one side of the page he wrote in Hebrew and the other side in English, he included the phrase from Isaiah that after the redemption and return of the people of Israel to Jerusalem, it would no longer be desolate and abandoned but called *Chefzibah* (Eng. Hepzibah):

Nevermore shall you be forsaken,
Nor shall your land any more be called desolate,
But you shall be called "I delight in her." (Heb., *Chefzibah*)

Origins of the Names: Zion and Jerusalem

While Zion and Jerusalem are interchangeable names, the origins of the names are not clear. Jerusalem seems to be connected to the word *rushalimum*, probably translated as "Shalem the Syrian God has founded this city."[7] Nevertheless, the Hebrew root of the word "Jerusalem" can also be distilled as *s-h-l-m* from the word *shalem* (whole, or "complete"). Because Hebrew words can have multiple meanings, it could also connect to the word *shalom* ("peace"), though this usage of peace is likely poetic and dates much later.[8] The origin, and precise meaning, of the name "Zion" is not known. Suggestions have included a rock, a stronghold, a dry place, or running water. It was named Zion by King David after he captured Jerusalem from the Jebusites.

The first time the name "Jerusalem" is alluded to in the Bible, albeit indirectly, is in the Book of Genesis, where the city of Salem, representing another name for Jerusalem, is mentioned. Here, the priest-king of Salem, *malki zedek* (Heb., king of righteousness), greets Abraham with bread and wine and blesses him in the name of *el elyon* (highest of gods).[9] The name "Jerusalem" is first mentioned directly in the Book of Joshua, where King David consolidated Israelite rule around 1064 BCE and the city became known as *Ir David* ("City of David"). Following this conquest, the Book of Samuel reports that David ruled in Jerusalem for 33 years[10] (all told, he ruled for 40 years). From that point on, the Bible refers to Jerusalem or Zion 825 times.[11]

Jerusalem has been the central point in Judaism and Christianity and the third most important site in Islam. In ancient Israel, it was considered extraterritorial – not belonging to a specific tribe. A similar designation in U.S. history and geography, is that Washington, D.C. belongs to no one state. Similarly, Jerusalem became the province of David, who first conquered it from the Jebusites and then used it to unite all 12 tribes. In short, Jerusalem fell within the boundaries of no single tribe – not even David's tribe of Judah, despite its being often referred to as the City of David.

From a Judeo-Christian literary perspective, Jerusalem plays a central role. For example, as we have seen, a moving example of the place that Jerusalem occupies in the Western psyche is evident in Blake's epic poem Milton where the poet referred to London as the new Jerusalem. Here, Albion (a literary name for England) is the Holy Land, and London, its "sister city," serves as a metaphor for Jerusalem:

> England! Awake! Awake! Awake!
> Jerusalem thy sister calls!
> Thy gates beheld sweet Zion's ways;
> Then was a time of joy and love.

Or, as recited often in churches and synagogues:

> By the rivers of Babylon there we sat and also wept, when we remembered Zion .... How can we sing the song of God on alien soil? If I forget thee, O Jerusalem let me forget my right hand (*eshka'chech Ye'mini*). Let my tongue adhere to my palate, if I fail to recall you, if I fail to elevate Jerusalem, above my foremost joy. (Psalm 137)

If we are to understand the psychological meaning of the psalm in Judaism, we must be aware of the Hebrew meaning of the word "forget." For rather than the more widely used translation of "cunning," or "wither," forget is a more accurate translation of the word (Heb., *eshka'chech*). Some rabbinical commentaries explain the use of the word forget as meaning that the people, in exile in Babylonia and longing for Zion, could not remember the joy needed to sing. It is written that they could not use their musical instruments to rejoice. Taken in this context, the expression "let my right hand forget" refers to the use of the right hand as in strumming the strings of a musical instrument (let my right hand forget how to make music, or rejoice).[12]

The exile from Jerusalem and the destruction of the Temple are integral parts of Jewish tradition; they indicate that there is a piece of us missing as long as

Jerusalem is not rebuilt. Similarly, from a psychological standpoint, the Individuation process is never complete. The inner work is never finished. Jung, in a famous interview with John Freeman of the BBC, refers to this when discussing the dreams of old people. Jung, replying to Freeman's question as to whether the dreams of old people, closer to death, are any different from the dreams from when they were young, said: "The psyche acts as if it will go on indefinitely; it is only the Ego that deals with death as a finality . . . . The Self is always incomplete."[13]

The Ideal Jerusalem: Archetypal Symbol

Christianity and Judaism deal extensively with a concept that they identify as the "heavenly Jerusalem." In the talmudic and kabbalistic tradition, the term used is *Yerushalayim shel ma'alah v'yerushalayim shel matah* ("Jerusalem of above and Jerusalem below"). The Jerusalem we strive for – Jerusalem above – is the ideal that Jerusalem plays in our psyches, the Jerusalem of the future, connected with the heavenly Jerusalem and the heavenly Temple. This is similar to what Jung describes as an inner manifestation of centeredness – the spirituality within, not necessarily connected with earthly, literal actions.

In the legends, the Jerusalem above is located directly above the earthly Jerusalem; Jewish and Christian legends both speak of the heavenly Temple being fully prepared before the world was created. An example can be found in the Apocryphal Book of Baruch, where God says that "the heavenly Jerusalem is prepared beforehand here from the time when I took counsel to make paradise."[14] The legend is meant to be experienced symbolically – a metaphor for our individual attainment of a higher level of spirituality. This theme, whose words are best embodied in the hymn "The Holy City," has been embraced by Jews and Christians and conveys the theme of a higher spiritual realm inspired by Jerusalem – one that we strive toward throughout our lives:

> *The Holy City*
>
> Last night as I lay sleeping,
> There came a dream so fair,
> Stood in Old Jerusalem,
> Beside the Temple there.
>
> Jerusalem, Jerusalem,
> Lift up your gates and sing,
> Hosanna in the highest,
> Hosanna to your king!

The hymn is a metaphor for Individuating and achieving a level of inner spirituality that will then raise us from the mundane to the sacred, from what Jung calls the biological in the first half of life, to the spiritual and philosophical in the second half. It has to do with our own centeredness, which is what the Individuation process is all about. It represents a search for an inner spirituality through a connection with what Jung termed the Self, the center of the totality of our personality, conscious and Unconscious. It is a unifying theme of the spiritual and the mundane; it hints at a higher level within us, as in the myth of the Jerusalem of above. This call is archetypal – dating at least as far back as the preaching of the Prophets in the Bible who call on their fellow Israelites to be a "light unto all the nations."[15] A higher standard of morality and ethics is expected as part of Jewish tradition. In this regard, on a collective level, Jerusalem symbolizes the opposite aspects of the Archetypes of light and Shadow, positive and negative.

Legends of Jerusalem

Jerusalem's Beauty, Wisdom, and Miracles

"The citizens of Jerusalem were renowned for their wisdom," R. Yose said. "Wherever a Jerusalemite went, a soft seat would be spread out for him, and he would be placed on it so that his wisdom could be heard." The designation is archetypal – borrowed to offset a Greek tradition that referred to the inhabitants of Athens. The midrash (legend) has a story about Athenians who came to Jerusalem and were impressed by the people's wisdom. Additionally, the Rabbis referred to Jerusalemites who visited Athens, surprising its inhabitants by their wisdom. To understand the power of the archetypal wisdom emanating from Jerusalem, an Aramaic expression in the Talmud relates that *avira d'Yerushalayim maḥkima* ("the air of Jerusalem makes one wiser"). In addition, we are told: "Jerusalemites were distinguished for their beauty," as was the city itself. There is no beauty like that of Jerusalem . . . . Of the ten measures of beauty that came down to the world, Jerusalem took nine."[16] Finally, as if these expressions of wisdom and beauty were not enough, according to legend ten miracles are associated with Jerusalem. Among them: "No person was stricken in Jerusalem, no person ever stumbled in Jerusalem, no building ever collapsed in Jerusalem, and no fire broke out in Jerusalem."

Jerusalem: Atop a Mountain and at the Center of the World

Like many sacred spaces in ancient religions, Jerusalem was thought to stand at the center of the world and, like other sacred sites, is located on a mountaintop, signifying a connection with God and spirituality. In the Judeo-Christian tradition, examples include God's covenant with Noah after the ark came to rest on Mount Ararat; God appearing to Abraham as he was about to sacrifice Isaac on Mount Moriah; Elijah defeating the false Prophets of Ba'al on Mount Carmel; Moses receiving the Ten Commandments on Mount Sinai; Jesus in a visionary state on a mountaintop; and Mohammed who is said to have been inspired to write many of the Koran's verses from atop Mount Hira. From an archetypal perspective, mountains play an important role in many spiritual traditions because of the association that a mountain, due to its height, is closer to God, and on a higher spiritual realm; this is true of Mount Moriah, one of the higher mountains surrounding the Old City of Jerusalem.

Mount Moriah

Many legends surround the derivation of the name Mount Moriah. Some say it is derived from the Hebrew word *l'horot* (to teach) while others say it is from the word *yir'eh* (he will see). An example is Abraham, following the angel's appearance, stopping him from sacrificing Isaac, and then naming the location *Adonai Yireh* ("God will see" or "God will be seen"). Another possibility is that the name *Moriah* is derived from the Hebrew word whose root is *yir'ah* ("awe" or "fear") following Abraham's readiness to sacrifice his son Isaac.

> For now I know that you fear [in awe of] God, since you have not withheld your son, your favored one, from me . . . . Because you have done this and not withheld your son, your favored one, I will bestow my blessing upon you and make your descendants as numerous as the stars of heaven and the sands on the seashore.[17]

Another legend about Mount Moriah is that inside the "Golden Dome," which lies atop the Temple Mount, lies the "foundation stone" of the world – an archetypal description that plays a central role in Jewish as well as Muslim myth. In Jewish legend, underneath this stone lies the entrance to the Garden of Eden. Also, God is said to have dropped a big rock in the waters there "and from thence the world expanded," following the version in Genesis of God separating the heavens from the earth. In an unusual interpretation of why a stone would be linked to water, is that this stone and water are interconnected because this stone is "the hidden source of all the springs and fountains in the world" – the place from which all the world drinks its waters.[18]

A parallel, archetypal example can be seen in an Islamic myth, in which a similar foundation stone exists, though this stone is placed in Mecca, not Jerusalem. The Archetype is the same, however, with both traditions placing a foundation stone at the center of the world. In this context, the foundation stone is crucial to the legends of both Jewish and Islamic myth as the most important stone in Islam is the *kabah*, a black stone that once dropped from the sky. This stone, similar to the Jewish myth surrounding the foundation stone on Mount Moriah, is said to have been positioned directly below the gate of heaven and, like the stone atop Moriah, have caused a hole in the sky that now makes heaven more penetrable by the prayers of people on earth. Added to these archetypal parallels and notwithstanding the importance of the *kabah* in Islam, Muslim legend says: "At Resurrection Day, the Ka'bah Stone in Mecca will go to the foundation stone in holy Jerusalem, bringing along with it the inhabitants of Mecca, and the two foundation stones shall be joined."[19]

In Jewish myth, the foundation stone lies inside what later became a Muslim site, today known as the Dome of the Rock, or the Golden Dome. This site, historically identified as the site of Solomon's Temple, is situated on what was probably the "Holy of Holies" which is described in Jewish lore. Other myths in Jewish legend associated with Mount Moriah include the sacrifices of Cain and Abel to God; Cain's subsequent killing of Abel, and Adam's skull, said to have buried there or at a nearby site known today as Golgotha, by Noah's son Shem. While the exact location of Golgotha is disputed (some place it on Mount Moriah, while Christian legend places it slightly outside the walls of the Old City), there is consensus that the name is connected to the Hebrew word *gulgolet* ("skull") though Golgotha (or Calvary) is the place, according to Christian myth, where Jesus was crucified. Finally, another myth connected to Mount Moriah is that the waters of the Flood gushed out from beneath the foundation stone on Mount Moriah before they receded into the abyss and were sealed by the stone at Mount Moriah, in Hebrew, *even hashtiyah* – considered the first solid thing in creation that God made on earth from the primeval waters.[20]

A Talmudic Explanation of Jesus' Miracles

In Jewish tradition, sited atop Mount Moriah were the First and Second Temples. Within both was the *kodesh hakodashim* (Holy of Holies), a room that only the high priest could enter. Once each year, on Yom Kippur, the holiest day in Jewish tradition, the high priest would enter and pray for the Israelites while pronouncing aloud the name of God, which only the high priest was privy to. During the period of the First Temple, known as Solomon's Temple, this room, an inner sanctuary, contained the Ark of the Covenant. When the Temple was rebuilt, following the end of the Babylonian exile, the ark, which had been lost or destroyed in the destruction, was replaced by a table adorned with a menorah of gold, loaves of bread, and an altar. The exact pronunciation of God's name was known only to the high priest since such knowledge carried the ability to harness the powers of God.

King David began to dig the foundation for the Temple (begun by David but completed by Solomon) and found a stone resting on the mouth of the abyss with the "divine name" (likely the YHVH, as traditionally translated) on it. Later, when his son Solomon continued the task of building a Temple, he placed this stone into the Holy of Holies. In this context, a discussion in the Talmud regarding how Jesus may have performed the miracles he was credited for adds an interesting perspective:

> The sages of Israel began to fear lest some young men might learn the divine name and destroy the world. To prevent this, they made two brazen lions, which they placed on iron pillars by the door of the Holy of Holies, one on the right and the other on the left. If anyone entered and learned the divine name, these lions would roar at him when he exited, so that through terror and fright, the name would be utterly driven out of his mind and forgotten.

Jesus of Nazareth went secretly to Jerusalem and entered the Temple, where he learned the holy letters of the divine name. He wrote them on parchment, and, uttering the name to prevent pain, he cut his flesh and hid the parchment therein. Then, again pronouncing the name, he caused the flesh to grow together. As he left the door, the lions roared, and the name was erased from his mind. When he went outside the city, he cut his flesh again and drew out the parchment, and when he had studied its letters, he learned the name again . . . . Thus was he able to perform all his miracles and wonders.[21]

Moriah was chosen as site of the Temple and the legend I like best as to why Mount Moriah was chosen as the site of the First and Second Temples is one that my father told me when I was a child (the eldest of six children in our family). It is a legend he made sure we all knew and whose moral was not lost on us: it is the story of two brothers, one married with a family and the other living alone, with lands adjoining each other. One year, when there was a plentiful harvest, each thought about how fortunate he was. The brother with a family of wife and children thought: "My brother lives alone and has no one to care for him. When he is old, or becomes sick, there would be no one, so I will bring him extra wheat during the night and leave it in his field." At the same time, the brother who lived alone thought: "How lucky I am to have such a harvest, but I have no family and do not need so much. My brother, who has many mouths to feed, is too proud to ask me for help, so I will go in the middle of the night and leave some extra wheat in his field." Each did so, but in the dark they came across each other, each with hands full of wheat, and realized the love they had for each other. They dropped their sheaves of wheat, took each other in their arms, and wept. The angels, and even God, were so moved that God said: "On this spot, I will build my temple."

Clearly, my father's motive in telling this legend was to ensure that all six of us would care for and help one another. While he knew nothing of Jung, he would, similar to Jung's emphasis on an Archetype also embodying the opposites, also relate a parable as to why the Temple was destroyed. It was because of Kamtza and Bar Kamtza – once the best of friends – who had a falling-out. The version that my father told is that Kamtza was about to marry off his daughter and hold a large celebration, to which all the notables of Jerusalem were invited. His former friend was mortified not to be invited. Why, Bar Kamtza asked, since he had known the bride since she was a little girl, couldn't his former friend overlook the past bitterness between them and invite him as well? Not being at the wedding would mean his being humiliated publicly. Feeling hurt, he even offered to pay for the food at the wedding, but Kamtza would not relent. Looking down on this scene, God turned to his angels, saying, "People like this do not deserve to have a temple." The legend, no matter which version one reads, has been related by the Rabbis as an example of *sinat ḥinam*, hatred for no cause. Cited frequently over the centuries, the mean-spirited attitude that people could have toward one another was the reason the Temple was destroyed and the Jews sent into exile by the Romans.

In relating to legends as to the Temple site, a popular song by Naomi Shemer (considered by many the modern poet laureate of Israeli song) was *Hakotel*, the Western Wall. In the song, the stones of the Western Wall are said to have human-like qualities while some people have hearts of stone: *Yesh anashim im lev shel even, v'yesh avanim im lev adam* ("There are people with hearts like stones and stones that have a heart like man").[22]

Pilgrimage: An Archetype Linked with Jerusalem

In Judaism, from Biblical times, the people were instructed to bring their offerings to God three times a year.[23] These periods coincided with what still are the three main festivals of the Jewish year: *Pesaḥ* (Passover), *Shavuot* (Pentecost), and *Sukkot* (Feast of Booths, Tabernacles). The tradition has come to be known as *aliyah l'regel* – associated with the Israelites' thrice-yearly pilgrimage to Jerusalem, where they offered their sacrifices to God. The tradition ended with the destruction of the Second Temple by the Romans in 70 CE and the exile of its inhabitants.

Meanwhile, worldwide, the tradition of a pilgrimage to a holy site is very much alive, with Jerusalem the destination for millions of Jewish and Christian pilgrims. Psychologically, pilgrimage to a sacred site represents a search for centeredness or wholeness and, from a Jungian perspective, related to the Individuation process. As Jung sees it, this process is a lifelong search for inner meaning. For Jews and Christians, Jerusalem represents an outer manifestation of an inner connection to help us in our search for meaning and spirit. Jung described this inner search, using Jerusalem as a metaphor for this journey, as one he himself had undergone following his break with Freud. In his introduction to the "Seven Sermons of the Dead," for example, Jung begins: "The dead came back from Jerusalem, where they found not what they sought."[24] Geographically and politically, Jerusalem was seen as the center of the earth, a motif that Jung describes as a "symbol of the Self." From this archetypal and symbolic perspective, Jung also points out that Jerusalem can be seen as the "heavenly bride," representing a longing for wholeness and an archetypal image of the mother Archetype.[25]

Anthropologists have pointed out that pilgrimage comprises three stages that are a classic rite of passage: separation – the start of the journey, when one separates from ordinary life and place; the liminal stage, which includes the journey and encounter with the Archetype; and, from a Jungian perspective the most important aspect – the return, the homecoming, when one should incorporate the inner meaning of the experience into daily life.[26]

Being "gripped" by an Archetype is similar to being in the throes of a pull stronger than gravity – like being in an orbit – with the momentum of the orbit continually propelling us. Similarly, a connection with the Archetype of pilgrimage captures the imagination of those who embark on it. Symbolically, after returning from our pilgrimage, we are transformed, though one cannot help but feel that the very act of embarking on such a journey propels us to a higher spiritual level. A pilgrimage to Jerusalem represents a ritual act that furthers one's search for spirit.

As with all Archetypes, where there is light, there is Shadow, the positive and negative sides of the Archetype. Seen through a Jungian lens, we can see the negative, Shadow side of pilgrimage in such examples when, in the name of religion, hundreds of thousands were slaughtered by the Crusaders en route to Jerusalem. Upon reaching Jerusalem, more were slaughtered in the battles for the city, leaving what historians have described as a city knee-deep in blood. This fanaticism, what we would term the acting out of an inner drive, the need for literal expression, has unfortunately been evident throughout Western history. From a Jungian perspective, such fanaticism can be understood as an overidentification with the negative side of the Archetype, which can manifest itself at the expense of a true inner spirituality.

Also associated with pilgrimage to Jerusalem is a state of psychosis observed by Israeli psychiatrists in a number of individuals visiting Jerusalem for the first time. This syndrome, which appears only in Israel, is connected with the Archetype of pilgrimage and is classified by Dr. Yair Bar-El, director of Jerusalem's municipal psychiatric hospital, as "Jerusalem Madness."; its symptoms were described by him as delusions of messianic grandeur, with the patient believing that he is one of "a range of figures from the Bible . . . including biblical Prophets, King David, Samson, Jesus, the Virgin Mary, and John the Baptist," among others.[27] Manifested by those who have arrived in Jerusalem on their own quests, most often during their first visit to the city, these individuals are caught up in the Archetype of spirituality – what Jung refers to as an overidentification with the Archetype, which can often result in psychosis if one's Ego is not strong enough.

In addition, some of the greatest American writers who have traveled to Jerusalem on personal journeys and quests and written of their quest include Herman Melville, in search of material to write about; and Mark Twain, describing highlights of a trip that ultimately resulted in his book *Innocents Abroad*. Both were disappointed in their visits to Jerusalem. Melville, "seeking to revive his spirit," complained of Jerusalem being "surrounded by cemeteries, and the dead are the strongest guild," concluding: "No country will more quickly dissipate romantic notions than Palestine, particularly Jerusalem."[28] Mark Twain was equally cynical. As his usual acerbic self, after arriving in Jerusalem, Twain poked fun at the pilgrimage experiences of various denominations of Christians after their visits to Jerusalem, following a visit to the Church of the Holy Sepulchre in Jerusalem:

> It is a singular circumstance that right under the roof of this same great church . . . Adam himself, the father of the human race, lies buried. There is no question that he is actually buried in the grave, which is pointed out as his – there can be none – because it has never yet been proven that that grave is not the grave in which he is buried . . . I leaned upon a pillar and burst into tears. I deem it no shame to have wept over the grave of my poor dead relative. Let him who would sneer at my emotion close this volume here, for he will find little to his taste in my journeyings through the Holy Land.[29]

Conclusion

Why is Jerusalem, as Archetype and living symbol, so important to our psyches? The answer is mystical; there is no simple answer. Jerusalem has been sacred especially to Judaism and Christianity and, to a somewhat lesser degree, Islam. Indelibly linked with the city of Jerusalem are the phrases and concepts of Messiah, hope, death, and rebirth. The Archetype of Jerusalem is a paradox – this city, like an Archetype, has a duality. Understanding the paradox from a Jungian perspective, for Jews, Jerusalem has always been known as *Ir David*, the City of David; and David's place in the history of the city is paramount. Seen through a Jungian lens, David embodied and represented a number of opposing, archetypal attributes: masculine and feminine, warrior and poet, light (as the greatest of kings in Israel) and Shadow (in his less than honorable seduction of Bathsheba). Still, in David we see messianic hope and redemption – for Jews, reappearing as a forerunner of the Messiah, for Christians connected with the lineage of Jesus and from a Jungian perspective, we could say that Jerusalem represents the Archetype of the Self.

In any case, as in all Archetypes, there is the potential – that is what this Archetype is about: the potential for healing and reconciliation, a development that all reasonable people would welcome. Like any powerful Archetype, Jerusalem is able to contain and hold the opposites for over the centuries, Jerusalem has been represented as:[30]

- A city portrayed as both pure and a harlot
- A city that represents both the exile and the return – death and rebirth
- A city seen as God's dwelling place yet where he has repeatedly abandoned his people
- A city of immense beauty and light, with a history of violence and bloodshed
- A city of mourning and a city of joy

Jerusalem, like our individual and collective psyches, is a complex, multilayered being. Our psyches contain many layers and levels; on a religious level, from the individual to the collective; and psychologically, from the personal to the collective Unconscious. Within the city lies layer upon layer of different cultures and different traditions, all archetypally linked. In trying to decipher what Jerusalem means to us all, there is no distinct answer.

It is important to understand the Archetype of Jerusalem as a living symbol – one, observed from a Jungian perspective, that clearly contains the opposites – both outer and inner. Jerusalem, an Archetype and living symbol, is a wonderful, powerful, and mysterious metaphor – what Jung has referred to as a symbol of the Self, a metaphor for the Individuation process.

Notes

1 Jung, *Collected Works*, 11:149.
2 *Encyclopaedia Judaica*, 9:1555.

3 At first, in their prayers, Muhammad instructed Muslims to face toward Jerusalem. When he realized that the Jews were not willing to adopt his new faith, he stopped the practice and instructed Muslims to turn instead to Mecca when praying.
4 2 Samuel 5–7.
5 *Forward*, November 25, 2011, p. 10.
6 William Bradford, "The Diary (1620–21), the History (of Plymouth Plantation), and the Hebrew Studies," in *Culture and Language at Crossed Purposes: The Unsettled Records of American Settlement* (Chicago: University of Chicago Press, 2022), pp. 35–49.
7 Karen Armstrong, *Jerusalem: One City, Three Faiths* (New York: Knopf, 1996), p. 7.
8 *Encyclopedia Judaica*, 9:1370.
9 Gen. 14:18.
10 Samuel II, 5:4.
11 Manfred Lehman, *Jerusalem Post*, July 15, 1995, p. 14.
12 See commentary, Psalm 137, *Tehillim* (Psalms), Art Scroll Series (Brooklyn, NY: Mesorah, 1987), p. 1620n.
13 Jung interview with John Freeman, *BBC*, 1959.
14 Baruch 4:2–7.
15 Isa. 42:6.
16 *Encyclopaedia Judaica*, 9:1557.
17 Gen. 22:12, 16–17.
18 Zev Vilnay, *Legends of Jerusalem* (Philadelphia: Jewish Publication Society, 1973), p. 8.
19 Armstrong, *Jerusalem*, p. 221.
20 Vilnay, *Legends of Jerusalem*, p. 28.
21 Vilnay, *Legends of Jerusalem*, p. 9.
22 The last remnants surrounding Mount Moriah and the Temple, is known in Hebrew as *Kotel hama'aravi*, the Western Wall; the term "Wailing Wall," is a name describing the place where Jews came to weep, and considered derogatory by those who understand the origins of the name "wailing wall"- a term associated as a "place of weeping" – where Jews came to and wept.
23 Lev. 23:14.
24 See C. G. Jung's reference to the *Seven Sermons to the Dead* in C.G. Jung, Memories, Dreams, Reflections, Vintage Books, published by Random House; New York, 1963, p. 308
25 Jung, *Collected Works*, Aion, Volume 9- part 1 par. 256.
26 Jean Dalby Clift and Wallace Clift, *The Archetype of Pilgrimage* (City: Paulist, 1996), p. 12.
27 *New York Times*, November 28, 1999.
28 Meir Shalev, *Moment* (March–April 2008): 35.
29 Mark Twain, *Innocents Abroad*, quoted by Stuart Schoffman, *Jerusalem Week*, August 6, 2010, pp. 5–6.
30 Amos Elon, *Jerusalem, City of Mirrors* (Boston, Toronto, and London: Little, Brown and Company, 1989), pp. 19–20.

Chapter 7

To Forgive, or Not to Forgive

Figure 7.1 Aleksander Gierymski, Święto Trąbek I (Tashlich), 1884, painting, National Museum in Warsaw.

Forgiveness is a charged issue – a struggle relevant on both personal and collective levels. It applies to countries as well as to individuals who were wronged by family, teachers, friends, or colleagues – some on such a deep level that permanent scars remain. In dealing with this difficult question, the question arises whether it is a theological, or a psychological issue. Is it an indication of mental health to forgive or the reverse? Do our religious beliefs encourage us to always forgive? What happens if we prefer not to forgive? On a psychological plane, the jury is out. One study, for example, focused on the population of Northern Ireland during the years the Irish refer to as the "troubles" and came to a conclusion that may be difficult for some to digest. Its findings were that those who held grudges and were unable to forgive were generally more neurotic and angry, even after a long period of time has passed. Alternatively, the study concludes, those who tended to forgive were "happier and healthier than those who hold resentments."[1]

As I see it, notwithstanding the findings of this study, forgiving is an individual issue which, from both religious and Jungian perspectives, is complicated, confusing, and contradictory. Moreover, the conclusions often conflict with one another and leave one more perplexed. For example, "Researchers at the University of Missouri found that forgiving others helped protect older women from depression, even when they felt unforgiven by others. Men, however, felt worse when they forgave others but didn't feel forgiven."[2]

On a personal level, I still think of incidents that occurred as far back as my childhood and wonder whether I should forgive and move on or is it acceptable to hold a grudge. Two examples that come to mind happened when I was nine and 11 years old. During those years, I was enrolled in Orthodox, religious Jewish schools, with teachers in one and an assistant principal in the other who were mean-spirited and sadistic toward me. In the first school, when I was nine, my fourth-grade teacher, Mrs. Eisenstadt, would hit me with a ruler if she felt I misbehaved or was not paying attention. With the passage of so many years, I cannot remember what prompted one particular onslaught but I do remember that she hit me so hard that my chair toppled backward onto a fellow student, whose chair promptly toppled over as well – causing not only me but my fellow fourth-grade students to break out laughing. Mrs. Eisenstadt became enraged and started pounding me again with her ruler. As a Jungian analyst, I realize that her anger at me was in all likelihood an Unconscious displacement of other issues in her life. Nonetheless, for me, a nine-year-old child, it was real in how it affected me. Can I forgive her? Must I forgive her?

An even more humiliating occurrence took place in the second school, when I was in the sixth grade. During our lunch period – which the entire school had at the same time – we were seated in the gym of the school. The assistant principal, Mr. Weiss, overheard a comment I made to a friend sitting nearby which so incensed him that he yanked me out of my seat in front of the entire school and punished me by relegating me back to the fifth grade – resulting in what we called being "left back." I felt shamed in front of the entire school and, later, before my new, younger classmates. Mr. Weiss apparently forgot about me, but fortunately the fifth-grade teacher intervened. After I had been in her class for a week, she told Mr. Weiss that it was inappropriate to have done what he did. When she confronted him, his response was that he "forgot" about me and that I could now be returned to the sixth grade where I belonged. Looking back on these events, over 70 years later, when neither is probably still alive, I still cannot forgive Mrs. Eisenstadt or Mr. Weiss. Even many years after this incident, I accept that I will always carry this bitterness. While I have moved on and try not to let these feelings occupy much emotional space in my psyche, the memories of the emotional hurt inflicted on me at the time do sometimes crop up.

At this late date, it is too late to confront either of them and demand an apology. And, given that it is a practical impossibility for them to appear on my doorstep and apologize, I will continue to hold this justifiable anger toward them. Not coincidentally, in researching and dealing with the topic of forgiveness, I have come to understand my feelings and reluctance to forgive at times. This struggle is continually playing out in my own psyche; yet from a Jewish perspective I feel validated in that anger as, in the view of Maimonides, among the greatest Rabbis and scholars in Jewish history, one of the sins that can never be forgiven is shaming someone in public.[3] Moreover, even from a distance of over 70 years, I understand that in both these instances, not just shame was the issue but that sadism was involved in publicly shaming me, especially through the punishment inflicted by Mr. Weiss, the assistant principal. For while I can understand that Mrs. Eisenstadt may have continued hitting me as a by-product of her own Unconscious anger, Mr. Weiss had the conscious aim of humiliating me. Nevertheless, perhaps if they were to suddenly appear on my doorstep and ask forgiveness, I could forgive them, but barring such an unlikely (and impossible) occurrence, they will not be forgiven.

Still, one could ask why, since my life has turned out well despite these incidents, I cannot bring myself to forgive these educators. For me to forgive my teacher or the assistant principal who abused the trust placed in them by my parents, I would be betraying myself. Part of my own Individuation process over the years has included staying true to my feelings and ensuring that no one denigrates me or undermines my self-esteem. The sin of humiliation, shaming another, is such a terrible sin that in one talmudic discussion one of the Rabbis declared that it is "better for a man to drop himself into a burning oven than to shame another in public for even in the afterlife there is no forgiveness for shaming another."[4]

A more difficult scenario which I encountered later in life is what if the wrong or hurt that a person inflicted on you turns out to be a turning point for the better? For example, a former brother-in-law (thankfully, my sister ultimately divorced him) was dishonest and necessitated my mother and the rest of our family giving up lucrative shares in a business – the firm my father, had built and, as a gift to my sister, had taken this former brother-in-law in as a partner. Once my father passed away, my brother in law at the time, forced my younger brother out. My brother, who had been hoping to enter the family business, ultimately thrived and flourished, far exceeding what he would have achieved had he remained in the family business – to say nothing of the loss of soul he would have had to face had he remained a partner with my former brother-in-law – a selfish, mean-spirited individual. For me, the loss of potential income made my financial situation more pressing and for years I needed to work far more hours than I would have otherwise done. As it turned out, however, both my brother and I have accomplished far more in life than would have been the case had the family not been forced out of the business – a situation brought about by our father's untimely and early death.

Should we forgive our former brother-in-law? After all, if our lives have turned out far better than would have been the case, should we then forgive the person who necessitated the change – even thank the person? From a theological perspective, some would say that the person inflicting the hurt was the instrument that God had chosen to move us forward in life – analogous to the concept of the "fortunate fall." But if the person has not only no intention of apologizing or owning their own Shadow, what then? Should we forgive such people "for they know not what they do"? For instance, if I do not know how to swim but someone throws me overboard from a boat and I learn to swim as a result, should I thank the person for enabling me to learn to swim when I might have drowned?

From a Jewish perspective, in some instances forgiveness can only be granted by God, albeit with specific sacrificial rituals carried out through priests: "The priest shall make atonement for him for his sin, and he shall be forgiven."[5] Nevertheless, there are wrongs we may have committed that are either unforgivable or can be forgiven only by the person whom we wronged – not even by God. In such a situation, even if one were to go to a priest, he cannot grant forgiveness. Moreover, when it comes to asking forgiveness from another person, the issue is complicated. For example, what if we ask for forgiveness and the person we are asking refuses to forgive? In Judaism, there are rituals to deal with that possibility.

Perhaps, in certain circumstances it is healthier not to forgive or, at times, just to "accept" and move on. From a Jungian perspective, we need to be true to ourselves and stand our ground, even if our religion has a different message. In Judaism, the issue is nuanced; it is not always necessary to grant forgiveness – attested to by Lord Rabbi Jonathan Sacks, former chief Rabbi of the U.K., who writes that "Forgiveness is too important to be confined to places of worship."[6] Moreover, from a Jungian understanding of how the psyche works, we do ourselves a disservice if we adopt a religious attitude that might exhort us to forgive in the name of God but does not feel right to us personally.

In Jewish tradition, differentiation is made between wrongs that can be forgiven – those that make the cut, so to speak, and others that are unforgivable. Some wrongs concern the collective community; others are strictly personal. In Judaism, forgiveness can be seen as on three levels: the collective, the personal, and the theological. Some issues and wrongs apply to relationships between individuals, others between the individual and God, and yet others between the individual and the community – the collective. For example, transgressions of a religious nature, between man and God, are a major part of the Yom Kippur service and clearly delineated, dating back to biblical times. This is evident in the Book of Leviticus where a scapegoat is sent into the wilderness carrying the sins of the collective – a portion of the Bible that is read on Yom Kippur.[7] Additionally, especially on Yom Kippur, prayers in the synagogue for forgiveness are recited from a collective position yet also are applicable to our individual sins and guilt – a duality of the collective and the individual, a tension that runs throughout the Jewish tradition.

From a Jungian perspective, this duality, what Jung would term "holding of the opposites," can be seen in our daily life. In some situations, community mores may stand in opposition to the need to respect our own Individuation process. However, when such a conflict manifests itself, the priority is clear: our first allegiance is to ourselves, not the collective. We can see this expressed in the *Mishnah* (authoritative part of Jewish Oral Law) through the teaching of Hillel, who stated: "If I am not for myself, who will be?"

In Judaism, forgiveness is not a given. For example, the Israelites are instructed never to forgive the tribe of Amalek, a refrain that can be seen in several sources – from the Books of Numbers and Deuteronomy, to the Prophets of old. Moses instructed the Israelites to "neither forgive nor forget" what the tribe of Amalek did to them when they were vulnerable and wandering in the desert: "Blot out the memory of Amalek from under heaven. Do not forget!" Or, in the Book of Samuel, a wrathful God commands Saul to kill every last Amalekite. When Saul neglects to do so, he is stripped of his kingdom by the prophet Samuel, who then slays Agag (the Amalekite king) himself. Amalek cannot be forgiven, Samuel tells us.[8]

In the Book of Genesis, Jacob and Esau are brothers, and rivals. In Jewish legend, Esau was considered the first enemy of Israel (Jacob's name after he wrestled with the angel). Subsequently, in the genealogical outline that unfolded, we are told that Esau was the father of Eliphaz,[9] who was the grandfather of Amalek, whose king was the same Agag who was spared by Saul. According to contemporary Jewish legend, Agag's descendants led to Hitler. In Jungian terms, Amalek is the archetypal enemy of Jews (the Israelites) from biblical times through today, the nature of an Archetype, and forgiving them is out of the question.

As seen in the Bible and Jewish myth, God is not predictable; he is sometimes forgiving and sometimes not. The forgiving aspect of God can be seen in the story of the Golden Calf that awaited Moses when he descended from Sinai with the first set of the Ten Commandments. At first, God declares that he will wipe out the Israelites for their transgression, but when Moses petitions God to change his mind, God relents and forgives.[10] Alternatively, the not-forgiving aspect of God does reach the limits of patience. We see this first in the destruction of Sodom and Gomorrah and later as portrayed by the prophet Amos, who warns the tribes of the Northern Kingdom of Israel as well as those of Judah: "For three transgressions of Judah [I will forgive, but] . . . for four I will not go back [forgive] . . . . I will send down fire upon Judah, and it shall devour the fortress of Jerusalem . . . . For three transgressions of Israel, I will forgive, but for four, I will not go back [forgive]."[11]

In Christian tradition, Jesus exhorts his followers to forgive, as seen in the parable of the Prodigal Son, whose father forgives him even if his siblings are resentful. Also, in the Book of Luke, we are told that if someone hits you, do not hit him back but, rather, turn your other cheek and let him hit you again, or if someone has wronged you, he must be forgiven: "Forgive and you will be forgiven."[12] Even more powerful is the story of Jesus on the cross telling his followers: "Forgive them for they know not what they do." Through the life and death of Jesus, God will forgive. This approach to forgiving is very much unlike the Jewish attitude.

Nevertheless, in Judaism as well as in Christianity, asking God for forgiveness through an intermediary is an acceptable part of the tradition – not only acceptable but customary. In Christianity, Jesus is the intermediary; in Judaism, an individual praying to such luminaries as Moses, Abraham, and Daniel is not unusual. For example, what is practiced by every Jewish community worldwide is the custom on

Rosh Hashanah and ten days later on Yom Kippur, to appoint a representative of the community to lead prayers on their behalf (Heb., *sheliah tzibur*, "representative of the community"). Some of the liturgy of these High Holy Days includes one of the most powerful prayers in the service, *Hineni he'ani mima'as*, which the individual leading the services recites aloud:

> Here I am, poor of worthy deeds, frightened in your [God's] presence, who has come to plead before you on behalf of your people Israel, who have appointed me the messenger, though I am not deserving or qualified for the task . . . . God of Abraham, God of Isaac, and God of Jacob.[13]

Nevertheless, when it comes to praying for forgiveness through an intermediary, there is an important distinction between Judaism and Christianity. For Christians, by supplication through Jesus, one's sins and wrongdoings will always be forgiven; in Judaism, God is not bound to comply and can reject forgiveness. When one's transgressions have exceeded the limit of God's tolerance, neither repentance nor forgiveness is an option. As in the prophecies of Amos, even God has his limits of tolerance.[14] This can also be seen in the Book of Jeremiah, where the prophet berates the Israelites for turning away from God: "Even if Moses and Samuel were to intercede with me, I would not be won over to that people." Or, as the Prophet Ezekiel made clear when the people of Israel sinned: "Even if these three men – Noah, Daniel, and Job – should be in it, they would, by their righteousness, save only themselves, declares the Lord God."[15] These can serve as examples in Judaism of why one need not always forgive. In a similar vein, there are times and incidents for each of us when the pain inflicted by another, whether physical or emotional, may be too hurtful to absolve. There are limits to be reached.

Issues concerning the Jewish collective waver on a spectrum – between man and God, between man and his responsibilities to the community, and between man and man. In Orthodox Judaism, if one informs the civil authorities on another Jew, it is considered not pardonable by the collective, though it is not clear whether this betrayal can be forgiven by God. This issue has been an important one as evidenced as recently as during the Holocaust when some Jews betrayed others in order to save their own lives or families. After the war, when concentration camps were liberated, a question that was extremely stressful for the Jewish community, especially for survivors of the Concentration Camps, was whether anyone guilty of such a betrayal could be forgiven.

Ironically, the same issue still exists today among the ultra-Orthodox Jewish community, who consider it unforgivable to report anyone in the community to the civil authorities – even when child abuse is involved or in a case of domestic violence. The attitude in this group is that "we will deal with it – but only in our community; we do not turn to the civil authorities to do so." One who hands over another Jew to the authorities is called a *moser*, one who "gives over" (reports on) a fellow Jew – in which case, Maimonides tells us that he will not have a portion in the "World to Come" (in Jewish eschatological terms, attain salvation).[16] Other examples among the ultra-Orthodox include the unwritten, but strongly enforced, tradition that if a person in the community were to seek a divorce in civil court, as opposed to letting the Rabbis handle such cases in a rabbinical court, he or she is ostracized or even excommunicated by one of the Rabbis.

Fortunately, although the ultra-Orthodox community is the fastest-growing segment in the Jewish world, it still does not represent the majority of Jewish communities. Most Jews are far more tolerant and diverse, ranging from totally secular, nonobservant Jews to partly observant or the more modern Orthodox. For me, the appealing aspect of Judaism is that there is not just one way to see things. One's relation to both God and others is complicated. In Jungian terms, we might say that each of us has light and Shadow, the ability to forgive and the choice of not forgiving. Maimonides is considered to be the greatest of Jewish philosophers and Rabbis, but not all Rabbis or scholars agreed with him concerning forgiveness. To place the greatness of Maimonides in Jewish tradition, one needs appreciate the Jewish adage that "from Moses to Moses, there was none like Moses," meaning that from the Moses of the Bible to Moses Maimonides, there was no greater figure in Jewish history than Maimonides (in Hebrew, known as *Rambam*, an acronym for Moses, the son of Maimon).

Author of the seminal work *Hilkhot teshuvah* (Laws of Repentance),[17] Maimonides listed some sins that could not be forgiven. Nevertheless, some Rabbis had the courage to disagree with him – even on issues of Jewish law. One such Rabbi was Don Yitzḥak Abravanel. An all-important religious as well as secular leader in medieval Spain (and, later, following the expulsion of Jews in Spain in 1492, a leader in Portugal's Jewish community), Abravanel listed his disagreement with some teachings of Maimonides. He venerated Maimonides but disagreed with some of Maimonides' writings and is said to have told his students: "This is the opinion of Rabbi Moses [Maimonides] but not that of our teacher Moses of the Bible." Or, more recently, in the words of Abraham Joshua Heschel, "The way of man is not God's way. If a person has been hurt with words, he may or may not be forgiving. But if someone has sinned, words will suffice for God to forgive [and] he who commits a sin and is ashamed of it will be forgiven all his sins."[18]

The Talmud tell us that if one truly repents, he will always be forgiven. Consequently, if someone sins toward God and his commandments, though not against a fellow man, a person who repents is always forgiven, a position that a midrash (legend) in the Talmud reinforces: "Says the Holy One, even if [one's sins] reach to heaven, if you repent I will forgive." Also in the Talmud, a numerical figure is given to God's empathy based on a portion in the Book of Exodus that tells us that "God's quality of forgiveness is five-hundred-fold that of his wrath."[19]

Seen from a theological perspective, some would say that the person inflicting the hurt was the instrument that God had chosen to move us forward in life. However, if the person has not only no intention of apologizing or owning their Shadow, and/or insists on always seeing themselves as the victim – what then? Should we forgive such people "for they know not what they do"? Jewish tradition is clear that this is not something we are required to do.

In his book Answer to Job, Jung understood that God's dual, seemingly contradictory, personality is mirrored in our own psychology. God represents both light and Shadow, good and bad, rewarding and punishing, forgiving at times and not forgiving at others. Parallel to this struggle, God can be said to have his own struggles concerning forgiveness. Approaching this duality from a Jungian model, we could say that God wrestles with himself, trying his best to hold the "tension of the opposites." This tension can be readily understood as fluctuating between an alliance with mercy – in Jungian terms, the feeling function – as opposed to identifying with the need for justice, the rule of the law, which would be represented by our thinking function. In fact, there is an interesting parallel to Jung's view which is expressed by one of the discussants in the Talmud where there is a representation of God as "praying to himself that his mercy should prevail over his anger."[20]

On the evening of Yom Kippur, an interesting tradition that is observed in many Orthodox synagogues is that just before services begin there is a ritual of going from one person to another in the congregation and asking for forgiveness. To those not familiar with the rituals of Yom Kippur, one often-overlooked aspect of this day is how Jews deal with the wrongs that one commits toward one's fellow man. They fall into a different, though no less important, category than sinning against God. For in Judaism, forgiveness also applies to misdeeds toward our fellow man (*ben adam l'ḥavero*) but not in the same category as between the individual and God (*ben adam la makom*). In sinning toward God, we are assured that through prayer, repentance, and charity, God will forgive us. For wrongs committed by one person toward another, God cannot forgive; only the wronged person can forgive, and must be approached directly. A request for forgiveness between people is generally phrased: "If I wronged you in one way or another, intentionally or unintentionally, or without knowing I wronged you, I am asking for your forgiveness." I remember my father approaching a number of people in the synagogue, just prior to services on Yom Kippur evening, asking for such forgiveness. It is a memory etched in my mind – one which I found moving and meaningful even as a child. For wrongs committed by one person toward another – for example, cheating someone in business, stealing from someone, or lying to or insulting someone – forgiveness can be granted only by the wronged party.

Maimonides devoted an entire book to the themes of repentance and forgiveness. Gathering rules and customs from all sources, he lists sins that can be forgiven and those that cannot. Interestingly, in the context of wrongs between one person and another, if the wronged person does not agree to forgive, he must be approached a second and even a third time in front of witnesses. If the wronged person still resists forgiving, he becomes the one considered to be the sinner. For, as Maimonides emphasizes, "It is forbidden for a person to be cruel and refuse to be appeased. Rather, he should be easily pacified and slow to anger . . . . This is the path of the seed of Israel and their upright spirit."[21] For the most part, just as God forgives, so must we, as individuals though even forgiveness by God is predicated on a request by the individual (sinner) to be forgiven.

Nevertheless, the question remains as to whether forgiveness is a religious obligation or an issue better described as a personal struggle left to the individual to decide. The most important goal in life is what Jung termed "Individuation." For some people, this process may call for transcending anger and moving directly to forgiving; others might need to follow their own religious tradition to define and govern their actions and forgiving even when it is not easy to do so. For example, in the words of the Dalai Lama, the Buddhist way is to forgive, albeit not forget, the wrongs done.[22] From both Jewish and Jungian perspectives, forgiveness is not a given for every situation and, most important, should not be considered a theological issue.

From a Jewish as well as a Jungian position, the challenge of forgiveness is ever present. Rabbi Sacks traces a fascinating progression of wrongs done in the Book of Genesis, and amplifies them as progressing from punishment to acceptance to forgiveness. For him, the tension and task of forgiveness are evident throughout the Bible, especially in Genesis, which includes the story of Ishmael and Isaac, rival firstborn sons, coming together for the burial of their father, Abraham; Esau forgiving Jacob upon his return from self-imposed exile to escape the wrath of his brother for "cheating" him of his rights as firstborn; and in the story of Joseph forgiving his brothers for selling him to the Midianites.[23]

Despite contradictory views among some of the Rabbis, for Maimonides the tradition and laws of forgiveness are clear and all-encompassing. He tells us that the guideline for forgiveness between wrongs done by one person toward another do not apply if the person wronged his teacher. In that scenario, the person who seeks forgiveness must persist and keep returning to ask forgiveness – even a thousand times. In the Talmud, we find the story of Rav, a leading Rabbi, who once insulted Rabbi Ḥananiah. "For thirteen years, he would come to him on Yom Kippur eve to beg forgiveness."[24]

Maimonides describes almost every possible permutation revolving around the issue of forgiveness. For example, if the person who was aggrieved is no longer alive, there is still a remedy for forgiveness. In such a situation, the person seeking forgiveness should gather ten people (a *minyan*, the minimum number needed for group prayer in Jewish tradition) and go to the grave of the person from whom one is seeking forgiveness and say the following prayer: "I sinned against God, the Lord of Israel, and against this person by doing the following to him." Or, if the penitent owed the deceased money and did not repay it before the wronged party died, the amount owed should be given to his family. If he cannot locate the family, he should hand the money or goods owed to a court, though he must confess openly to the court what he did to wrong that person. Without such a confession and public admission of guilt, there can be no forgiveness; with it, he will be forgiven.[25] Put in a Jungian context, the goal is consciousness, an acknowledgment of the issue (owning up to one's Shadow) with witnesses as a stand-in for confessing. The ultimate goal in the rituals surrounding forgiveness is similar to the reason one enters analysis: raising to consciousness what has been denied or repressed. This, as much as or more than the restitution of the money owed to the wronged party, lies behind the admission of one's wrongdoing. Restitution of the funds is not enough. Apologizing without owning up as to why the apology is needed is not sufficient in Judaism – or, from a Jungian perspective. We must do both: accept responsibility and make restitution.

The story of how, why, and when Joseph was able to forgive his brothers illustrates the importance of consciousness. As the scenario unfolded in the Book of Genesis[26] Joseph, clearly and intentionally, took his time in granting forgiveness. In the various interactions when his brothers came to Egypt to purchase grain for Jacob and their families, as the tale unfolded one might have expected Joseph to have more easily forgiven his brothers, especially given that at the start, he declared that it was God's will it should happen. All this took place for a reason, Joseph tells his brothers. One would think that Joseph could have told them right from the start that he not only recognized who they were but that he forgave them. However, Joseph first had to hear from his brothers that they understood the wrong that they had done him on a personal level. Only after Judah acknowledged what they had done and accepted responsibility for their action could Joseph forgive them. As seen through a Jungian lens, we know that this is true for us today as well. It is not enough to say "I am sorry." One needs to go into greater detail and explain why one is sorry, to "own" the wrong we have done. This is a point made by the clinical psychologist Janis Abrahms Spring, author of *How Can I Forgive You? The Courage to Forgive and the Freedom Not To*: "If the other person isn't sorry and hasn't made meaningful amends, the hurt party often can't and won't forgive."[27]

Seen through an archetypal lens, several examples in the Bible of not forgiving come to mind. Such important figures in Jewish history as Jacob and David did not forgive wrongs done to them. Jacob, even on his deathbed, did not forgive his sons Simeon and Levi for bringing shame on him and his family – shame for slaughtering the entire tribe of Hivites in revenge for Shechem first raping Dinah and then taking her as a wife. For Jacob, his honor was at stake since the killing took place even though a bargain had been struck to accept the marriage if all the Hivites were circumcised. This unwillingness to forget, or forgive, is clearly understood when Jacob, as he lay dying, in dispensing "blessings" to his children, addressed Simeon and Levi and let them know that they were not forgiven: "Accursed is their rage for it is intense, and their wrath for it is harsh; I will separate them within Jacob, and I will disperse them in Israel."[28]

King David, from whose lineage, according to legend, the Messiah will emerge, on his deathbed instructs Solomon to remember the wrong that his general, Joab ben Zeruiah, did to him and to two of his generals (Abner, son of Ner; and Amasa, son of Jether), by killing them, as well as Joab's execution of Absalom, David's favorite son. For despite Absalom's rebellion and attempt to take over the kingship by force, David was ready to forgive him as well as the two generals, who had at one time helped David. Nevertheless, David would not forgive his leading general for disobeying him, though it seemed as though he was executing men guilty of treason. On his deathbed, David tells Solomon that forgiveness was not an option: "You shall act according to your wisdom and not let his white hair go down to the grave in peace." In other words, David is telling him to make sure Abner does not die a natural death.[29]

For me, the tension between staying true to myself or living a life within the Orthodox community has been a lifelong challenge. Individuation is a goal I have strived toward and I prefer not to be bound by some of the religious restrictions of orthodoxy. In this context, I remember being brought to tears upon first hearing the song in the Broadway musical *Les Misérables* that included the verse "Who cares about your lonely soul, we're fighting for a higher goal." Yet, while Individuation should be our priority, we also need to connect to others, including community. Jung described it perfectly with his insistence that we do not Individuate in a vacuum. Still, no matter how much I value my own individuality, I will always feel an inner conflict between wanting to be part of the Jewish community or being a person in my own right. Long ago, I made the choice not to follow the letter of the law; rather, I have allowed myself to be guided by what I perceive as the spirit of the law. I am intent on finding my own path without subscribing to the dogma of the Orthodox environment. To this day, each time I participate in services in a synagogue, I feel a tension between wanting to be a part of the community and follow all the rules and customs inherent in being an Orthodox Jew or living a spiritual life in my own way.

The rituals of Jewish forgiveness are important components in my own development and emotional well-being, whether I am leading an Orthodox Jewish life or not. In Judaism, Individuation is not a goal; but being part of a larger community is. The link to community is an archetypal one and, like all Archetypes, goes back centuries. For Jews, the connection to community is deeper than just our own personal needs. For Jungians, this tension between individuality and community is important, though they need not necessarily be exclusive of each other. When it comes to forgiveness, this distinction is important, albeit a difficult path to adhere to as can be extrapolated from the prayer many Orthodox Jews recite just prior to going to sleep each night:

> I hereby forgive all who angered me or who denigrated me, or who sinned against me, be it physically or economically; be it toward my honor or toward anything connected with me; whether they were forced to do so, or whether they did so of their free will; whether accidentally or purposely; whether through words or through deeds, and may no person be punished on my account

As if to contradict Maimonides' long list of offenses that are not pardonable, others, from the Prophets of old through some Rabbis today, think that people can be forgiven by God for whatever wrongs they committed if they truly repent. This view can be extrapolated from the Yom Kippur liturgy which tells us that just as a father can more easily forgive his child, so can our sins be forgiven by our Father (God). In the same spirit, Jonathan Sacks points out that "Forgiveness comes from the idea of a God who loves us as a parent loves a child." In fact, he points out, the Hebrew word for mercy, *raḥamim*, comes from the word *reḥem* ("womb").[30]

The question that still requires a definitive consensus among Rabbis and Jewish scholars is: what is the rationale for thinking that God will always forgive his people and not allow their destruction? The clearest explanation is biblical – and archetypal. We start from the premise related in the Book of Genesis describing a compact that God made with Abraham. What is key is that God promises Abraham and, by extension, the people of Israel, Abraham's descendants, "an everlasting covenant throughout the ages, to be God to you and to your offspring." If we accept this rationale, we can understand why traditional Orthodox Judaism takes the position that "God's honor is at stake in the world if he does not forgive." If Jews (descendants of Abraham) were obliterated, it would be seen as God's inability to fulfill his covenantal obligations.[31]

The Jewish month of Tishrei begins what is known as the Ten Days of Awe, a period when we take stock of who we are and how our lives are being lived. This period begins on Rosh Hashanah (Jewish New Year) and closes on the night that Yom Kippur ends. On Rosh Hashanah, according to legend, our fate for the coming year is inscribed in a book in heaven, and on Yom Kippur, our fate is sealed. In amplifying this legend, some believe that three books are actually opened in heaven on Rosh Hashanah: the Book of Life, where the righteous are listed; the Book of Death, for those who are truly bad or evil; and a book for those in between – neither good nor bad and whose fate is not yet decided. On Yom Kippur, our fate is sealed and, as expressed in the prayers it will be determined

> How many will pass from the earth, and how many will be created; who will live, and who will die . . . who will rest, and who will wander; who will live in harmony and who will suffer; who will be poor and who will be rich; who will be degraded and who will be exalted.

Seeing the three scenarios – books of life, death, and in between – from a Jungian perspective, we could say it is an example of holding the opposites until a third, transcendent option arises.

Finally, in dealing with forgiveness, it would be negligent, from Jewish and Jungian perspectives, not to include the issue of the Holocaust. It is a daunting, impossible task to represent any one view that reflects what the Jewish, Christian, and Jungian communities think about forgiveness for the crimes committed by Nazi Germany. My presumption is that none of the "survivors" would forgive the Nazis or the concentration camp guards; I know that I wouldn't. However, some do not agree. Moreover, many believe that the German population and average German soldier of the time should not be held responsible, since not all were Nazis. This view holds that most civilians were not Nazi party members, that most German soldiers were not Nazis or Nazi sympathizers, and that Germany as a country should not be held responsible.

However, in Daniel Goldhagen's well researched book *Hitler's Willing Executioners*, he points out that "tens of thousands of ordinary Germans – not just the SS or Nazis – took part in the Holocaust."[32] Understandably, over seven decades later, forgiveness for those who supported the Holocaust, actively or passively, still evokes powerful emotions. From a personal as well as a Jewish perspective, I do not believe that all sins can be forgiven – certainly not those perpetrated in the Holocaust. Christianity and Buddhism, and even some streams of Judaism, may preach forgiveness for all sins or crimes; but the aspects of Jewish tradition of forgiveness that I resonate with do not take the position that all sins can be forgiven – certainly where there is no admission of guilt to accompany the request for forgiveness.

In this regard, complicating the issue further is the question of what attitude should we take toward those who helped many Nazis escape justice after the Holocaust? For, sadly, research and writing by historians has shown that the Catholic Church as well as the U.S. government were both complicit in helping many highly placed Nazis escape justice and prosecution. For the U.S., the fear and threat of communism was apparently more important than bringing Nazi criminals to justice. Many of these Nazis had expertise to offer the U.S. government in terms of identifying communist sympathizers and spies and that many among the scientists were helpful in furthering U.S. military goals. For example, among those secretly brought to the U.S. soon after the Holocaust was Wernher von Braun, who brought with him many German scientists who had helped Germany develop the V-2 rockets which terrorized London during the war. The U.S. government was more intent on utilizing their expertise than bringing them to justice.

In addition, the Catholic Church is also known to have helped many Nazi officers and SS officials escape to South America through a system now known as the "rat line." The Vatican has still not opened all its files to researchers, so it is impossible to prove whether the Pope and other highly placed leaders of the Church were aware of what was transpiring. However, it has been established that many who escaped Europe were helped by highly placed anti-Semitic priests and bishops in the Church who not only knew the identities of the Nazis they helped but actively helped them hide in South America. These Nazis included, among many others, such infamous criminals as Klaus Barbie, head of the Gestapo in Lyon, France; Adolf Eichmann, one of the main architects of the "final solution"; Walter Rauff, who perfected the Nazi mobile gas chambers; and Joseph Mengele, the sadistic physician in Auschwitz who carried out his experiments on Jewish inmates. In addition, between rampant corruption and overt anti-Semitism, several countries in South America gave refuge to leading Nazis – including Argentina, Brazil, and Chile.[33] Because of this, very few of the leading Nazis had to pay for their crimes. Although a few were ultimately extradited to face trial thanks to the work of Simon Wiesenthal, only Eichmann, who was kidnapped by Israel's Mossad, brought to Israel to stand trial, and hung, truly paid for his crimes (though there is no capital punishment in Israel except for Nazi war crimes, and no other person has ever been executed in Israel).[34]

Nevertheless, can anyone forgive these Nazi murderers? Do not the crimes committed by Nazi leaders go beyond the realm of forgiveness? Are these crimes even forgivable? And if so, by whom? What of the U.S. government that not only neglected to bring many Nazis to justice but enabled them to start new lives in the U.S., gave them new identities, and helped them escape justice? And what about the Vatican, which looked the other way when some of its priests and leaders helped Nazis escape to South America by providing new identities and funds for travel? Can we forgive them? For me, Jews, and for Jungians, forgiveness must go hand in hand with repentance, a conscious admission of wrongdoing, if it is even possible to forgive some crimes.

Some individuals might feel that it is morally wrong not to forgive; I disagree. It is not an issue of faith but of personal perspective: not all crimes can be forgiven. The prerequisite for any forgiveness is repentance, which requires admission and ownership of one's guilt. Such repentance, accompanied by admission of guilt, parallels the Jungian emphasis on consciousness, though given the horrors of what was perpetrated during the Holocaust, in good conscience one could choose not to forgive. Examples of the least one could hope for in exacting some satisfaction before granting forgiveness are the "truth and reconciliation" commissions in South Africa and Canada's Truth and Reconciliation Commission.

Simon Wiesenthal and Elie Wiesel, both survivors of concentration camps, and whose families were murdered by the Nazis, authored important works dealing with this theme. Wiesenthal and Wiesel spent much of their remaining years dealing with the consequences of the Holocaust. Both raised an all-important question: Can those who were Nazi criminals ever be forgiven – and, if so, by whom? Wiesenthal's response to the horrors of the Holocaust, in which most of his family was murdered, was to devote the rest of his life to tracking down Nazi war criminals, bringing them to face trial. Wiesel, on the other hand, whose father, mother, and siblings were murdered in concentration camps, devoted his remaining years to writing about the Holocaust in a more unemotional, yet powerful, way. Both were effective; ultimately, both were awarded Nobel Prizes. Interestingly, neither Wiesenthal nor Wiesel lost their faith in God, although both questioned how God could have allowed such atrocities to exist.

Sadly, Wiesenthal and Wiesel had a falling-out, but both came to the same conclusion: it was not up to the living to grant forgiveness to those Nazis who had perpetrated the crimes. Wiesel, in many interviews and – as but one example in a response to the question of forgiveness by the *Deseret News*, a Mormon newspaper in Utah – was of the view that "only God can forgive." Since those who were murdered need to be the ones to forgive, and a prerequisite for forgiveness is repentance, Wiesel made clear that he was unqualified to forgive, even if he wanted to.[35] Wiesenthal raised the issue of forgiveness to consciousness in his book *The Sunflower: On the Possibilities and Limits of Forgiveness*, where he used the experience of a dying Nazi soldier asking him for forgiveness. The soldier wanted to confess to a Jew, Wiesenthal, and be forgiven for being part of a group of Nazis who had murdered hundreds of Jews in a village in the Ukraine. Wiesenthal's response was silence but, in looking back, he wondered whether he should have granted the Nazi forgiveness.

Posed as a challenge to a number of leading theologians, philosophers, and Holocaust survivors, the responses to Wiesenthal's question naturally varied, from the Dalai Lama (whose response segued from the Holocaust to the atrocities committed by the Chinese government toward the people of Tibet) to theologians of different persuasions. The Dalai Lama thought that all people should be forgiven, with the distinction made between forgiving but not forgetting – and that not forgiving "is not the Buddhist way."[36] Alternatively, leading Christian theologian Matthew Fox states: "Some sins are too big for forgiveness, even for priests. Public penance is required."[37] From a Jewish perspective, and one I identify with, is the response of Abraham Joshua Heschel: "It is preposterous to assume that anybody alive can extend forgiveness for the suffering of any one of the six million who perished."[38]

Writing about forgiveness has given me the opportunity to deal with this issue from a personal, Jewish, as well as Jungian perspective. It has pushed me to differentiate between those who might be forgiven – including, at times, myself – and those I don't care to forgive. It has helped me understand that I needed to come to terms with whether I wanted to forgive some in my life who did not ask for forgiveness (some of the people may not be alive anymore) or toward others who did not wrong me intentionally and might be surprised that I held anger toward them. It has highlighted the tension I often feel in furthering my Individuation process with the need to honor and stay connected to the Jewish collective that I was raised in. Most important, it has helped me better appreciate the depth and nuances of Jewish tradition and culture regarding the issue of forgiveness.

Notes

1 Robert Enright, "Forgiveness Is a Choice," American Psychological Association presentation, 2001; J. Maltby et al., *Journal of Research in Personality* 42 (2008): 1088–1094.
2 Diane Cole, "The Healing Power of Forgiveness," *Wall Street Journal*, March 21, 2016.
3 Maimonides (Rambam), *Hilkhot Teshuvah: The Laws of Repentance* (Brooklyn, NY: Moznaim Publishing Company, 1990), 3:14, p. 86.
4 BT Baba Metzia 58b.
5 Lev. 4:22–35.
6 Jonathan Sacks, *From Optimism to Hope* (London: Bloomsbury, 2004), p. 67.
7 Lev. 16: 7–10.
8 Num. 13:29; Deut. 10:16, 25:17–19; 1 Sam. 15:19.
9 Genesis 32:22–32, 36:10–12.
10 Exod. 32:14.
11 Amos 2:5–5.
12 Luke 6:37, 23:34.
13 *Maḥzor* (special prayer book for holidays) for High Holidays; see Musaf service.
14 Amos 1:3–11.
15 Jer. 15:1; Ezek. 14:13–20.
16 Maimonides, *Hilkhot Teshuvah*, chapter 3, pp. 82, 84.
17 Maimonides, *Hilkhot Teshuvah*, chapter 4.
18 Abraham Joshua Heschel, *In This Hour: Heschel's Writings in Nazi Germany and London Exile* (Philadelphia: Jewish Publication Society, 2019), pp. 104, 144.

19 Exod. 34:6–7; BT: Tractate Tosefta Sotah 4:1.
20 *Encyclopaedia Judaica*, 6:1435; BT Bereshit 7a.
21 Maimonides, *Hilkhot Teshuvah*, 2:1, p. 46.
22 The Dalai Lama, in Simon Wiesenthal, *The Sunflower: On the Possibilities and Limits of Forgiveness* (New York: Schocken Books, 1998), pp. 129–130.
23 Jonathan Sacks, *Covenant and Conversation* (Jerusalem: Koren, 2009), p. 326.
24 Maimonides, *Hilkhot Teshuvah*, 2:10, 46, 46n.
25 Maimonides, *Hilkhot Teshuvah*, 3:48.
26 Genesis: (42–45).
27 Quoted in Cole, "The Healing Power of Forgiveness."
28 Genesis 34 and 49:5.
29 1 Kings 1:2:6.
30 Sacks, *From Optimism to Hope*, p. 103.
31 Gen. 17:7; *Encyclopaedia Judaica*, 6:1435.
32 Stanley Hoffman, book review of Daniel Jonah Goldhagen's *Hitler's Willing Executioners*, *Foreign Affairs* (May–June 1996).
33 See Philippe Sands, *The Rat Line* (New York: Alfred A. Knopf, 2021) and David G. Marwell, *Menglele: Unmasking the Angel of Death* (New York: W.W. Norton, 2020).
34 Moreover, the primary goal of putting Eichmann on trial for Israel was educational – to illustrate to the younger generation in Israel, and the world at large, what happened in the Holocaust. Otherwise, Eichmann could have been assassinated in Argentina and not brought to Israel to stand trial.
35 Interview with Simon Wiesenthal, *Desert News*, May 20, 2006.
36 Wiesenthal, *The Sunflower*, pp. 129–130.
37 Wiesenthal, *The Sunflower*, p. 145.
38 Wiesenthal, *The Sunflower*, p. 171.

Chapter 8
Scapegoating and Shadow

Figure 8.1 Artist and date unknown, Joseph's brothers throw him into the pit, engraving.

In Jungian terms, scapegoating is understood as projecting the Shadow – shifting negative feelings, or guilt, from accuser to accused. In everyday language, scapegoating can be defined as identifying an individual or a group and accusing them of causing a negative feeling that one is experiencing. The scapegoated individual or group is shunned, ejected, or – as is the case in pogroms and mob rampage – murdered. On a collective level, the scapegoating of Jews was, and still is, a classic example of this phenomenon. On a personal level, it can also be experienced as responding to the envy someone feels, stimulating feelings that are difficult to contain. These feelings are then projected onto another person or collective and often acted upon.

From an archetypal perspective, in the Judeo-Christian world, the term "scapegoat" is associated with the account in the Book of Leviticus describing the ritual of sacrificing two goats on Yom Kippur, one released into the desert and the other ritually sacrificed. Both goats served as carriers of the sins ostensibly committed by the people.[1] Scapegoating can take place on several levels, the individual as well the collective. In the Book of Genesis,[2] the tale of Joseph as scapegoat for his brothers is an example of scapegoating on a personal level. It was only later, on a collective level, that the Israelite experience in the desert included the introduction of a ritual responsible for incorporating the term "scapegoat" into our vocabulary. In Jewish history, the story of Joseph and his brothers traverses the personal and the collective levels and encompasses Joseph's experiences personally as well as the role he plays as part of the Jewish collective experience.

The Personal: Joseph and His Brothers

In Jewish myth, two heroic individuals are associated with the coming of the Messiah: *M'shiah ben David* (Messiah, son of David) and *M'shiah ben Yosef* (Messiah, son of Joseph), one a descendant of the House of David, and the other a descendant of the House of Joseph. Messiah ben Joseph was generally understood as a forerunner Messiah who would prepare the way for Messiah ben David (the ultimate Messiah).[3] The story of Joseph and his brothers is discussed extensively in Jewish legend: "few biblical figures have inspired more extensive and more universal literary testament than Joseph. . . . He appears in poems and plays, including Jewish, Christian, and Islamic literature music and art . . . and dozens of plays in Spanish, French, Italian, Latin, German, Dutch, and Hebrew literature."[4]

During the festival of *Sukkot* (originally a harvest festival, known as Tabermacles), one of the three major festivals in Judaism, Jews are commanded to dwell in a *sukkah* (a temporary booth) for seven days to commemorate the exodus from Egypt and the life of the Israelites during the 40 years they wandered in the desert. During the holiday of *Sukkot*, each day one of the important figures in Judaism, the shepherds of the people, is symbolically invited to join the family as *ushpizin* (Aramaic, "honored guests"). Joseph is one of those honored guests (the others being Abraham, Isaac, Jacob, Moses, Aaron, and David) with each of the seven being invited into the *sukkah* at the start of the meal with the following words: "Let us invite our guests. Let us prepare the table. Be seated, guests from on high." These icons of Jewish history and tradition are considered helpful partners with God.[5]

The sukkah becomes what Jung would describe as a *temenos*, a sacred space where one can connect to an inner spirituality while performing the commandment of honoring the forefathers of Judaism. Joseph is one of these fathers and serves as a helper in our inner quest. These iconic figures in Judaism represent a higher level of spirituality and put us in touch with what Jung termed the "numinous" – an experience of inner spirituality, our soul. When seen through a Jungian lens, Joseph and the other fathers represent inner figures of wisdom.

The story of Joseph and his brothers precedes the well-known portion in Leviticus that describes Aaron as high priest who, on Yom Kippur, designates two goats to carry the sins of the people. One goat is sent into the wilderness, to Azazel, and the other is sacrificed as an offering to God. Aaron's role is to take one goat "and confess over it all the iniquities and transgressions of the Israelites, whatever their sins, symbolically placing them on the head of the live goat," before setting it free in the wilderness. The other goat is sacrificed on the altar as an offering to God.[6] The Hebrew word for "scapegoat" can be understood as derived from combining two words: *se'ir* ("goat") and *azazel*, a word used only once in the Bible, and which appears in the context of this ancient Yom Kippur ritual. Despite many interpretations, there is no definitive understanding or translation of exactly what *azazel* means. Is it a place? Is it a concept? In spoken Hebrew, it connotes hell; but biblically, one cannot be certain of how the ancient Israelites related to the word.

Scapegoating rituals are archetypal. They are evident not only in Judaism but in Greek, Roman, and other civilizations among others. In ancient Greece, for example, the ritual of scapegoating, known as *pharmakos*, was also part of the culture. This custom may well have influenced the Jewish tradition, and it manifested itself through an animal or person carrying the projections of the collective. "In Athens, in exceptional times, such as a drought or a famine, certain ugly people were selected and sacrificed." Or, at the Thargelia, a festival for Apollo, "a man with white figures around his neck was expelled from the city as a purification for the men, and another man with black figures for the women."[7]

In the story of Joseph, we see how he was scapegoated by his brothers, prompted by their envy of him. Later, in Egypt, Joseph is scapegoated again after he resists the sexual overtures of Potiphar's wife. Spurned by Joseph, she accuses him of initiating this interaction which results in his master, her husband, having him imprisoned. In both instances – the brothers' envy and Potiphar's wife feeling scorned – Joseph became the scapegoat. Both represent the projection of their own Shadow Joseph.

From a Jungian perspective, scapegoating is the manifestation of one's Shadow, a repressed, Unconscious aspect of their personality projected onto another person, or, as has been evident in the spread of anti-Semitism, onto another collective. A legitimate question is whether Joseph was somehow responsible for inviting these projections. In describing how projections work, Jung's view was that where there is projection, there is also a hook to catch it, meaning that there often is something in the person who is the object of a projection that provides fertile ground for – indeed, almost invites – the projection. Projections onto another person do not come out of nowhere; in the legend of Joseph, we see that he provided quite a hook. Joseph plays a significant role in becoming the object of his brothers' scapegoating. June Singer, in *Boundaries of the Soul*, connects the scapegoat role that some people find themselves in with the role of victim. She notes that until there is a consciousness that can break the cycle, the person who is scapegoated plays a role in the process as victim contributing to, and inviting, the projection.[8]

While we have been conditioned to see the story of Joseph as one in which his brothers are jealous of him, the Hebrew text begins by relating that the brothers hated him (*vayisne'u oto*), and it is only a few verses later that we hear his brothers were jealous of him, *vayikan'u oto*. In Jewish tradition, the Rabbis say that there are no extra words in the Torah – no words without meaning. The tale of Joseph and his brothers begins with Joseph relating two dreams. In the first, he and his brothers were gathering sheaves of wheat when his sheaf stood up and remained standing. Then, his brothers' sheaves gathered around and bowed down to his sheaf. In Joseph's second dream, the sun and the moon and 11 stars were bowing down to him, which prompted even his father, Jacob, to berate him: "Are I and your mother and your brothers to bow down to you?"[9]

How can we reconcile the messianic figure of Joseph with the scapegoat that he became for his brothers? A natural place to begin is to understand why his brothers resented him, blaming him for being his father's favorite child. After the first dream, we read that his brothers hated him; it is only after relating the second dream that the Hebrew text describes the brothers as being jealous of him. What turns hatred into jealousy? One commentator noted that, at first, they hated Joseph because he was Jacob's favorite; but after the second dream, they experienced him as narcissistic, which brought on jealousy.[10] Nor was Jacob blameless, as we can extrapolate from the text in Genesis: "Now Israel [Jacob] loved Joseph more than all his children because, Jewish myth tells us, Joseph's features were like his," an example of narcissism on the part of the father as well as his son, not an uncommon phenomenon in families, even today.[11]

Moreover, Jacob made Joseph a *ketonet passim* – translated in most Bibles as a coat of many colors. However, *pasim* is not "many colors"; rather, the correct translation of *pasim* is "stripes" or "lines." In this context, *Rashi* (in Judaism, the most authoritative commentator on the Bible) translates it as "a garment of fine wool," "a long-sleeved embroidered tunic, made of variously colored strips of fine wool"; somehow, it morphed into a coat of many colors. However, Rashi notes,[12] another implication of the long sleeves is that it was not meant for work since Joseph, unlike his brothers, did not have to do physical labor – in all likelihood, contributing to the brothers' jealousy of him.

Nevertheless, at one point Jacob sends Joseph, who, alone among the brothers, was given a "special coat," to check on them when they were working and tending the flocks. From a distance, the brothers noticed Joseph coming and conspired to kill him. According to legend, they wanted to have dogs attack him, which would not be considered murder.[13] Brother Reuben, however, persuades the other brothers not to kill Joseph but rather to throw him into a pit, with Reuben's intention being to return later and rescue him. For some reason, Reuben walks away, but before he returns, the other brothers decide to sell Joseph to a group of Midianite traders who were passing by. The Midianites, in turn, take Joseph to Egypt, where they sold him as a slave. In Egypt, Joseph becomes servant to Potiphar, chief steward of Pharaoh, who recognizes how gifted Joseph is and puts him in charge of his household. Potiphar's wife, not referred to by name in the Bible (Jewish and Islamic legend give her name as Zuleika), tries to seduce Joseph. Resisting her advances, Joseph runs away, though not before she tears his coat from him, a coat she shows as proof of her accusation that Joseph tried to seduce her. Joseph is then thrown into prison as a punishment.

Coats play an important symbolic role in Joseph's story: first, the coat arousing his brothers' envy; then the coat that Potiphar's wife pulled off him when he resisted her advances and then used as proof to condemn him. If viewed as a symbol, a coat – indeed, clothing in general – can be seen as representing one's persona, the outer part of our personality, the face we show the world. In Joseph's case, as we shall see, it took multiple changes of clothing for him to shed his persona, his narcissism, and to stop approaching life on an Ego level. It is Joseph's persona that gets him into trouble – which inevitably occurs if the Ego is allowed to play a dominant role in who we are as individuals.

In Jewish myth, Joseph is far from the untarnished icon he is often seen as – practically a saint. In fact, rabbinical commentators have described Joseph as overly concerned with his looks and dress. In the legend, Joseph, "though only seventeen years old . . . walked with a swagger, and he styled his hair [and] he painted his eyes, and dressed his hair carefully," though the most glaring critique of Joseph was his habit of "bringing evil reports of his brethren to his father," that is, he gossiped.[14] When he approached his brothers out in the field, Joseph "came strutting like a peacock, which was his wont," which undoubtedly sealed his fate with his brothers and encouraged them to first throw him into a pit and then sell him to the Midianites.[15]

One could say that for Joseph, the descent into the pit into which his brothers threw him began a process of self-reflection. Symbolically, descent represents going down into the Unconscious, confronting and coming to terms with one's Shadow. An illustration, and a parallel to Joseph's descent, can be gleaned from the myth of Inanna, Sumerian goddess of heaven and earth, descending to the underworld and confronting her "dark sister" Ereshkigal, and then returning from the underworld with a raised level of consciousness.[16] In Joseph's case, this process started with his brothers throwing him into a pit and continued to develop after he had been thrown into prison in Egypt. Only later, after his imprisonment, did he begin to claim his own Shadow. These experiences of descent began what Jung would term Joseph's inner transformation. But true change and inner transformation and consciousness do not develop in a linear fashion or in a straight line. After Joseph attained high stature in Egypt, he went back into denial mode and fell into the habits of his younger years. According to legend, "When Joseph found himself so comfortably situated, he began to eat and drink well, to frizz his hair," which prompted "The Holy One, to say to Joseph: Your father is in mourning for you in sackcloth and ashes, and you eat and drink well, and frizz your hair – you pampered brat! As you live, I shall sic a she-bear upon you. At once, it came to pass that his master's wife cast her eyes upon Joseph."[17]

Joseph is depicted as vain and self-involved. It was not until after being thrown into prison and stripped of his coat, symbolically his persona, that Joseph was able to start to Individuate and become a real person and develop into the Jewish icon he became. First, Joseph had to spend two years in prison before he could begin to grow into the role destined for him – a forefather of Judaism and a role model for his people. Before that, he was dealing with first-half-of-life issues, concerned with his looks and appearance and unable to relate to others. From a Jungian perspective, his suffering brought growth, which is the positive side to one having to suffer in life. If we look for meaning in our life struggles, alchemically speaking, if we are fortunate, we are able to extract gold from the lead.

Individuation is a lifelong process. The Hebrew expression *ma shelo ya'aseh hasekhel, ya'aseh hazman* means that, at times, what we cannot achieve with our thinking, time helps us accomplish. Psychologically, it took Joseph a few more years to begin to truly Individuate. Until then, his identity had been wrapped up in being Jacob's favorite son. His father, Jacob, was a hard act to follow, as evidenced in his successful wrestling with the angel and being renamed Israel by God with the blessing: "A nation, yea, an assembly of nations, shall descend from you,"[18] with his new name coming to represent the identity of future generations of Jews. Joseph, following his time in prison and insightful interpretation of Pharaoh's dreams, was appointed to the most powerful position in Egypt. Only then, after his descent and reemergence, did Joseph begin to develop into an individual with his own identity and start living his own life apart from family and tribe.

Notwithstanding Joseph's new and important role in society, albeit Egyptian and not the Israelite tribe of his birth, Joseph was left with a residual anger at his father as well as his brothers. With great insight, Lord Rabbi Jonathan Sacks poses a perceptive and analytical question, one that a good psychoanalyst would ask: Why didn't Joseph send for his beloved father, Jacob, earlier? Why did he wait all those years, until his brothers came to Egypt, needing to purchase food for Jacob's flock and family? After all, Sacks has pointed out, Joseph was already in a safe position in Egypt and could easily have done so. Rabbi Sacks' response to this question was that Joseph was angry at his father for exposing him to his brothers' jealousy.

> Joseph did not communicate with his father because he believed his father no longer wanted to see or hear from him. His father had terminated the relationship.... He could not have known that Jacob still loved him, that his brothers had deceived their father by showing him Joseph's blood-stained coat.[19]

If we follow this train of thought, we can understand that Joseph was projecting his own anger on to his father; this is how projections work. When we do not have a reality check to draw on, we tend to fill the void with our own, usually negative, projections. Joseph's experiences, from the betrayal of his brothers to his enslavement in Egypt, would logically have had the effect of a life-changing trauma. As a result, while Joseph, the dreamer and interpreter of dreams, becomes a leading official in Egypt, second only to Pharoah, the price he paid for this achievement was an emotional one – a denial and suppression of his past life. Indeed, Joseph's name was changed from the Hebrew Joseph to the Egyptian name *Zaph'nath-Pane'ah* (a person to whom hidden things are revealed). Following his elevation to second in command in Egypt, Joseph marries the daughter of the Egyptian priest of On and does his best to put his past life behind him. Moreover, he named his firstborn son Manasseh, in Hebrew, meaning that God had made him forget his hardship and parental home.[20]

Eventually, Joseph matured, as was evidenced in his finally acknowledging who he was to his brothers. Still, it was not easy for him to forgive and move on. If we follow the story closely, we see that until he reached the point of forgiveness and was able to reclaim his past connection to his own tribe, he teased and tormented his brothers. We could even make the case that Joseph was sadistic toward his brothers, first denying them the purchase of grain and then insisting that they bring Benjamin (his younger, full brother) to Egypt. Before Joseph revealed his identity, it took his brother Judah to approach him and plead the case that would sway Joseph. In Judah's reaching out to Joseph, the biblical text is clear that Judah approached Joseph and offered himself as ransom in place of Benjamin.

In Judaism, one must acknowledge the wrong that one has done to another as a step toward receiving forgiveness. In this case, Judah noted that their father was under the impression that Joseph was no longer alive and that if Benjamin did not return, their father would surely die, since Jacob's soul was bound up with Benjamin's soul. By describing Jacob's connection to Benjamin as a soul connection, Judah was acknowledging the reality of Jacob preferring the children of Rachel (Joseph and Benjamin), to the other brothers – a jealousy that had prompted the scapegoating of Joseph in the first place. By doing so, Judah broke the emotional barrier between the brothers and enabled Joseph to access his long-suppressed feelings and break down in tears. By finally accessing these feelings, previously masked by anger and denial, Joseph was able to ask about his father's welfare and reestablish his ties to the tribe that he had been a part of. Joseph's reintegration into the tribe was finally complete, as described in the Book of Exodus when Moses, as his last act in leaving Egypt with the Israelites, fulfilled Joseph's wish to be buried in the land of his fathers. "And Moses took with him the bones of Joseph, who had extracted an oath from the children of Israel, saying, 'God will be sure to take notice of you: then you shall carry up my bones from here with you.'"[21]

The Collective Jewish Experience

In addition to the individual example of the envy and jealousy of Joseph's brothers as fertile ground for his scapegoating, from a Jungian perspective scapegoating can also be seen as manifesting itself on a collective level. Here, too, scapegoating can also be seen as emanating from a denial of the Shadow – a projection of the Shadow onto another nation or people. Most of us associate Western anti-Semitism as a Church-inspired vendetta directed toward the Jewish people for rejecting the divinity of Jesus and contributing to his crucifixion. In reality, anti-Semitism predates Christianity by hundreds of years – one better described as an archetypal, anti-Jewish bias. It is important to understand anti-Semitism as specifically referring to Jews, since Arabs, like the Jews, are also a Semitic people. The reality is that a great deal of what is referred to as anti-Semitism exists in the Arab world as well and is directed specifically at Jews – so much so that the historian and Holocaust studies scholar Deborah Lipstadt (a leading Holocaust historian) "advocates the use of 'antisemitism' as one word rather than anti-Semitism, because the term was invented specifically to describe a hatred of Jews."[22]

Anti-Jewish bias dates as far back as the Egyptian, Greek, and Roman Empires, indicating that anti-Judaism is not simply a European phenomenon that arose following the death of Jesus. This bias toward the Jewish people is archetypal and can be traced to lies spread by Greek and Roman historians well before Christianity appears on the scene. Demonizing the Jews and the Jewish religion by ancient peoples such as Greeks and Romans set the stage for the scapegoating of Jews by Christianity. An origin of this anti-Semitism, anti-Judaism, is indicated here:

> An Egyptian high priest of the temple at Heliopolis named Manetho was one of the first to popularize conspiracies and distortions about Jews and Judaism in the third century BCE. He claimed that Jews were originally the Hyksos who had invaded Egypt and then been expelled when the "leprous tribe" was accused of sacrilege and impiety, stories repeated not long after by Lysimachus (third-century BCE Macedonian general) and Chaeremon of Alexandria (first century CE Egyptian historian). What this leprosy libel really implies is a dehumanized condition . . . just as the Nazis argued centuries later with accusations that Jews were vermin, a dangerous underclass requiring elimination.[23]

What is important about these libels is to understand the archetypal nature of anti-Semitism – in effect, anti-Judaism. These early prejudices by Romans, Greeks, and Egyptians enhanced and laid the groundwork for the prejudices of later generations that spread anti-Jewish myths that became catalysts for the persecution of Jews in Europe.

Part of what served as motivation for this ancient aspect of anti-Judaism was that from biblical times, Jews not only denigrated the gods of their neighboring tribes but kept a distance from them socially as well. The Israelites were described as a "nation apart" – an "other," from which naturally emerged the projection onto Jews that they believed that they were superior. One need look no further than the Bible, where the Midianite prophet Balaam was hired by the king of Moab to put a curse on the Israelites. The incident, a fascinating tale, which included a donkey who spoke, describes Balaam as blessing the Israelites instead of putting a curse on them. In the course of his assignment to put a curse on the Israelites, Balaam's famous phrase was that the Israelites were "a people that dwells apart, not reckoned among the nations."[24]

Whether one accepts the biblical version of how the Israelites escaped their enslaved status in Egypt and made their way through 40 years in the desert, or reads the story as a combination of history and myth, what developed over time was that many passages in the Bible were cited and utilized in anti-Jewish tracts that were written and promulgated over the centuries. In this regard, bias toward the Israelites, the tribes that ultimately transformed into the Jewish nation, carried the projected anti-Jewish dogma of previous centuries. This anti-Jewish prejudice became potent from the time the Israelites left Egypt and made their way back to their homeland of Canaan. From that point, the Bible and Western history tell us that the people of Israel became a nation in its own right. In this regard, according to Paul Johnson: "the Exodus was an act of political separation and resistance; but it was also, and above all, a religious act."[25]

These ancient Israelites abstained from eating at the same table or drinking wine with non-Israelites and they married only with others from their own tribe. Dining with only their own people may well have developed during the period of enslavement in Egypt. For the custom of not partaking in meals with other tribes or people was true of the ancient Egyptians as well – at least as extrapolated from the narrative of Joseph and his brothers. There, in the biblical text, we see that when Joseph gave orders for his staff to "serve the meal" to his brothers, "they served him by himself, and them by themselves, for the Egyptians could not dine with the Hebrews, since that would be abhorrent to the Egyptians."[26] Ironically, the same is true for most observant Jews today – especially regarding the drinking of wine not made by a Jew – which contributes to keeping them separate from the rest of people in whatever country they reside. Psychologically, when there is such a distance between people, socially and politically, it presents fertile ground for projecting the Shadow on to the "other." From a Jungian perspective, these projections naturally lend themselves to the anti-Jewish feelings since it gives the impression that they (the non-Jews) are not good enough to dine with or marry someone who is Jewish. Indeed, since ancient times, anti-Semites have used this trope to emphasize that Jews believe that they are superior to other people – that Jews believe that they are the "chosen people," better than the people and nations around them.

One of the earliest assaults on Judaism, a politically motivated attempt to suppress the Jewish religion, was driven by the Syrian-aligned Greeks during the time of Antiochus Epiphanes (175–164 BCE). It was political, religious, and cultural. The (Syrian) Greeks defined themselves as the torchbearers of Hellenistic ideals, and the antagonism of Judaism to every other religion was an obstacle. However, the attempt to suppress Judaism backfired when King Antiochus Epiphanes ordered the sacrifice of pigs on the altar of the Temple in Jerusalem, which led to a revolt.[27] Diodorus, a Greek historian, in the first century BCE, stated that Antiochus believed that "if he could break Jewish habits regarding pork, he could break the Jewish religion."[28] Another point of animus toward Jews was the custom of circumcising all males in the tribe. This particular antipathy toward the Jewish custom of male circumcision also dates back to Antiochus, who devoted himself to the spread of Hellenism. An example of denigrating Jewish custom and tradition can be seen in the poems of Juvenal, a Roman satirist in the first and second centuries, who portrayed Jews as "unprepared to guide a person who has lost his way if he is not an observer of the law of Moses, and as unwilling to give a person a drink if he is uncircumcised."[29] Following the attempt at the political, cultural, and religiously inspired policy of humiliating the Jews, a rebellion resulted in expelling the Greek army of Antiochus. The revolt, led by the Hasmoneans, ultimately gave us the holiday of Hanukkah.

For Jews, eating pork has always represented a glaring rejection of God's commandments, an expression of the religion that is archetypal and has always been an essential part of Jewish dietary laws. This dietary restriction came to symbolize Jewish separateness from the nations around them and was used as another rationalization for the scapegoating of Jews. Where Jewish tradition holds the pig to be an unclean and disease-carrying animal, Jews' refusal to eat pork was turned into the opposite of what was intended. For example, Petronius, the first-century Roman writer who is credited as the author of *Satyricon*, referred to Jews as "worshippers of a 'pig god,'" and their refusal to eat pork was twisted into evidence of a Jewish fondness for pigs."[30]

Scapegoating Jews for their refusal to eat pig meat and for their insistence on circumcising males continued throughout medieval times and took wing with the spread of Christianity. This dehumanization of Jews was manifested not only in the writings of the church fathers but in the art and sculpture that often appeared on the doors and paintings of cathedrals and churches. These anti-Jewish images are known as *Judensaus* – images of Jews in obscene contact with large female pigs – and are found in some churches of Europe to this day. One such example is a *Judensau* in a church in Wittenberg, Germany, a sculpture lauded by no less a religious figure than Martin Luther. The sculpture, which portrays Jews participating in obscene acts with a pig, has remained there since Luther's time, despite attempts by some in the Jewish community to have it removed – efforts that have been denied by courts in Germany. A communication by Luther transmitted this message:

> Here on our Church in Wittenberg, a sow is sculpted in stone. Young pigs and Jews lie suckling under her. Behind the sow, a rabbi is bent over the sow, lifting her right leg, holding her tail high and looking intensely under her tail and into a Talmud placed under her as though he were reading something acute or extraordinary.[31]

Luther's loathing of Jews seems to have had no bounds. For, in addition to his comments extolling the virtues of the *Judensau* sculpture above his church, he wrote pamphlets aimed at the Jews of Europe, which were filled with hatred and such vitriol toward Jews as:

> The Jews are brutes.... Their synagogues are pigsties; they ought to be burned, for Moses would do it, if he came back to this world. They drag in mire the divine words, they live by evil and plunder, and they are wicked beasts that ought to be driven out like mad dogs.[32]

While the scapegoating and persecution of Jews dates back to ancient times, in Europe it took hold and spread exponentially beginning with the spread of Christianity in the late fourth century. What began in the ancient Greek, Roman, and Egyptian civilizations as nationalistic, political, and economic bias toward Jews developed into a theological movement, a stimulus for violence and persecution. Before Constantine declared Christianity the religion of the land, the early Christians were considered to be another sect in Judaism and were themselves persecuted. Ironically, while anti-Semites have accused the Jews of killing Jesus, he lived and died as an observant Jew, and the first Christians were themselves Jews.

Starting in the late fifth century, the Church as an institution made anti-Judaism a principal part of Christian doctrine throughout Europe. However, as we have seen, the origins of this anti-Jewish bias date back to ancient Egypt, Greece, and Rome; only with the spread of Christianity did it became accepted religious dogma. In this regard, it is important to note that the persecution and prejudice against Jews developed primarily in countries that were originally part of the Roman Empire – areas where Christianity took hold and flourished. Over time, Egyptian, Greek, and Roman anti-Judaism progressed to active Christian persecution of the Jews and was transformed from a nationalist to a theological stance, one that was a continuation of the archetypal anti-Judaism of ancient times. Although ancient civilizations found Jewish tradition and customs abhorrent to them, they had no use for the Bible, something that Christians had in common with Jews. Yet ironically, Christianity was built on the biblical foundation of Judaism; its development depended on a theology calling for the rejection of Judaism, to be replaced by a "New Testament" and a rejection of its own past history. By the fifth century, Christianity no longer saw itself as part of Judaism, with the result being that it was necessary to demean the religion it had grown out of. From this point, Jews carried a projection of the Christian Shadow that rejected, and was in denial of, their own Jewish roots.

Sylvia Perera, in *The Scapegoat Complex*, points out that "In Jungian terms, scapegoating is a form of denying the Shadow of both man and God. What is seen as unfit to conform with the ego ideal, or with the perfect goodness of God, is repressed and denied, or split off and made unconscious."[33] Seen in this framework, "the scapegoater feels a relief in being lighter, without the burden of carrying what is unacceptable to his or her ego ideal, without the Shadow."[34] Jews, by their very existence, carry the Shadow of Christianity, and, as a result of dismissing their own Jewish roots, they have scapegoated Jews.

Other Shadow projections Jews carried included being labeled as materialistic worshippers of gold – justified by pointing to the Israelites building and worshipping the Golden Calf while in the desert – as well as being the murderers of Christian children for the baking of *matzo* for Passover.[35] These accusations were particularly virulent around Easter with anti-Semitic rabble-rousers, at times priests, encouraging assaults on Jewish communities. Unsurprisingly, these blood libels were fueled by rumors that grew out of the ignorance of Jewish ritual, since Jewish dietary law restrictions preclude using even the smallest amount of blood in food, including, of course, *matzo*, which is made from wheat and flour. An example of the lack of knowledge about Judaism is that in order to be deemed kosher and edible by Jews, even meat and chicken, let alone bread or matzo, require enough salting to eliminate any blood left before consumption.

Nevertheless, it is important to note that the scapegoating of Jews, including the blood libels that Jews endured, were archetypal and can be traced back centuries – well before Christianity took hold in Europe and at least as far back as the third and second centuries BCE. For example, Antiochus VII Sidetes of Syria (ruler of the Hellenistic Seleucid Empire from 138 to 129 BCE), another villain in Jewish history, is said to have fabricated a story that dehumanized Jews and, in effect, portrayed them as cannibals. Amazingly, he is reported to have said that he entered the Israelite Temple in Jerusalem and found "a non-Israelite fattened up and prepped for human sacrifice." As if that were not enough to slander Judaism, yet another myth associated with this Seleucid king, one which he or his court disseminated, was that he entered the Temple and came across a "golden donkey that was being worshipped in the inner sanctum."[36]

While blood libels date back to ancient times, similar accusations continued to surface throughout medieval Europe. These allegations contributed significantly to the pogroms and violence directed at Jewish communities. For example, in the first part of the twelfth century, a monk named Theobald – paradoxically, a Jewish convert to Christianity – popularized a conspiracy theory that Jewish leaders gathered in Narbonne, France, to select a Christian child to sacrifice.[37] Similar slanderous stories continued to circulate throughout Europe. The setting for one of the most infamous of these rumors was in Norwich, England, in 1144, when the mutilated body of a young Christian boy, William of Norwich, was discovered. William was hailed as a martyr, with associations to the crucifixion of Jesus, and his grave became a pilgrimage site in England with masses of people flocking there, leading to his being declared a saint by the Church of England. Leading up to this sainthood, the Jewish community of Norwich was scapegoated and accused of his death as part of a "ritual murder" – a rumor that resulted in hundreds of Jews being tortured, forced to falsely confess to crimes they did not commit, and murdered.[38]

Most disturbing about the martyrdom of William of Norwich is that it fueled rumors that became a model for the blood libels and accusations that Jews engaged in such rituals in their religious observances. For example, in 1255 in England, it was dredged up by the local English authorities and used as justification to arrest and hang 18 Jews for the alleged crime of fattening up "Little Hugh" of Lincoln, killing him and using his blood to bake *matzo*.[39] These blood libels persisted throughout Europe and England in the following centuries, even as recently as the twentieth century. Accusations of Jews committing crimes of killing Christian children and using their blood for baking *matzo* continued, even surfacing in the U.S. as late as 1928. That year, the Jews of Massena, New York, were accused of the kidnapping and ritual murder of a Christian girl and using her blood for Passover *matzo*. The leaders of this small Jewish community were rounded up for questioning and, incredibly, state troopers investigating the incident interrogated the Rabbi of the town and asked: "Is it true that your people in the Old Country offer human sacrifices?" It was only after the child was found (apparently, she had wandered into the woods, fallen asleep, and lost her way) that an apology was issued by the mayor of the town.[40] Scapegoating of Jews and blood-libel accusations generally led to the violence, murder, and expulsions of entire Jewish communities. In this regard, it is easy to understand that the logical progression of the pogroms aimed at Jews would ultimately lead to the extermination of Jews by the Nazis – a natural outgrowth. "Anti-Jewish violence was particularly rabid in Germany, where it had been preceded by a dark half century of anti-Jewish persecution in conjunction with a succession of blood libels and accusation of host desecration."[41]

In addition to the rumors of Jews engaging in ritual murder was the common bias that Jews worship money, have no spiritual values, and place the highest value not on spirituality but on the accumulation of gold. This bias can likely be traced as far back as ancient Egypt, in the third or fourth century BCE. At the time, Jews were the leading traders between Egypt and the northern kingdoms of Assyria and Babylonia. Jewish success led to what was termed *invidia auri Judaici* (Latin, "Jew gold envy").[42] Envy, as we have seen in the story of Joseph and his brothers, can be a catalyst for scapegoat projection, an association linking Jews and money to this day. Even in contemporary times, the infamous forged *Protocols of the Elders of Zion*, probably the most widely seen anti-Semitic publication in history, is accepted as fact by ignorant anti-Semites. Within this publication is the assertion that Jewish bankers are said to control the world economy, Jewish financiers are said to control stock exchanges, and Jews control the media.

Shockingly, I learned how widespread this image of Jews still is today. A fairly well-educated contractor who was recently working in our home opined that the banks in the U.S. were controlled by Jews. When I asked him for an example, he hesitated and then blurted out that it was the Rothschilds. When I responded that there were no Rothschild banks in the U.S., he told me that they secretly controlled all the banks, which is why I was not aware of any. An even more outrageous comment I heard recently, to my mind in the tradition of medieval and ancient blood libels, came from a barber I went to in Florida to have my hair cut. Completely serious, he told me that he knew for a fact that there was a secret cabal (a euphemism for Jews, I realized) that not only controlled the financial world in our country but worshipped the devil. When I asked him to give me an example of this devil worshipping, he said that they sacrificed children to Baal and Moloch.[43] When he was surprised to realize that I knew who they were and was steeped in biblical texts and Jewish history, he changed the subject.

Sadly, blatant anti-Semitism is not something of the past, nor limited to the uneducated and prejudiced. Years ago, before I entered the academic world, when I engaged in a business transaction in one of the southern states, when the person I was negotiating with, a person with both college and MBA degrees, did not get what he wanted, I was told in no uncertain terms to go back to "Jew York" since that was where the Jews live and where money was the highest value in their lives. The fact that our disagreement was about his not wanting to fulfill a written contract that he had signed seemed not to register in his consciousness – a classic anti-Semitic attitude.

The linkage of Jews and money is an anti-Semitic embellishment that became particularly popular beginning in medieval times – and, unfortunately, not only accepted by many today but becoming all too popular once again. In this regard, the linkage of Jews and money has its roots in medieval Europe, since moneylending was one of the professions that Jews were allowed to engage in. Most Jews did not have enough gold or money to be in the business of lending to others; most were poor themselves. Nevertheless, anti-Semitism did not need much to instigate mob violence, since one advantage of forcing Jews to leave town was that any debts to a Jew would then be uncollected so one could say that the Shadow of greed, not having to repay debts, was projected by these Christian communities on to the Jews. Moreover, there still exists a misapprehension that Jews were only moneylenders – a fact that many historians have overlooked or intentionally ignored. For, in addition to lending money at interest, Jews were skilled craftsmen, traders, physicians, and financiers for some of the leading princes and rulers in Europe. However, Jews were also often appointed as tax advisors and collectors for the local rulers and, in many instances, helped facilitate the tax collection levied on the local population, an occupation that did not endear them to the local population.

For centuries, and in many countries contributing to Jewish anguish, a situation that often arose occurred when the ruler who had welcomed them to his land died or was replaced. When that happened, Jews were often expelled with an added incentive being that those who owed a Jew money would then be relieved of the obligation to pay back a loan or fulfill a contract that they had entered into with a local Jewish merchant or trader. Added to this angst was that when such situations arose, the entire Jewish community then needed to find a new place to settle which also contributed to scapegoating them as wanderers, a shiftless people being punished for their sins. Some of the better-known expulsion of Jews – for religious or economic reasons – was France in 1182; Belgium in 1261; England in 1287; and of course Spain in 1492, and Portugal in 1496 as a result of the Inquisition.

Finally, in medieval times, and contributing enormously to the scapegoating of Jews, was the accusations that Jews were responsible for the Black Plague. Driven by rumors and gossip, Jews were accused of causing this pandemic, which ravaged Europe in the mid-fourteenth century and resulted in millions dying. Jews were scapegoated, with many massacred and accused of causing the epidemic by poisoning the wells of their Christian neighbors. To worsen matters, a belief has developed that Jewish communities were spared from the ravages of this disease – a belief that has taken root among some historians and accepted as fact.[44]

In the centuries following this catastrophic period in European history, a time when an estimated third to half of the entire population perished from the plague, the scapegoating of Jews continued unabated. The ignorance and intolerance of Judaism by Church clergy added to the scapegoating and persecution of Jews. One rationalization was that the Talmud contained not only an anti-Christian bias but "an allegation that Jews murder non-Jews, especially Christians, in order to obtain blood for the Passover or other rituals." In response to this accusation, in 1240 in France, the Talmud itself was "put on trial" by King Louis IX and found guilty; two years later, he issued a decree to burn every copy of the Talmud that could be found. This ban provided a stimulus for several popes to carry out similar book burnings, including Popes Gregory IX and, around the same time, Innocent IV in 1244, Honorius IV in 1286, John XII in 1320, and Benedict XIII in 1415.[45] Just as the blood libels and indiscriminate massacres of Jews were a model for Nazi Germany, book burning became a model for Nazi Germany. With a similar emphasis on eliminating Jewish culture and tradition, a most infamous burning of books, including the Talmud, was the public burning of Jewish religious texts in Berlin in 1933.

Scapegoating of Jews had no limits and extended even as far as the written word. Historically, Jews are often referred to as the "people of the book" (meaning the Bible), so perhaps it is not so surprising that anti-Judaism reached the point where they were not only accused of using Christian blood for ritual purposes and forever tainted as moneylenders, but also had their books burned, a symbol of Jewish culture. From a Jungian perspective, Jews did not fit in to what Sylvia Perera described as the Ego ideal of Christianity. In general, over the centuries, Jews have resisted conforming to what the Church promulgated in the name of religion and God yet was actually their own Shadow – a part of them that was repressed, denied, fragmented, fell into the Unconscious and was acted out in the form of scapegoating.

Notes

1 Lev. 16:1–34.
2 Genesis 37–47.
3 Howard Schwartz, *Tree of Souls* (New York: Oxford University Press, 2004), p. 484.
4 Howard Schwartz, *Tree of Souls*, p. 299.
5 Howard Schwartz, *Tree of Souls*.
6 Lev. 6:21–22.
7 Jan Bremmer, "Scapegoat Rituals in Ancient Greece," *Harvard Studies in Classical Philology* (1983): 301.
8 June Singer, *Boundaries of the Soul* (New York: Anchor Books, 1994), p. 362.
9 Gen. 37: 9–11.

10 *The Torah: Five Books of Moses*, Artscroll Series, ed. Stone (Brooklyn, NY: Mesorah Publications, 1993), p. 201 (11n).
11 *The Book of Legends*, ed. Bialik and Ravnitzky, Eng. trans., p. 51n.
12 *Five Books of Moses*, ed. Stone (Brooklyn, NY: Mesorah Publications, 1993), p. 200 (Rashi comments on Gen: 37:2).
13 *Five Books of Moses*, p. 51.
14 Louis Ginzberg, *Legends of the Bible* (Philadelphia: Jewish Publication Society, 1992), p. 196.
15 *The Book of Legends*, ed. Bialik and Ravnitzky (New York: Schoken Books, 1992), p. 51.
16 Sylvia Perera, *Descent to the Goddess: A Way of Initiation for Women* (Toronto: Inner City, 1981).
17 *The Book of Legends*, ed. Bialik and Ravnitzky, p. 53.
18 Gen. 35:8.
19 Jonathan Sacks, "Does My Father Love Me?," in *Covenant and Conversation*, pp. 315–322.
20 Gen. 41:51.
21 Exod. 13:19.
22 Israel B. Bitton, *A Brief History of Antisemitism* (Jerusalem: Gefen, Publications, 2022), p. 7.
23 Bitton, *A Brief History of Antisemitism*, p. 37.
24 Num. 23:9.
25 Paul Johnson, *A History of the Jews* (New York: Harper & Row, 1988), p. 29.
26 Gen. 43:32.
27 *Encyclopaedia Judaica*, 3:88.
28 *Jewish Journal*, March 28, 2022.
29 *Encyclopaedia Judaica*, 3:95.
30 Bitton, *A Brief History of Antisemitism*, p. 61.
31 Bitton, *A Brief History of Antisemitism*.
32 Bitton, *A Brief History of Antisemitism*.
33 Sylvia Perera, *The Scapegoat Complex* (Toronto: Inner City, 1986), p. 9.
34 Perera, *The Scapegoat Complex*, p. 11.
35 See chapter 2, the Golem of Prague- note 1n.
36 Bitton, *A Brief History of Antisemitism*, p. 38.
37 Bitton, *A Brief History of Antisemitism*, p. 58.
38 Bitton, *A Brief History of Antisemitism*, p. 56.
39 Bitton, *A Brief History of Antisemitism*.
40 Robert Rockaway, "American Blood Libel," *Tablet*, September 19, 2021.
41 *Encyclopaedia Judaica* 4:1064.
42 Bitton, *A Brief History of Antisemitism*, p. 56.
43 First Kings 18:19–40.
44 Although there has been no way to prove the validity of this anecdotal acceptance, if fewer Jews died of the Black Plague, it could be attributed to Jewish sanitary practices and isolation from the Christian community at large. Jewish custom calls for washing one's hands before eating, burial of the dead within 24 hours. These and other customs, if it were to be proven, could have contributed to fewer in the Jewish community dying of the Black Plague.
45 Bitton, *A Brief History of Antisemitism*, p. 58.

Chapter 9

Hope, Resilience, and Humor
The Jewish Experience

Figure 9.1 Noah Receives the Dove, from The Story of the Bible from Genesis to Revelation, Charles Foster, 1883, engraving.

DOI: 10.4324/9781003511908-10

Our hope is not yet lost
The ancient hope,
To return to the land of our Fathers
The land of Zion, Jerusalem.

Jewish existence for over 2,000 years is an archetypal example of survival. Jews have endured despite exile, and wandering – not only survived, but thrived, despite being persecuted, expelled, and often massacred. Other, more mighty civilizations have come and gone but despite being banished from their country of origin and spread throughout the world, Jews are still here, and Judaism is still alive and vibrant.

From a Jungian perspective, one reason Judaism survived is that, to use an alchemical term, they were able to turn the lead into gold, to transform the negative aspects of isolation and persecution into the positive aspects of insulation and community. In a sense, the persecution and isolation of Jews validates the popular phrase that "what doesn't kill you makes you stronger."

How have Jews endured destruction of their country, exile, slaughter, pogroms, and the Holocaust? Why have they survived when other, more powerful and advanced, civilizations such as the Assyrians, Babylonians, Greeks, and Romans, have disappeared? Why have Jews flourished in the very countries trying to annihilate them? In this chapter, I will explore the themes of resilience, hope, and humor, and how these factors enriched Judaism and enabled Jews, to be transformed into a nation that has experienced a rebirth.

What fosters resilience? Is it innate in an individual or a community, or can it be developed? Why is it that some, on personal or collective levels, are able to bounce back after major setbacks, often becoming stronger, while others cannot seem to survive life's disappointments? Why are some able to overcome adversity, yet not allow it to define them forever? The Jewish experience of survival, over two millenia of persecution, had resilience, hope, and reliance on humor as ingredients that offset their despair and persecution during bleak periods of their history.

Decades ago, Jung recognized that we live in political, economic, and spiritually distressing times and that the hope of the planet would ultimately depend on the inner work that we, as individuals, do. Now, even more than when Jung articulated it, "the future of mankind hangs on a single thread."[1] On the level of an individual, self-reflection can give greater meaning to one's life. Similarly, on a collective level, doing what Jung terms the "inner work," can help a country or a culture to transcend personal obstacles and collective anxieties. James Hollis, a leading Jungian analyst, is of the opinion that through the paths of inner exploration – the tools of Depth Psychology, classical literature, philosophy, dream work, art, and myth – we gain access to our "locus of knowing," a wellspring of deep resilience.[2]

This ability to transcend stress, anxiety, and collective obstacles carries the hope that we all have to effect positive change. Even in the extreme environment of a Nazi concentration camp, as Viktor Frankl articulated in *Man's Search for Meaning*, individuals who could find meaning or hope stood a better chance of survival than those who lacked those attributes. The hope that there is a better future and the ability to laugh can help manage stress, anxiety, and coping with adversity – on both individual and collective levels. For Jews, these factors contributed to the continuity and well-being of the community.

Jewish culture and community, from earliest to contemporary times, is full of outrageous jokes and stories – many with a subtle, psychological bent. For example, a section of the Talmud (known as *Aggadah*, legend) relates that what helped Joseph resist the seduction advances of Potiphar's wife was that an image of his father appeared before him as he was about to be seduced, causing him to realize that he should not destroy himself by acceding to Potiphar's wife. Leading to the seduction, commentators state: "Once he became a success in his master's home, Joseph became preoccupied with his appearance and began to curl his hair," a manifestation exhibited by many a teenager today.[3]

Another talmudic legend, dating to the second century CE, contains a combination of serious debate and humor. Rabbi Eliezer, one of the most respected Rabbis at the time, was discussing with his peers whether a particular type of oven was kosher. Eliezer ruled that it was. His fellow Rabbis and scholars disagreed and overruled him, a rebuke that angered Rabbi Eliezer. To prove his point, he brought about a miracle by saying, "Let the carob tree that is outside the study hall prove that I am right" – at which time the tree uprooted itself and flew into the air. His colleagues' response was that miracles do not prove anything. To further his point, Rabbi Eliezer declared: "Let the river of water outside this study hall prove that I am right" – after which the river began to flow in the reverse direction. The Rabbis, equally stubborn, declared that no river or tree can prove anything. With uncharacteristic anger, the Rabbi then commanded the walls of the study hall to collapse on the Rabbis gathered there – at which point, another noted scholar, Rabbi Joshua, turned to the walls and declared: "When scholars are in disagreement, what right do you have to interfere?" At this stage, a voice from heaven cried out: "Rabbi Eliezer is right." In response, Rabbi Joshua turned toward heaven, quoting Deuteronomy: *Lo ba'shamayim he* (meaning that the Torah was given by God to the people and is not in heaven; rather, it is here on earth). In other words, the Rabbis were telling God to mind his own business, that God had given them the Torah and that it is up to them interpret it, not God. Upon hearing the story, the legend continues, Rabbi Nathan, said to have been a mystic, met Elijah the prophet and asked him, "What did God do when, in effect, he was pushed out of the study hall?" Elijah's response was that God "laughed with joy" and said, "My children have defeated me!"[4]

Resilience

An important issue is whether the Jewish people – and, by extension, Judaism, constitute a religion? A nation? A civilization? The answer is that they are all three. The reason Jews have been able to survive was their resilience, fueled by hope, and with a good sprinkling of humor. Over the centuries, Jews developed the ability to adapt and thrive in the many different cultures they have been a part of, despite, or perhaps even because of, the persecution they endured in almost every country where they lived for the past 2,000 years.

In exile, Jews always maintained a sense of community (Heb., *kehillah*); each community was organized to offer support, charity, and help for fellow Jews. In whichever place they lived, the *kehillah* provided a sense of order and collective responsibility in the face of persecution by the local populations. Jews, individually and as a community, from religious as well as secular perspectives, were educated from childhood to look after one another. As far back as the fifth century, when the Talmud was collated, one phrase uttered by the Rabbis was *kol yisrael arevim zeh lazeh* (all of Israel, meaning the Jewish people, are responsible for one another). Adhering to this communal outlook helped ensure that the poor and destitute in the community were provided for, rabbinical courts established to insure order, Jews taken hostage were redeemed and ransomed whenever possible, and members of the community taxed to insure its viability.

Still, Jews did not take their persecution lightly or accept their fate without complaint. Even Rabbis and leaders of the community complained to God about their circumstances. Elie Wiesel, in fact, recounts a Hasidic story of a famous Rabbi who protested to God about Jewish suffering: "If you think you can bring your people back into the fold by making them suffer, then I, Leib, son of Rachel, swear that you will not succeed. So why try? Save your children by giving them joy." And, in response to a famine in the land, another Hasidic Rabbi, known as the "Grandfather of Shpole," protested to God: "Lord, save your people before it is too late. Otherwise, there will be no one left to save." He then gathered ten talmudic scholars to sit as a court in judgment of God. The trial is said to have lasted three days before reaching a talmudic-style verdict: "Whereas the Father of all creatures is responsible for their sustenance, let Him put an end to the famine."[5] Among other factors, what enabled Judaism to survive, and made it unique, has been this attitude: a combination of determination, spirit, and humor.

Another contributing factor to Jewish survival over the centuries was the fact that Jews were compelled to wear different clothing in order to be easily recognized by the local population. In some Islamic areas, as far back as the ninth century, Jews had to wear special clothes or badges so that the local population could identify them on sight; the design and style these varied. Under Caliph Haroun al-Rashid (807 CE), Jews in Baghdad had to wear yellow belts or fringes; under Caliph al-Mutawakkil (847–61 CE), Jews wore a patch in the shape of a donkey; in 1005, Jews in Egypt were ordered to wear bells on their clothes.[6]

Similarly, just as some Islamic countries singled out Jews through their dress, in Christian Europe at the Fourth Lateran Council (1215), a policy was established ordering all Jews to display special symbols on their clothing so that they could be easily differentiated from local Christians. Issued as Canon 68, the decree became the basis of the subsequent imposition of a so-called Jewish badge in Christian kingdoms.[7] The Nazis, by forcing Jews to display the yellow Star of David badges on their outer dress, revived this ancient custom.

Ironically, decrees that Jews must wear different clothing dovetails with Jewish legend and enables some to turn this negative aspect into its opposite – a classic example of an Archetype having an opposite. In this view, in a number of rabbinic commentaries and legends the explanation given is that the Israelites were redeemed from slavery in Egypt because they did not change their names, their language, and their way of dress. In other words, the Israelites were distinct and able to survive because their clothing, food, and language were different from those of the Egyptians and they kept themselves apart; that is to say, they were identified and known as a separate nation even while living among other people and countries.

To this day, in Europe, long after the clothing requirements and other anti-Semitic decrees fell into disuse, many Hasidic and other ultra-Orthodox Jews voluntarily choose to continue the custom of wearing different clothing. Perhaps, we might surmise, this custom of wearing different clothing and speaking a separate language at home (Yiddish in Eastern Europe and the U.S.; Ladino and Judeo-Spanish in many Sephardic families) could be categorized as a form of what Jung would term a compensatory aspect toward the secular world. By voluntarily keeping themselves apart through dress and language, the ultra-Orthodox Jewish population is able to ensure a continuity of identity and resist being part of the secular world – a world which, paradoxically, by and large excludes them so that the end goal is the same.

Despite the contributions to Jewish survival through maintaining different dress and language, another component in keeping the history of the people alive is an homage to the memory of ancestors and past family history. This manifests itself through the custom of naming children after departed family members.[8] Doing so has helped keep the memory and history of the family alive. In addition, there has always been an emphasis on education in the Jewish world, albeit primarily in the areas of Jewish and religious studies, which has contributed heavily to Jewish literacy. Such scholarship ensured a consciousness among Jews, as it most often pertained to keeping alive the history and culture of the people. From the age of three or four, boys are taught to read and write. They are mainly taught Hebrew and religious texts though by the beginning of the Enlightenment, many Jews had begun to learn how to read and write in the language of the culture and country they lived in. In this regard, a great many became proficient in science, mathematics, and literature, as well. Not surprisingly, despite many of the Rabbis discouraging the acquisition of secular knowledge, by the late eighteenth century, enlightened Jews began to read newspapers and learn about and participate in the world around them.

In this regard, one still-prevalent myth is that Jews were moneylenders and bankers. In fact, over the centuries, they were engaged in many other occupations with medicine being one of the professions most open to Jews. In Christian and Muslim countries, for example, despite many professions being closed to Jews, medicine was not one of them. Even some women, though they specialized in women's health issues, became physicians although primarily working as midwives. While most universities would not accept Jews, men and women could circumvent this by studying independently and passing an examination that certified them to practice medicine. Moreover, a number of Rabbis were also physicians with the most well-known among them being Maimonides (1138–1204) and Nachmanides (1194–1270). Furthermore, as far back as the fifth century, the Talmud cited many Rabbis as being physicians, including Rabbi Ḥanina, Rabbi Ishmael, Rabbi Ḥiya, and Rabbi Ashi. Even later, in medieval times, some of the most widely used medical textbooks were written by Jews.[9] On an archetypal level, health and medicine were emphasized in the Bible and the Talmud through regulations concerning hygiene. Of the 613 *mitzvot* ("commandments,"), 213 are of a medical nature and cover such issues as "prevention of epidemics, dealing with venereal diseases, frequent washing, care of the skin, strict dietary and sanitary regulations, rules for sexual life, and isolation and quarantine."[10]

Nevertheless, medicine was not the only field Jews engaged in. Ancient Israelites, for instance, were also warriors, even hired as mercenaries by the Egyptians in sixth century BCE, and worked as farmers, priests, and craftsmen as well as being leading traders, businessmen, and scholars. And, on the Iberian Peninsula, from the twelfth to the fifteenth centuries (an era still recognized as a Golden Age in Jewish history), Jews were engaged not only as physicians, but were recognized leading poets, philosophers, astronomers, mapmakers, teachers, and printers. Simultaneously, in southern France and northern Spain, where the kabbalah is said to have originated, there were Jewish alchemists and kabbalists. Following the expulsion of Jews from Spain and Portugal at the end of the fifteenth century, many Jews migrated to the Italian city-states where they engaged in trading, banking, and shipping, as well as to the Ottoman Empire, where they became renowned physicians, philosophers, writers, and theologians.[11]

Historically, Rabbis were not priests or ministers in the Christian sense. In fact, until the fourteenth century, Rabbis were not paid; rather, like the majority of Jews, they worked as shoemakers, tailors, surveyors, businessmen, and physicians. For example, as far back as the fifth century, many of the most revered Rabbis mentioned in the Talmud were engaged in other professions. For example, Hillel was a woodchopper, Shammai the Elder was a builder, and Abba Shaul was a gravedigger. The Talmud states: "Great is the labor for it honors the workman," with the lesson that manual labor is an occupation to be respected.[12]

In this regard, a Rabbi was originally not a paid position or even given a formal title. Historically, Rabbi originally meant "teacher," someone who did not exercise official religious or spiritual authority simply by being addressed as Rabbi. In talmudic times, one would say *Rabi* (pronounced *rah-bee*), meaning my teacher or my master. His importance depended not on an official position but rather on being learned in Jewish law and noted in the community as a scholar. Among other occupations, Rabbis were judges – primarily because they were deemed respected scholars. In the *Mishnah* (Jewish Oral tradition – codified in the third century

CE), we read that one should love work and hate the rabbinate – meaning that one should not use Jewish law, the Torah, as a spade to make a living.[13] A Rabbi did not lead religious services; any respected layperson could serve that function. The paid position of Rabbi, as we know it today, emulated Christian practice, and Jews likely began a similar custom around the fourteenth century. In effect, being a paid Rabbi in the community dates back not to biblical or talmudic, times but likely to the Christian tradition of a paid pastor.

Another area that contributed to Jewish survival was the emphasis on education – an emphasis that cannot be overestimated. For example, despite quotas on Jews being accepted by leading universities in the U.S., Jews became outstanding medical researchers, lawyers, and judges, In addition, thanks to their emphasis on education, Jews have contributed disproportionately to the fields of arts, finance, law, medicine, music, and entertainment. Recent examples include such renowned writers as Elie Wiesel, Victor Frankl, Isaac Bashevis Singer, Saul Bellow, Philip Roth, and Cynthia Ozick. In psychoanalysis, in addition to Freud, in the world of analytical psychology there were many leading Jungians who were Jewish, including James Kirsch (a founder of the Los Angeles Jung institute); Aniela Jaffe (coauthor of Jung's autobiographical book *Memories, Dreams, Reflections, Reflections*); Gerhard Adler (one of the coeditors of Jung's *Collected Works*); and Erich Neumann (a giant in the field of Jungian writings, famous for his groundbreaking Jungian treatise books *Depth Psychology and a New Ethic*; *The Great Mother*; and *The Origins and History of Consciousness*) in Israel. In addition, an illustration of this can also be seen in the number of Jews who have been awarded Nobel Prizes in medicine, physics, and literature among other fields.[14]

One accusation against Jews, which could be categorized as part of an archetypal pattern of persecution, is the "chosen people" label. Enlightened Jews, and many well-educated Christian theologians, understand the concept as not denoting a feeling of superiority but, rather, that Jews were chosen by God to receive the *Torah* (Bible, Pentateuch). Nevertheless, even if some Jews do consider themselves "chosen," it should be interpreted psychologically as being a compensatory attitude. The concept of being "chosen" by God, a phrase that appears in some of the Jewish prayers, likely evolved to compensate for collective feelings of inferiority and persecution. In this regard, a contributing aspect to Jewish survival can be understood as emanating from persecution and forced separation – often legislating the local Jewish community to live apart from the Christian or Muslim host countries where they resided. Seen in this context, we can understand it as a compensatory attitude toward being treated as inferior by Christianity and Islam. On a humorous note, one is reminded of the scene in the film Fiddler on the Roof when Tevya turns to God and declares "next time You choose a people, choose someone else!"

Finally, a powerful element contributing to the resilience and survival of Judaism is collective memory – remembering, telling, and retelling the history of the people. Some of this is achieved through books – for example, studying the Talmud and the Bible over and over again. Additionally, the same major holidays that were observed in biblical times – Passover, Sukkot (booths), and Shavuot

(Pentecost) – have remained an essential part of the contemporary Jewish tradition. In this context, the ritual of the Passover *seder* is especially poignant, with its emphasis on remembering. For as part of the festive meal, on the first night of the holiday, we read the *Haggadah* (from the word *le'hagid,* to tell), a booklet designed to remind both adults and children to remember their Jewish heritage. Moreover, to ensure that all in the community be alert to potential danger, the *Haggadah* exhorts Jews to remember that in every generation (*b'khol dor v'dor*), there has been an attempt to destroy us – for Judaism to cease to exist. However, along with remembering this threat, the Haggadah also contains hope – a certainty that God will keep his promise – an assurance that Jews and Judaism will survive, *barukh shomer havtahato (Blessed is God – who keeps his promise).*

Hope

Resilience alone cannot sustain a people for over 2,000 years. Hope for a better future must accompany resilience. Given the persecution of Jews throughout history, there had to be hope that something better or different awaited. During the Holocaust, even in the darkest days of those incarcerated in concentration camps, hope sustained many and the hope that they would someday be free kept many alive emotionally. A moving illustration of this is evidenced in some of the research done with survivors of the Concentration Camps. For example, in one such study, when Auschwitz survivors were asked about the nature of their dreams while in camps, it seems that those dreams were "generally more optimistic and less devastating than the postwar dreams."[15] In other words, the Unconscious produced positive images to compensate for the horrors and despair they were experiencing.

In Judaism, we experience this hope daily; it is enmeshed and instilled in prayer, literature, and ritual. In prayer, three times a day for thousands of years, Jews have recited the hope of returning to Jerusalem, to Zion (another name for Jerusalem), and end the annual Passover seder with the words "next year in Jerusalem." For Jews, Jerusalem has always signified hope, a longing to return to ancient days when we had our own country and were whole as a people. A derivation of the name "Jerusalem" (Heb., *Yerushalayim*) can be said to be wholeness, from the root of the word *shalem* ("whole").[16] Without a return to Jerusalem, Jews will always be incomplete, a message etched on Jewish collective memory.

In this vein, some of the greatest Jewish poets wrote about Jerusalem. One of the most renowned of Jewish poets, Yehuda Halevi, captured this feeling in a poem written in the twelfth century: "My heart is in the East [Jerusalem], but I am in the far corners of the West [Spain]." This poem, one of many by Spanish Hebrew poets of medieval Jewish Spain, has been a staple of Jewish poetry for centuries. Its significance lies in maintaining an archetypal longing for Jerusalem. Over the centuries, poetry, along with other writings and prayers, has reminded Jews to keep alive the hope that the Jewish people would one day return to Jerusalem – a dream that materialized after thousands of years, when the State of Israel was established in 1948.

In 1897, 51 years prior to the State of Israel becoming a reality, Theodor Herzl inspired the first Zionist Congress in Basel, Switzerland, with the phrase: "If you will, it will not be a legend." Keeping alive the hope for a return to Zion was the impetus for making the hope of thousands of years a reality. Almost miraculously, 51 years later, the State of Israel came into being, and the song that was adopted as the national anthem of Israel was "Hatikvah" ("the hope"). Written in 1878 by Naftali Herz Imber (1856–1909) and set to music by Samuel Cohen in 1888, it is the National Anthem of Israel yet was composed well before the State of Israel came into being. Moreover, the song carried such a powerful, archetypal message that for a time it was briefly banned by the British (League of Nations custodian of what was then called Palestine) because of England's anti-Zionist attitude. Its words capture the hope that sustained Jews for thousands of years and illustrate a compelling testimony to the power of the Archetype of hope:

Hatikva (The Hope)

As long as deep within the heart
A Jewish soul stirs,
With eyes facing East,
To Zion, an eye looks

Our hope will not be lost,
The ancient hope, the hope of two thousand years,
To return to the land of our Fathers
To the land of Zion, Jerusalem

Humor

For Jews, along with hope and resilience, comes the ability to laugh – to make fun of ourselves and others. As we have seen, an important tool in maintaining psychic equilibrium is what Jung describes as the compensatory function of the psyche. He applied this as the ability of our psyche to bring to consciousness the opposite of what our Ego is displaying to the world. The ability to reflect on, and compensate for, feelings of depression and despair is manifested in various forms in our psyche – in dreams and through humor and satire. We could describe this as a self-regulating aspect of our psyches, be it conscious or Unconscious, on the personal or the collective level. This compensatory function allows us to tolerate what otherwise might be hurtful or unbearable situations.

The ability to laugh, including laughing at oneself, is an important component of mental health. Psychologists such as Freud, Maslow, and Rollo May have noted this. Norman Cousins, author and editor of *Saturday Review*, in writing about a life-threatening illness, attributed a great deal of his healing process to laughter.[17] Archetypally, laughter has been manifested in the figure of the trickster, a role respected, albeit at times just tolerated, for raising to consciousness what might be too dangerous to state openly. Through humor, the trickster points out some aspect of a personal or collective situation that might otherwise be unsafe, or too painful to face directly.

In this manner, humor, comedy, and satire were manifested in Jewish culture as a means of compensation. It is said that Jung once remarked that without an ability to laugh, including laughing at oneself, there is no hope for healing. Marie Louise von Franz, one of Jung's most distinguished disciples, made clear how important she and Jung thought humor was as an element for healing in the psyche.

> Schopenhauer once said that the sense of humor is the only divine quality in humans. Jung often quoted this saying. Once, he told me that he made it a great point to see if his patients had a sense of humor. People who have no sense of humor are very difficult to treat.[18]

Jung was not the only one of the founding fathers of psychoanalysis to note the importance of humor in the treatment of patients. Freud, as well, took note of this in his work on *Jokes and Their Relation to the Unconscious*. In addition, Theodor Reik, one of Freud's earliest and most important disciples, was also interested in the role that laughter played in the analytic process and has been credited with "stimulating Freud's interest in laughter and Freud's analysis of the unconscious dynamics of wit."[19]

In the Judeo-Christian tradition, the concept of laughter first appears in the Book of Genesis, with Sarah laughing at the idea that she would give birth at her age (in Jewish legend, Sarah was one hundred at the time). After the messengers (angels) tell her that she will conceive and give birth by the following year, she first laughs and then tries to hide her laughter. But a year later, she gives birth. The child was named Isaac (Heb. *Yitzchak*), derived from the word *tzchok* (laughter), with Sarah saying, "God has brought me laughter: everyone will laugh at me."[20]

Notwithstanding Sarah's view that people would laugh at her, the ability to laugh, to make fun of oneself or the environment around us, can serve as a psychological compensation for feelings of inferiority, prejudice, persecution, and hopelessness, all of which Jews have experienced for thousands of years. As a way of sustaining some semblance of positive feelings, even in the darkest days of persecution, Jews could still laugh and joke – what today we would call "dark" humor.

For example, that silver lining of laughter helped Jews keep alive their connection to humanity – one which the Nazis tried to obliterate. An illustration of this can be seen in the following joke that made the rounds in Germany during the period of the 1930s. Articles with classic anti-Semitic tropes appeared in each issue of *Der Stürmer*, a Nazi propaganda newspaper. In this popular weekly paper there were continual diatribes against so-called Jewish control of the world media and financial institutions. However, despite the ant-Semitic articles which appeared, some Jews were still able to use humor as a compensatory coping mechanism to offset the despair that they felt in 1930s Germany as can be seen in the following example:

> During the Nazi era, a Jew is sitting in a café reading *Der Stürmer*, a Nazi newspaper. A friend of his comes to the café and sees him reading the newspaper and asks him how he can read such an awful, propaganda-filled, anti-Semitic paper. He responds, "It makes me feel good with all the terrible things happening to us Jews. I read that we are so powerful, that we control all the banks and stock markets and newspapers in the world."

For Jewish humorists, no person or institution was taboo; even Rabbis, cantors, and leaders of the community are made fun of. Broad categories of Jewish humor include, to name but a few:

- Jokes about other nationalities that oppress Jews
- Jokes about anti-Semitism
- Jokes about Jews of different countries from one's own, e.g., German Jewish jokes about Polish Jews
- Jokes about leaders of Jewish institutions: Rabbis, cantors, presidents of synagogues
- Jokes about God
- Jokes about funerals and mourning
- Jokes about religion (Orthodox vs. Reform Judaism)

Frustration and feelings of persecution were elements of Jewish life that were a given, no matter the country or situation. In these situations, Jewish humor served as a vehicle for dealing with the foibles within the community as well as the world at large. Russian, Polish, other Eastern European Jewish, and more recently American Jewish humor, helped compensate for the persecution or prejudice that Jews faced. This humor makes fun of the pretentiousness of the rich and famous, as well as important public figures. Shortly after World War I, for instance, when Woodrow Wilson was working with other heads of state to establish a League of Nations and redefine boundaries of areas previously under control of the Axis powers, the following two examples made the rounds in Jewish circles – first, following World War I and the second during the Soviet era:[21]

> Ignace Paderewski, Poland's post – World War I premier, was discussing his country's problems with President Woodrow Wilson: "If our demands are not met at the conference table, I can foresee serious trouble in my country. My people will be so irritated that many of them will go out and massacre the Jews."
> "And what will happen if your demands are granted?" asked Wilson.
> "Why, my people will be so happy that they will get drunk and go out and massacre the Jews."

In short, Jewish humor always thrived despite an atmosphere that discriminated against Jews and left them feeling hopeless about any improvement in their situation. For example, in Soviet Russia, during the years of Stalin, if one did not actively support the communist party there was no hope for advancement; any indication of non-compliance with the party was duly noted and poked fun at, as illustrated in the following witticism:

> "Comrade Rabinowitz, why were you not at the last meeting of the Communist Party?"
> "No one told me it was the last meeting. Had I known, I would have brought my wife and children, too."

Jews did not hesitate to poke fun at one another – or to make fun of Rabbis, cantors, and synagogue services. One such account includes a report in the synagogue that the Rabbi had a heart attack. The synagogue's board of directors met to discuss the implications and designated the synagogue president to call on the Rabbi in the hospital the next morning and tell him of the meeting. The president visits the Rabbi and tells him: "I have good news for you. The board of directors of the synagogue met last night and by a vote of 12–10 wished you a speedy recovery."

Jewish humor, especially the ability to laugh at ourselves, has not only made its way into the mainstream of American comedy but has introduced Yiddish expressions into our vocabulary, for example *oy vey*, *chutzpah*, *pisher*, *shlep*, *nebbish*, kosher and *meshuga*, to name just a few. Additionally, in the U.S. many leading comedians and people in the entertainment industry are Jewish. In show business, Jewish writers and comics have stood out with comics leading the way – especially Jewish comedy writers, comedians, and producers. One of the first successful radio shows, *The Goldbergs*, featured a Jewish family. On radio and television, many of the most successful comedians were Jewish. The list of American Jewish comedians reads like a "who's who" of American comedy and includes Jack Benny, Fanny Brice, Mel Brooks, Lenny Bruce, George Burns, Sid Caesar, Groucho Marx, and Gilda Radner, among many others.

In the U.S., especially in the twentieth and twenty-first centuries, Jewish humor has been thriving, having become mainstream. We can see this by the popularity of such comedians as Woody Allen, Billy Crystal, Larry David, Madeline Kahn, Jon Stewart, Sarah Silverman, and Jerry Seinfeld. Jewish humor, including the ability to laugh at ourselves, is part of the Jewish tradition. One of the most interesting examples of humor for my generation can be seen in the work of the Jewish comedian Sid Caesar, from his highly successful *Show of Shows* on television to his comic routines in person.

> On his early *Your Show of Shows* . . . Caesar surrounded himself with all-Jewish writing teams who were personally experienced in the traumas of modern Jewish history. Caesar's head writer on *Your Show of Shows* was Mel Tolkin, born Shmuel Tolchinsky in a shtetl near Odessa, Ukraine, where he experienced

anti-Semitic pogroms. Later analyzing this persecution which drove his family to North America, Tolkin described it as creating a "condition where humor becomes anger made acceptable with a joke." .... In the *Jewish Chronicle*, Caesar remarked that "Jews appreciate humor because in their life it's not too funny. We've been trodden down for a long time, thousands of years. So we had to turn that around because if you take it all too seriously, you're going to eat yourself. And we're very good at being self-deprecating. Either we do it or somebody's going to do it for us. We might as well do it first."[22]

Even as outstanding an intellect as Albert Einstein was an admirer of Sid Caesar, and a list of Caesar's writers over the years reads like a comedy all-star team.

A wonderful aspect of Jewish humor has always been the ability of Jews to poke fun at aspects of themselves. Examples include:

- The definition of a Jewish telegram: "Start worrying, details to follow!"
- Definition of Jews at a wedding celebration: always saying goodbye but never leaving
- Example of a Jewish birth announcement: "Mr. & Mrs. Goldberg are pleased to announce the birth of their son, Dr. Jacob Goldberg"

Another genre is Jewish humor in literature, from the Yiddish stories of Sholem Aleichem and Isaac Bashevis Singer, to such contemporary American Jewish writers as Saul Bellow (*Herzog*); Philip Roth (*Portnoy's Complaint*), and, more recently, Howard Jacobson (*The Finkler Question*). On a more ironic, yet somewhat positive, note, Isaac Bashevis Singer, when he was awarded the Nobel Prize, was asked why he wrote in Yiddish, a dying language. He responded: "In Jewish history, between dying and dead is a very great distance."[23]

While there are so many examples of Jewish humor, some of my favorites are:

A Jewish mother goes to the beach with her five year old son; a wave comes in and washes the boy out to sea. The mother gets down on her knees and begs God to save her boy. Another wave comes in and brings the child back to safety. His mother looks him over and when she sees he is fine, thanks God but adds "thank you, but when he was swept out, he had a hat on!"

Or, one of my father's favorites is an exchange that is humorous but still satirizes the American custom of people having to pay for seats in the synagogue on the High Holy Days. Paying to attend Services is a custom that my father, who grew up in Poland and did not emigrate to the. U.S. until he was 19, found offensive and to the end of his days objected to despite that being a highly successful businessman finances were not an issue for him.

A man comes to the synagogue and wants to enter to give a friend who is attending Services there a message. The usher responsible for collecting tickets tells him "you can't come in without paying for your seat." The man protests; "I only want to go in for a few minutes; why should I have to pay?" Finally, after much back and forth and heated arguments, the usher relents and tells him "alright; you can go in for five minutes, but don't let me catch you praying!"

Through jokes and laughter, Jews were able to turn what would otherwise be overwhelmingly difficult situations and transform them into something tolerable. From a Jungian perspective, it is the trickster at work – the court jester, making light of a serious subject, presenting it in such a way that the psyche can tolerate it. Humor is what Jung would identify as a nonrational coping mechanism of the psyche, on both personal and collective levels. In effect, using an alchemical term as metaphor, humor helps turn the lead into gold, the depressing into a way to lighten the darkness. In conclusion, Jewish humor varies from satire to entertainment, from pathos to despair, from self-denigration to vignettes that make Jews look good. It transforms fear, depression, and anxiety into laughter makes a sad situation more bearable.

Notes

1 Jung interview with John Freeman, *Aired on BBC*, 1959 (filmed August 5–8, 1957).
2 James Hollis, *Living between Worlds: Finding Personal Resilience in Changing Times and Prisms: Reflections on This Journey We Call Life* (Louisville, CO: Sounds True Publication, 2020).
3 Gen. 39:7–12, Stone ed., p. 215n.
4 Babylonian Talmud (BT); Tractate Baba Metzia 59a.
5 Elie Wiesel, *Souls on Fire: Portraits and Legend of Hasidic Masters* (New York: Simon and Schuster, 1972), p. 47.
6 *Origins of the Badge;* United States Memorial Museum Holocaust Encyclopedia.
7 *Origins of the Badge*.
8 Primarily among Ashkenazi (Eastern and Western European) Jewry. In the Sephardic tradition (mainly Jews from Middle Eastern and Spanish and Portuguese descent), it is more acceptable to name a child after a living relative, usually a grandparent.
9 Julius Preuss, *Biblical and Talmudic Medicine* (London: Jason Aronson, 1993).
10 Jewish Virtual Library; American – Israeli Cooperative Enterprise, 1998–2023.
11 By the early twentieth century, millions of Jews had migrated to Western Europe, England, Australia, the U.S., and South America, where they have worked as physicians, bankers, attorneys, accountants, scholars, academics, musicians, and financiers.
12 BT Nedarim 49b.
13 *Pirkei Avot* 1:10.
14 "Jews . . . make up 0.2 percent of the world population . . . [but] 27 percent of the Nobel physics laureates and 31 percent of the medicine laureates. Jews make up 2 percent of the U.S. population, but 21 percent of the Ivy League student bodies, 26 percent of the Kennedy Center honorees, 37 percent of the Academy Award – winning directors, 38 percent of those on a recent *Business Week* list of leading philanthropists, 51 percent of the Pulitzer Prize winners for nonfiction." [David Brooks, "The Tel Aviv Cluster," *New York Times*, January 11, 2010].
15 Wojciech Owczarski, *Dreaming in Auschwitz: The Concentration Camp in the Prisoner's Dreams* (Newcastle upon Tyne: Cambridge Scholars, 2023), p. 14.
16 See chapter 6, "Jerusalem as Archetype and Living Symbol."

17 Norman Cousins, *Anatomy of an Illness* (New York: W.W. Norton, 1979).
18 Marie Louise von Franz, *Archetypal Patterns in Fairy Tales* (Toronto: Inner City, 1997), pp. 183–184.
19 Martin Grotjahn, *Beyond Laughter* (New York: McGraw Hill, 1957), p. 21.
20 Gen. 18:12, 21:3.
21 Rabbi Joseph Telushkin, *Jewish Humor* (New York: William Morrow (Quill imprint), 1992), pp. 112 and 120.
22 Benjamin Ivry, *Forward*, February 12, 2014.
23 David Wolpe, *The Jewish Week*, May 16, 2014.

Chapter 10

The Search for Spirit in Jungian Psychology

Figure 10.1 Gustave Doré, detail of Jacob Wrestling with the Angel, 1855, engraving.

> Not by might, nor by power, but by My spirit, said the Lord of Hosts.
> (Zecharia: 4:6)

Zecharia's words are particularly poignant for me; they were a section of my bar mitzvah portion and especially relevant personally in my gravitating to Jung's psychology and ideas now that I am an adult. I am still not sure how I, a boy born in Brooklyn and raised in an Orthodox Jewish home, ended up as a Jungian analyst. Throughout my childhood and high school, I studied in yeshivot (Orthodox, Jewish Day Schools) and led a typical modern Orthodox Jewish life. Although I was born and raised in the U.S., my family spent considerable time living in Israel. When I was ten, my parents tried settling in Israel, and then again when I was 17. Both times the experiment lasted but a few months. However, that last year, while my parents and siblings returned home, I was allowed to remain in Israel to complete my first year of college since classes had already begun. Years later, as an adult, along with my wife and children, I spent seven years in Israel where I completed a PhD program at the Hebrew University while simultaneously entering Jungian therapy with Dr. Rivkah Scharf Kluger. At the age of 35 I earned my Doctorate after which I enrolled at the Jung Institute in Zurich and earned a Diploma in Analytical Psychology. Those years were most important in my professional and psychological development. Thanks to my analytic work with Rivkah, and subsequently with René Malamud in Zurich, I developed the tools to understand myself as well as appreciate the depth of Judaism – especially its myths and legends – through a Jungian perspective.

During my years in Zurich, I was fortunate to work with leading "old school" Jungians who helped me foster my own inner work – a search for meaning and what Jung terms "Spirit." When I returned to the U.S., after a ten-year hiatus, I took on the role of Executive Director of the C.G. Jung Foundation of New York, a position I held for 11 years. Upon leaving the Foundation, Diana and I founded the New York Center for Jungian Studies, with the goal in mind of presenting the psychology and ideas of Jung through seminars and conferences. We have been fortunate to have been able to offer these programs for over 30 years – a labor that in itself has brought much meaning to my life.

In addition to the administrative work I have been engaged in, I have always devoted a day or two a week to working with patients as the Jungian analyst I trained to be. In both capacities, I have continued to explore Jung's psychology and ideas and further the Individuation process that I embarked on over 50 years ago, when I first entered Jungian analysis. Aside from devotion to my family, the most important aspect of my life has been the continual search for meaning – spiritually, personally, and professionally.

There is an anecdotal tale of a man who asked Hillel (first-century Rabbi and scholar) to summarize the *Torah* while standing on one foot. He did not dismiss this clearly provocative question and is said to have responded by summarizing what he believed was the essence of Judaism: "What is not pleasing to you, do not do to others." As I am far from the stature of Hillel, who was arguably the most important Rabbi in Jewish history, it would require much more space than I have here to explain what the psychology and ideas of Jung has meant to me – let alone if I were have to do so while standing on one foot.

In trying to understand and explain how Jung's psychology and ideas have been relevant to me, however, I have read much of what Jung has written, as well as books by other Jungians about spirituality, psyche, and soul. During the years of my quest, the question I have grappled with was whether Jung's approach to the psyche is compatible with my own experience as a committed Jew. This has not been an easy task. Most of what Jung has written about religion or spirituality has been connected to Christianity: the symbolism of the Mass, Jesus as a symbol of the Self, and the role that Mary plays in Christian theology. Being steeped in the Jewish tradition, I wondered if any of this was relevant for me.

The material I read ranged from Jung's writings, to books and articles on spirituality, written by highly respected Jungian authors, including an especially important book for Jewish Jungians edited by Jungian analyst Marvin Spiegelman: *A Modern Jew in Search of a Soul*.[1] In my search, I kept trying to focus on what we, as Jungians, mean when we refer to spirituality. And what about the soul? Religion? And what does it mean for me, a Jungian analyst who is proud of, and deeply connected to, his Jewish roots and culture? Most important, is being religious the same as being spiritual? Is the concept of "spirit" a separate entity from soul? In Israel, where I lived and studied for over seven years, I reconnected with my roots thanks to being able to view Judaism through a Jungian lens – especially its symbolic aspect, replete with myths and legend. At first, I found Jung too "Christian"; but through my own analysis with Rivkah, who had herself been in analysis with Jung, I began to understand how to apply Jung's ideas to Judaism and find meaning in it. Moreover, Rivkah related that during the course of her analysis with Jung, he had told her that his goal was not to make her a Christian but a better Jew. In any case, thanks to Rivkah, I realized that Jung's focus on the interface of theology, myth, and psychology, helped me appreciate my own Jewish tradition and its essential depth. If I did not take everything in the Bible literally, or the dogma foisted on me by some of the Rabbis I had studied with as a child, Judaism started to resonate in me.

The search for spirit is not exclusive to Jungian psychology. Moreover, given its injection into the realm of politics, it seems to be an American pastime – one that has continually resurfaced throughout American history and politics. Fundamentalism and an emphasis on religion have been reemerging as social and political forces in recent decades. Charismatic television preachers fill the air waves; fundamentalist ministers and politicians are influencing national and local politics, and PBS presentations and magazine stories on God are not uncommon.

Explaining what one means by the words "spirit" or "soul" is difficult. In my continued search, I decided to ask some of my Jungian colleagues to describe their own experiences with spirit or soul. Specifically, I wanted to hear their view on what "soul" was all about, as well as get their impression of Jung's view of the concept of soul. I questioned some leading figures in the Jungian world about what they perceived as a Jungian understanding of spirit or soul. The hurdle I faced from the start was the usual analytical position that they had all been trained to adopt: "Well, how do you see it?" They were throwing it back at me. Naturally, this made me uncomfortable: the reason I was asking them in the first place was that I was not able to articulate this. In the end, none gave a satisfactory answer that would help me in my inner search. It reminded me of an old Jewish joke: "Why does a Jew always answer a question with another question?" The answer is: "Why shouldn't he?"

Once I realized my colleagues were not going to be of help, I understood that I was on my own and had to come to terms with what spirit or soul meant to me from a Jungian stance. In this search, a person who finally helped was Adolf Guggenbühl-Craig – a Jungian analyst I had admired over the years for his down-to-earth approach to analytical psychology. Guggenbühl addressed the question of what is meant by "soul" from a Jungian perspective:

> "Soul" is a difficult term to use. Some psychologists avoid it, trying to create a psychology without soul. Others replace the religious-sounding "soul" with the more neutral "psyche." I am all for employing the word "soul"; yet when used too often, it sounds pompous or sentimental. There is no way out. If you don't use the word "soul," you avoid the basic issue of psychology; use it too often, and it becomes embarrassing.
>
> Soul is and remains a mystery. What is it? Where is it? How is it? We cannot catch it; we cannot locate it; soul is everywhere and nowhere. Because of its elusiveness, we have to experience and recognize soul mainly through projection. Projecting the soul enables us to deal with it.[2]

This made it easier to understand. The concept of soul cannot be defined, which brought me back to an intuitive definition: "I'll know it when I see it." Guggenbühl's treatment of soul, combined with realizing that Jung himself was not clear, freed me enough to begin to deal with it in Jewish oriented terms.

In Hebrew, the biblical words for "body" and "soul" are the same: *nefesh*. In the Book of Genesis, in describing the creation of Adam, the phrase written was that upon God breathing life into him, Adam became a *nefesh ḥaya*,[3] a living being, a living soul. In the Book of Exodus, in a combination of redemption and census taking, Moses was instructed by God to collect a half-shekel from each person, *kofer nafsho*, a ransom for himself, his soul – from the root of the word *nefesh*.[4] In short, in Hebrew, the word for "soul" and "person" can be seen as interchangeable. From a symbolic perspective, *nefesh* can constitute a dual process – one's inner connection with soul, as well as one's outer persona, meaning, a union between the divine and the human. Seen from this perspective, we can surmise that "soul" does not mean a spiritual entity separate from the body.

Nevertheless, the question remains: Where do we find soul? How can a person get in touch with it today? One place we look for soul is in psychotherapy, derived from the word "psyche" (Greek, "soul") and therapy, a treatment intended to relieve or heal a disorder. In this regard, we can extrapolate that the term "psychotherapy" means therapy of the soul. However, let's think about this on a contemporary, down-to-earth level. Why do we choose to go into therapy in the first place? There are many reasons: a crisis in our life; a major loss; an inability to function at work; anxiety; depression; problem in relationships; low self-esteem. The list goes on and on, but in principle, we say that a person is suffering in some way, or feels a lack of wholeness. Hopefully, whatever theoretical or orientational background of the therapist, the patient's symptoms will be alleviated, hidden complexes and negative patterns will have been explored, and he or she will function better in the outer world as well as find meaning on an inner level.

But why does a person enter a Jungian analysis, rather than choose a different modality of therapy? Is the reason different for those who have read Jung's writings or who have been exposed to Jungian thought through lectures, workshops, or seminars? In the 44 years that I have been a Jungian analyst, many of the individuals who I worked with analytically had specifically sought a Jungian analyst. More often than not, they said they were interested in a Jungian approach because "it is more spiritual." Or, at times, others have said to me that they wanted to get in touch with their creativity, with their more mystical side, or even to undergo a "dream analysis." The fact that they use these descriptions indicated that they were not in touch with, or not presenting, their real-life, outer-world issues. Most often, they were in need of something else first – a way to deal with or understand the suffering that propelled them to seek professional help.

Often, individuals in search of Jungian analysis are in need of basic therapy first, a grounding necessary for the search for spirit – the ultimate goal to be reached. The idea of searching for something as elusive as spirituality tends to attract many who use this concept as a defense against some of life's basic issues: intimacy, relationships, and the establishment of roots. One does not come into an analytical situation looking only for "spirit." Rather, one is coming for help – help in dealing with everyday problems, getting out of a bad relationship, a stagnating career, feelings of depression, and so on. Preferably, after they have made order in their lives, established themselves in the outer world – career and relationships, for example – they can more fruitfully connect to an inner need for meaning and soul. In Judaism, a comparable analogy would be the tradition that one should not study the kabbalah until the age of 40. The thinking behind this tradition is that before studying the kabbalah, an esoteric mystical text, a person should have made their way in the world, i.e. marriage, children, an occupation, being grounded in reality and able to take care of one's material needs. A powerful talmudic phrase that the Rabbis cite is *im ein kemah, ein torah* (if one does not have flour [i.e., is not able to put bread on the table], one cannot study Torah).[5] Making a living – being established in the world – takes precedence over studying Torah. Similarly, one needs to be established in the world before searching for soul or spirit.

Similarly, before delving into an in-depth Jungian analysis, one should first deal with outer, real-life issues. Only then, when they are grounded in life, should they be embarking on a search for spirit. Still, when people are in emotional or psychic pain, why should they seek out a mental health professional? Why not a Rabbi, a minister, or a priest? Perhaps they should – and many people do, though sometimes to no avail. Jung stated:

What is true of all my patients in the second half of life, over thirty-five, is that there has never been one whose problem in the last resort was not that of finding a religious outlook on life. It is safe to say that every one of them fell ill because he had lost what the living religion held with age had given to their followers, and none of them has been really healed who did not reconnect to his religious outlook.[6]

If we look to Jung for guidelines, does this mean that for an effective and meaningful therapy one has to be over 35, or that we need to encourage a "religious outlook"? And what does a religious outlook mean? Jung is not referring to organized religion; rather, he means spirituality and the search for inner meaning. Moreover, the age he mentions, 35, is not to be taken literally. Perhaps, just as in the tradition in Judaism that one should not study the kabbalah until one is settled in life, Jung used the age of 35 symbolically. I believe that what he meant was that a person first needs to resolve first-half-of-life issues – establish oneself in the world through career and family. And, what Jung meant by the absence of a religious outlook is a feeling that one's life has lost its meaning. This meaning, this faith or belief system, was, in earlier times, provided by organized religion. Their belief system bestowed meaning in their lives. If this need was not met, neurosis was inevitable. In Jung's words:

The absence of meaning in life plays a crucial role in the etiology of neuroses. Psycho-neuroses must be understood, ultimately, as the suffering of a soul that has not discovered its meaning . . . . These people were no longer able to believe, either because they could not reconcile scientific thinking with the tenets of religion, or because the truths enshrouded in dogma had lost authority for them and all psychological justification. If they were Christians, they did not feel redeemed by Christ's sacrificial death. If they were Jews, the Torah offered them no support."[7]

Or, in the words of Aniela Jaffe, they lacked the protection afforded by being rooted in a religious tradition. In Jung's experience, according to Jaffe, no one is really healed, and no one finds meaning 'who did not regain his religious outlook. This of course has nothing to do with a particular creed or with membership in a church.'"[8]

In reading this, I began to understand that what Jung meant by religious outlook was similar to what we loosely refer to as soul on an inner, personal dimension. It is this inner spiritual search for meaning in our lives that led me to appreciate Jung's psychology and ideas. Being raised in a so-called religious environment, I was aware that many so-called Orthodox people could be better described as "observant" but not necessarily "religious," or spiritual. They were living by the letter of the law, but dismissing what I held paramount: the spirit of the law.

Despite his own Jewish-bias issues due in part to his break with Freud, Jung's perception of some attitudes in the Jewish community at large were correct. In a letter to Gerhard Adler (later, leading figure in bringing Jungian psychology to England, and one of the editors of Jung's *Collected Works* in English) explaining some of his problems with Freud, Jung writes: "When a Jew forgets his roots, he is doubly and triply in danger of mechanization and intellectualization . . . . I think the religious Jews of our time should summon up the courage to distinguish themselves clearly from Freud, because they need to prove that spirit is stronger than blood."[9] Nevertheless, as Guggenbühl pointed out, we are often not aware of our own need for meaning until we experience it and see it in others. We become conscious of it first through our projecting it onto another individual, including but not limited to our therapists, teachers, and mentors.

The "soul" or "spirit" I have been able to connect to through Jung's psychology and ideas has been an appreciation of Judaism – my own heritage. I first entered therapy in search of help for everyday issues, albeit my first experience was with a Freudian therapist. I was raised in an Orthodox Jewish environment and the schools I attended were all-encompassing. In high school, the first part of each day was devoted to Jewish religious texts. Afternoons and the remainder of the day were spent in secular studies. In addition, throughout high school, Sunday mornings – not recognized as a day of rest by Orthodox Jews who observed Saturday as the day of rest – were spent in school, devoted solely to religious studies. With Friday evenings, Saturday mornings and evenings and Jewish holidays (and there are many) spent in the synagogue, I resented being cut off from the world outside this community.

Throughout childhood, my secret ambition was to discard all traces of connection to the Jewish world. To paraphrase Isaiah in reverse, who said that the Israelites should "not be like all the people," what I strove for was the opposite – to be just like all other people. Though I insisted, in a rare show of power toward a strong patriarchal father, on enrolling in Hofstra College, a secular institution, as opposed to Yeshiva University, I remained connected to the Orthodox Jewish world. I was not permitted to attend an out-of-town college so I lived at home with my parents throughout my college years. Marrying early, as was usual in this community, by the time I was in my early twenties I had entered the business world, become the father of two children, and was living in a lovely home in a suburban, predominantly Jewish, community. Upon reaching adulthood and financial independence, I began a secret "liberated life" – traveling on Saturdays, eating non-kosher food, and not praying daily. I avoided going to synagogue as much as possible and somehow made my way to (Freudian) therapy.

I understand now that what prompted me to enter therapy were issues relating to separation and Individuation. Marriage was the only respectable way one left home in that community. I found myself unhappy, discontented with the career path I had chosen, and in a marriage that was good enough but not meeting my inner needs. Something felt wrong. I realized I felt lost and needed help, even though everything appeared outwardly fine. After all, I owned a home, had two cars (even a sports car – before my expected midlife crisis), was married, and had two wonderful children I loved deeply. Still, I entered therapy. Why?

I can still trace what prompted me to seek help: a trip from Long Island to Manhattan early one morning during my usual commute to work, a discussion, in the car, with my cousin who was three years younger than I was and someone considered "troubled" by the family. By his early twenties, to the consternation and disapproval of family and friends, after completing two years of medical school, my cousin dropped out and went to work in theater and film. Yet, at this time, he seemed to me happier than I'd ever known him, enthusiastic about life, and certain that he would succeed. During our ride, I asked what had helped him take charge of his life. He told me that he had entered therapy – which, in the community I lived in, was associated with a place that only disturbed people went to, something to be ashamed of. His openness and sharing what was a secret at the time gave me the impetus to do the same – to seek professional help.

A few days after our conversation, I entered therapy through a referral of my cousin's therapist. Understandably, the attitude of the community I had been raised in had been imprinted so deeply in me that for the first year or so of my therapy, I was convinced that even the doorman in the therapist's building judged me a disturbed, even "crazy," patient, someone to be pitied. My initial therapy was with a Freudian psychiatrist – twice weekly, on the couch, with me doing all the talking and her sitting behind me, listening, with almost no input. This continued for a little over two years, during which time I reconnected to my love of history, which had been my major studies in college, enrolled in the MA in History department at New York University. I took in courses two evenings a week following full days at the office – not an easy task. Finding the time to study, working a full day, taking courses in the evenings, being in therapy twice a week and an involved father, required a commitment – a personal search, almost an obsession. Looking back, I realize I was searching for meaning to feed my soul, which it did. In 1970, I was awarded my MA and accepted a position in Israel – in the frozen food business, in which I had extensive experience in the U.S. for over five years. During this period, I developed enough inner strength and courage to stop pretending that I was still Orthodox and to live a more genuine, open, and honest life. To my mind, I had made all this progress because of therapy. Yet, in reminiscing, I don't remember my Freudian therapist speaking more than a dozen sentences to me over a two-year period. Still, something inside of me had moved. A spirit had been awakened.

Consciously, I had entered therapy because I was unhappy and unable to openly live a life of my own choosing. Ultimately, Jungian analysis turned out to be more closely linked to an inner search for spirit and meaning – enabling me to Individuate, to live a life that was true to my Self. Throughout my years in therapy, this search for spirit was ever present, albeit not consciously understood. In this regard, I am reminded of a statement of Jung's concerning the relationship between theology and psychology: "I am continually asked 'theological' questions by my patients, and when I say that I am only a doctor and they should ask the theologian, the regular answer is, 'Oh, yes, we have done so,' or 'We do not ask a priest because we get an answer we already know, which explains nothing.'"[10] That was my situation; I had no interest in consulting with Rabbis; I knew what their responses would be.

Over the years, I have spent much time exploring the role that religion should or shouldn't play in my life. At first, I related to religion on an outer, concrete level – for example, whether I should observe the Sabbath, keep kosher, and not distance myself from the community I had been raised in. It was only much later, through my Jungian work and analysis, that I was able to differentiate between religious practice and an inner, spiritual dimension. For many years, I tended to see life in a one-dimensional, concrete way. One was either outwardly observant, or one was not considered religious; an inner spirituality was not part of the equation. The situation was painful for me. Should I deprive myself from the all-encompassing warmth and grip of a community? Should I dare to eat in a non-kosher restaurant and embarrass, my family, or did I need to eat only in kosher establishments? Should I attempt to live my own life, which meant not attending synagogue, the center of the community, where one was expected to attend each week, or could I engage in athletics or sleep late on a Saturday morning?

Breaking away meant escaping from two sets of families: my nuclear family and the collective community. If I did not show up at the synagogue on Sabbath, my absence was duly noted. Invariably, a telephone call was sure to come on Saturday night or Sunday morning, wondering whether I was ill – why else would I not show up at the synagogue? My initial impetus for asserting myself had been to turn from my upbringing and deny anything that even reminded me of religion. By the end of this period, I decided to move to Israel and pursue an alternative lifestyle. Israel represented a healthy change from the Orthodox Jewish world – an acceptable way to assert my independence from the community, yet still maintain a connection to my Jewish roots. My Freudian analyst did not provide the answers to my questions, though I thought she had. Somehow, I was convinced that I had talked it through with her and had her approval. In retrospect, I realize I was the one doing all the talking – and agreeing. I was on the couch in her office twice a week for over two years, and I posed the questions and supplied the answers. She pretty much sat there like a blank screen, only occasionally offering an intervention. It is still surprising to me that one can be in an analysis with all the talking being one-sided and still make progress. Nevertheless, I must admit that as a result of this therapy, I was able to connect to a part of me that longed for meaning and enabled me to muster the courage to effect significant changes in my life. The answers were inside of me all along and she, like a good therapist should be, helped me give birth to myself – the person I wanted to be, to lead the life I wanted to live.

Nevertheless, a year or so after moving to Israel, I came to realize that some of my problems and issues had followed me across the sea. It was not long before I entered therapy again – this time, with a Jungian analyst, Rivkah Scharf Kluger. I had no particular knowledge of Jung – in fact, had never even heard of him – and chose my therapist purely on the basis of a recommendation from my then-brother-in-law, who was studying to be a Jungian analyst in Zurich. Upon entering analysis with Rivkah, I left the world of business and enrolled in the history department for a doctoral program at the Hebrew University of Jerusalem.

For all this, I am grateful. A Jungian approach has provided me with insights into my own life as well as propelling me into the very field I am now in – an occupation that has provided both material and spiritual rewards. Still, I often ask myself: Did I enter therapy with a search for spirit in mind? Was I looking for a connection to my psyche, my soul? Not consciously. Nevertheless, I have come to understand that I was trying to connect to an inner spiritual realm, one which could guide me in the outer world as well. In effect, I was searching for meaning in my life – from the personal to the collective, from the role that family and career played to my own inner needs. Why else would I have made such a commitment of time, money, and energy? It was being caught up in this archetypal force – what Jung describes as an instinct for spirit – that has kept moving me throughout the years, a drive that has been stronger than sheer logic.

Most analysts probably would have labeled my first passing up a lucrative career in business and then spurning the possibility of a tenure-track appointment at the Hebrew University in Jerusalem and moving to Switzerland to study Jungian psychology, as "resistance," a defense against being in the real world. Ironically, they would have been right. But being caught up in the power of an Archetype – in this case, spirit – leaves little choice. One feels a need to keep going through this experience regardless of the emotional cost to those one loves deeply. In retrospect, once out of the gravity spin of the Archetype and able to look back, I have an appreciation and respect for the power of the Archetype that I was caught up in. As has often been the situation, there was no conscious understanding that what I was fighting for was to claim my soul. In retrospect, I recognize that this was a search for spirit. It is a powerful, archetypal force that propels a person. Being caught in this archetypal pull defies dissuasion even from well-meaning friends and family. I made the major transitions and shifts in my life seemingly driven – without understanding why – propelled by the Unconscious.

Jung's psychology and ideas have helped me understand those aspects of my life that are spiritual, even if they lack clarity and definition. His psychology and ideas have enabled me to accept and understand not only the clients I have worked with, but life, history, and the people around me. This, in turn, enabled me to leave myself open to the mystical quality of the Unconscious. Freud and Jung understood from their work with patients that the idea that people who often thought that they knew why they made major decisions in their lives was an illusion. Both made clear that when it came to important turning points in one's life, decisions were made "on the basis of entirely unconscious and unknown criteria and conditions."[11] Appreciating the power of the Archetype of spirit has helped me understand much of what I have struggled with on a personal level; it has given me the tools to place Jung's work in the context of the message rather than focus on the messenger has enabled me to avoid rejecting his psychology out of hand because of his focus on Christianity and lack of knowledge about Judaism.

The psychology and ideas of Jung have enabled me once again to read Jewish texts but without abdicating the power of interpretation to the world of the Orthodox Rabbis. Those ideas have helped me participate in some of the moving ancient Jewish rituals while relating to them through a symbolic perspective; they have brought a religion I wanted to declare dead back to life, with much meaning. I can now see the world through different spectacles and appreciate the archetypal dimension in it. For instance, approaching the world through such a prism revolved around my decision as to where I should train to be a Jungian analyst. Rivkah, my analyst in Israel and a person I loved and respected dearly, wanted me to remain in Israel and train there. However, for reasons not clear to me at the time, I was determined to leave my safe haven in Jerusalem, which included a tenure-track position at the Hebrew University, and move to Zurich for my studies – a decision she opposed. In struggling with this decision, I had to confront the question: When does one listen to one's analyst, and when does one disregard that advice and move ahead on one's own? I found a parallel in Judaism. During the course of a talmudic discussion, a crucial question arose as to whether adherence to tradition means adherence to the authority of the carriers of that tradition. Are we to question our mentors, our Rabbis? The consensus that I came across indicated that while the ruling of one's Rabbi is to obey him, there is a dissenting opinion that this concept of absolute authority need not be followed when we believe that our Rabbi or teacher is mistaken.[12] I knew that I needed to leave Israel and train in Zurich, even if it did not make sense professionally or financially.

History seemed to repeat itself for me when this issue surfaced again. While in the process of editing a book on Jung and anti-Semitism, one of the leading Jungian analysts in the U.S. practically forbade me from publishing a book on this subject. I ignored the pressure and was able to complete this project – one that meant a lot to me personally and which I have written about extensively.[13] Both the conference, held in conjunction with several major institutions, and the books I had co-edited and edited (*Lingering Shadows: Jungians, Freudians and Anti-Semitism*, and *Jung and the Shadow of Anti-Semitism*) were successful and several valuable contributions to this topic emerged from both, including articles and presentations by notable analysts, academics, and authors.

For rather than simply idealize Jung, we were able to accept that Jung had personal shortcomings by drawing on the very tools that he had provided us with – a practical application of his psychology and ideas. Examining Jung's life and work helped me value the archetypal nature of my own struggle for spirit. I have learned to see the world through different lenses. An example of this is that, in re-reading the Bible, and in discussion with Rivkah, I understand that King Saul suffered from what we would today diagnose as depression because "the spirit of God" had left him.[14]

In addition, something that made me appreciate aspects of Judaism that I had been unfamiliar with has been the world of Hasidism. The Hasidic movement provides a refreshing and positive attitude toward Jewish tradition, one that until later in life I knew little about. The movement, which began in mid-eighteenth-century Eastern Europe, marked a departure from the strict, rigid, Orthodox rabbinical approach to Judaism. Hasidic culture greatly emphasized a joyful approach to life; compassion, outreach, love, and the mystical tradition were cornerstones of the movement. Hasidism generally stood in opposition to the rigid, legalistic, and rationalistic attitude prevalent in Jewish communities at the time. The founder of the Hasidic movement was a charismatic leader known as the *Besht* (*Baal Shem Tov*, "master of the good name"), and was known for using parables, myths, and storytelling to inspire his followers.

A prevailing attitude in Hasidism was the validation of emotion, music, and song in the practice of Judaism. The great majority of Rabbis at the time opposed the Hasidic movement. Fittingly, they went by the name of *Mitnagdim*, meaning that they opposed Hasidism; it was not what they espoused that defined them but, rather, what they opposed. In contrast to the joy of music and dance of the Hasidic movement, the economic and social situation of Eastern European Jews was dismal and depressing, mirroring the outlook of the leading Rabbis in Europe. With Jews being persecuted and denied the basic rights of the other citizens in their countries, Hasidism brought joy and a loving worship of God to the forefront of many Jewish communities, despite the resistance it faced from the rabbinical establishment.

Life, including the Individuation process, is not always rational; at times, it has a nonrational, mystical aspect. Even Freud, in an earlier period in his life, told Jung about his and Sándor Ferenczi's visit to a medium, admitting that "the woman medium did appear to have certain telepathic powers." Freud wrote to Jung: "In matters of occultism, I have grown humble since the great lessons Ferenczi's experiences gave me. I promise to believe anything that can be made to look reasonable. I shall not do so gladly . . . . But my [hubris] has been shattered." Years later, Freud wrote to a colleague: "If I were at the beginning, rather than at the end, of a scientific career, as I am today, I might possibly choose just this field [parapsychology] of research, in spite of all difficulties."[15] Clearly, following this experience, Freud's belief in the Unconscious became wider than merely the scope of the individual Unconscious he is generally associated with – a stance that would position Jung and Freud closer together than is generally realized.

For me, breaking away from tradition meant rejecting some of the cornerstone values of my parents as well as the broader, collective Jewish community I was raised in. I entered therapy looking for answers, hoping to find a mentor, teacher, or Rabbi to guide me but in the end, I realized I had the answers I needed within me. Ironically, although I was trying to break away from the Jewish community, I believe that through my Jungian work, I have become a better Jew. I have come to understand that the Orthodox Rabbis do not hold a monopoly on what constitutes a good Jew. I can now relate to the spirit of Judaism without living a so-called observant life within the Orthodox community. I have come to value the rich mythology and traditions in Judaism through my own, Jungian-oriented, lens. I have come to realize that it is not compatible, or honest, toward one's own roots to deny who we are meant to be. In a penetrating analysis by I.I. Rabi, one of Oppenheimer's most esteemed colleagues (who was awarded the Nobel Prize for Physics) wrote:

> Oppenheimer was Jewish, but wished he weren't and tried to pretend he wasn't . . . . The Jewish tradition, even if you don't know it in detail, is so strong that you renounce it at your own peril. [This] doesn't mean you have to be Orthodox, or even practice it, but if you turn your back on it, having been born into it, you're in trouble.[16]

For me, entering therapy, changing careers, countries, and a way of life were all done through the impetus of my Unconscious. Was I seeking to replace the communal aspects of Judaism with a new religious attitude – Jungian psychology? Was my work with Jungian analysts consciously a search for spirit? Ultimately, what was paramount was the search itself. Connecting to this Archetype of spirit has helped me understand much of what I've struggled with over the years. It has forced me to keep struggling with whether the search includes a reconnection to organized religion and community, or even a tacit acceptance of the existence of a God. Does Jungian psychology take for granted that the search for spirit – what Jung refers to as a reconnection to the religious attitude – includes an automatic acceptance of belief in God? Did becoming a Jungian analyst mean that I was joining a cult, a new religion to replace the community I was trying to distance myself from? I think not; if it were, I would run from it even faster and farther than I had distanced myself from the Orthodox Jewish community I was raised in.

Jung believed that each of us has an intrinsic striving for wholeness and integration in our psyche. The Individuation process is itself a search for spirit. It is a desire to understand why we struggle – a longing to see and be seen and, above all, to find meaning in our lives. In entering analysis, we are looking to be relieved of our pain, or shame. Hopefully, through our therapy, we find the answers to our questions and/or relief of psychological discomfort. Unfortunately, therapists do not have answers. Their role is to help us ask the questions; the answers lie within. We each have our own spiritual needs. The therapist can only be a guide or, better yet, a midwife, helping us give birth to our true Self.

This idea was expressed with great poignancy to me during one of my analytical sessions with Rivkah when she related a story that Martin Buber had written about a Hasidic master, Rabbi Zusya. Shortly before his death, Rabbi Zusya expressed a fear of being judged as wanting by God – as not having lived up to his potential as a good Jew. His students protested, telling the Rabbi that he was as great a person as Moses and had nothing to fear; shortly before his death, he said: "In the world to come, I shall not be asked: Why were you not Moses? I shall be asked: Why were you not Zusya?"[17] In short, Jung's concept of Individuation contains within it the same idea intuitively understood by the Hasidim who lived a century earlier: every person's foremost task is the actualization of their own Self.

What makes Judaism special for me is an ideological stream that allows the individual to be unique – an individual who stands alone, yet can still be connected to, and supported by, one of the many Jewish communities of choice (and there are many such possibilities from which to choose). This connection, along with many of the rituals, makes one responsible for his or her own actions and allows a connection to the community on another level. When this connection to community comes about, one does not just have a responsibility to the community; the community has a responsibility to help the individual. Thanks to Jung's approach to the psyche, I have been able to see the Jewish world through different spectacles, from the personal to the collective, from the role that community and tradition play to my own needs as an individual. While Jung had little or no understanding of the various streams of Judaism, or the depth of Jewish myth and tradition, my fantasy is that had Jung been able to explore this aspect of Judaism, he would have found kindred spirits to his own approach to the Individuation process.

I have come to appreciate the uniqueness of my own Jewish tradition through a wider, more inclusive attitude – one that is underappreciated. Jung's work has given me the tools to place the dictates of Rabbis and some of its dogma in the context of the message rather than the messenger. These tools have enabled me to read Jewish texts without abdicating the power of interpretation to the world of Orthodox Rabbis. They have encouraged me to delve deeper into, and discover the richness of, Jewish myth and tradition and appreciate many rituals on a symbolic level. Both Jungian psychology and the essence of Jewish thought involve turning inward, to have the individual look for answers within and avoid the concretization that inevitably arises when the Shadow of the institution takes over. When that happens, the original spirit turns into dogma, authority, and inflexibility. A true gift of Jungian psychology is in understanding the archetypal nature of our struggle for spirit. We see the biblical Jacob wrestling with the spirit of God, or King Saul suffering from depression because "the spirit of God" left him.[18] This search for spirit runs through the Jungian analytic experience as well as the Jewish world, whether or not the person is consciously aware of it or not. It does not have to be defined as such to exist – indeed, many people could never articulate it this way; but it is a basic archetypal presence in the field.

Like Odysseus, I needed to leave home and discover myself through my ten years of travels and studies in Israel and Zurich, to return with a greater understanding of my own Jewish roots. It has been through my analytic work, studies of Jung's psychology and ideas, and immersion in Jewish history, culture, and myth, that I have been able to find meaning and soul. It has not been an easy journey, nor is it complete. Individuation is a lifelong struggle and I am still working on it. This, and much more, I have learned from my Jungian work and my own analysis. It is a continued search for spirit from a Jungian and a Jewish perspective.

Finally, in prayers throughout the year, the following wording found in the daily prayers may provide a lesson in what Individuation means in Judaism – an attitude similar to the Jungian concept of Individuation. In Judaism, each of the forefathers (Abraham, Isaac, and Jacob) had his own separate experience of God, as seen in the daily prayer: "God of Abraham, God of Isaac, and God of Jacob." It would have been correct grammatically, and more efficient, for the prayers to read "God of Abraham, Isaac, and Jacob." By noting each of the forefathers separately, the prayers indicate that God is experienced differently and uniquely by each of us – as he was by Abraham, by Isaac, and by Jacob. And so it must be for us, even for those who believe in the existence of a God, or following the dictates of their church or Jewish orthodoxy. Similarly, a Jungian approach to Individuation is that we each have our own connection to God, our own path to lead – a personal spirituality.

Notes

1. Marvin Spiegelman and Abraham Jacobson, eds., *A Modern Jew in Search of a Soul* (Phoenix: Falcon, 1996).
2. Adolf Guggenbühl-Craig, "Soul and Money," in *Soul and Money*, ed. Russell Lockhart (Dallas: Spring, Publications, 1982), p. 83.
3. Gen. 2:7.
4. Exod. 30:12–13.
5. *Pirkei Avot* 3:21.
6. Jung, *Collected Works*, 11:34.
7. Jung, *Collected Works*.
8. Aniela Jaffe, *The Myth of Meaning* (Zurich: Daimon, 1983), pp. 12–13.
9. Jung to Adler (June 9, 1934), in *C. G. Jung Letters*, ed. Gerhard Adler and Aniela Jaffe (Princeton, NJ: Princeton University Press, 1973), pp. 104–105.
10. C. G. Jung, *Psychology and Western Religion* (Princeton, NJ: Princeton University Press, 1984), p. 282.
11. Mortimer Ostow, referenced in lecture delivered at 'Lingering Shadows: Jungians, Freudians and Anti-Semtism' conference at New School for Social Research, New York, March 28, 1989.
12. Jerusalem Talmud Horayot 2b.
13. See chapter 4: "Anti-Semitism: The Jungian Dilemma."
14. Rivkah Scharf Kluger, *Psyche in Scripture: The Idea of the Chosen People and Other Essays* (Toronto: Inner City, 1995), pp. 33–56.
15. *Freud – Jung Letters*, ed. McGuire, p. 429.
16. Kai Bird and Martin J. Sherwin, *American Prometheus: The Triumph and Tragedy of J. Robert Oppenheimer* (New York: Vintage Books, 2006), p. 76.
17. Martin Buber, *The Way of Man*, Paperback ed. (New York: Citadel Press, 1967), p. 16.
18. Rivkah Scharf Kluger, "King Saul and the Spirit of God," in idem, *Psyche in Scripture*, pp. 36–57.

Index

Note: numbers in *italics* indicate a figure

Aaron 27, 109, 110
Abba Shaul 129
Abel *see* Cain and Abel
Abner, son of Ner 101–102
Abraham, Karl 53
Abram/Abraham 18, 24, 25, 27, 103, 109, 152; burial of 100; God's promise to 103; Isaac and 79, 84–85; Jerusalem and blessing of 81; praying to 96–97
Absalom 101
Abulafia, Abraham 39
Adam: creation of 41, 142; as father of the human race 89; as *nefesh ḥaya* 142
Adam and Eve, expulsion from Eden of 28
Adler, Alfred 53
Adler, Gerhard 30, 59, 130, 144
Adlerian 8
Agag 96
Aggadah 35, 41, 126
Aḥashverosh see Ahasuerus (king of Persia)
Ahasuerus ("a Jew named Ahasuerus") 24
Ahasuerus (king of Persia) 66–68, 74
Al-Aqsa Mosque 79
Al-Buraq (Muhammad's white horse) 79
alchemist 40; Jewish 41, 129
alchemy 29, 30, 35, 37, 39, 40; *see also* gold from lead
Allen, Woody 135
al-Mutawakkil (Caliph) 127
al-Rashid, Haroun (Caliph) 127
Alger, Horatio 70
Amalek, Amalekite 96
Amasa, son of Jether 101
Amman, Peter 47, *60*, *61*, 64
analytical psychology 130
Analytical Psychology Club of Zurich 46–48, *62*

Antiochus VII Sidetes of Syria 119
Antiochus Epiphanes 67, 116–117
anti-Jewish bias 115
anti-Judaism *see* Judaism
anti-Semites 22, 44; Nazi-era priests as 104; Thaddeus the priest as 36
anti-Semitic: judgement 29; myths 25; phrases 27; pogroms 136; stereotypes 23–24
antisemitism, as term 115
anti-Semitism: blood libel and 36, 43n4, 119–121; "chosen people" and 116; cultural 31; *Der Stürmer* (a Nazi propaganda newspaper) 133–134; Jewish jokes about 134; Jews as killer of Jesus and 118; Jung accused of 3, 44–64, 149; linking Jews and money as form of 70, 120–121; Nazi 104, 133; of *Protocols of the Elders of Zion* 120; spread of 110; tax collecting by Jews and 30; Western 115
Aphrodite 40
Aquinas, Thomas (Saint) 40
archetypal: anti-Judaism 118; bias 115; context 4, 25; dimension 16; enemy 96; example of survival 125; force 4, 21, 148; longing for Jerusalem 131; makeup, of Christians 51; message 132; myths 18, 40; parallels 7; patterns 54, 67; patterns of persecution 130; roots, Jewish 3, 57; scapegoating of Jews 119; symbol, Jerusalem as 83–84; wandering 24; wisdom 84
Archetype, the 7, 16, 23; of being saved 38; of hope 132; of Jews as Wanderers 23, 28, 32; Jungian definition of 35; link to community as 102; opposites of 128; orphan as 70; pilgrimage 88–89;

power of 79, 148; Purim as 68–69, 71–72, 75 Shadow side of 42; of spirit 151; struggle for spirit 149 152; of Zionism 22; see Golem of Prague; Jerusalem
Ark of the Covenant 86
Artemidorus 11–12
Aryan race 54–55
'Aryan' unconscious 55
Aryeh 36
Aryeh Yehudah 36
Ashi (Rabbi) 129
Ashkenazi Jewry 137n8
Athena (goddess) 38, 40, 41
Auschwitz 104, 131
Automata 40
Avele, Johan Van den *65*

Ba'al 84
Baal Shem Tov 149
Babylonian Talmud 5, 12, 38
Baeck, Leo (Rabbi) 30, 57, 58
Balaam 11, 31, 32, 116
Barbie, Klaus 104
Bar-El, Yair 89
Bar Hedya 9
Bar Kamtza 87
bar mitzvah 29, 139
Baruch, Book of 83
barukh shomer havtaḥato (Blessed is God – who keeps his promise) 131
Bar Yohai, Shimon 7
Bathsheba 90
Beebe, John 48
Bellow, Saul 130; *Herzog* 136
Benedict XIII (Pope) 122
Benjamin (son of Jacob) 114
Benny, Jack 135
Bernstein, Jerome 48, 50
Besht, the 149
Bevin, Ernest 44
Bezalel of Worms (Rabbi) 37
Black Plague 36, 121, 123
Blacks (Negros) 54
black stone *see kabah*
Blake, William 82
blood 56; Jerusalem as city of 89, 90; spirit as stronger than 145
blood libel 36–37, 43n4, 119–122
bloodshed 74–75, 90
blood-stained coat *see* Joseph's coat
bloodthirsty *see* Kali
book burnings 122

Bradford, William 81
Braun, Werner von 104
Brice, Fanny 135
Brill (Rabbi) 6
Brooks, Mel 135
Bruce, Lenny 135
Buber, Martin 30, 151
Burns, George 135

Caesar, Sid 135, 136
Cain and Abel 24, 28–29, 80, 86
cantors 134
Čapek, Karel: *R.U.R.* 40
Carroll, James 81
Catholic Church and Nazis 104
Catholic Popes *see* Popes
C.G. Jung Institute, Zurich 45, 46, 54, *61, 63,* 140; *see also* Meier, C.A.
C.G. Jung Foundation, New York 15, 46, 47, 140
Chaeremon of Alexandria 115
Chagall, Marc 24
Chefzibah 81
City of David (Jerusalem/Zion) 80–82; *see also Ir David*
City on a Hill 81
Clinic and Research Center for Jungian Psychology in Zurichberg 61
cloning 42
Cohen, Samuel 132
collective history 35
collective Jewish experience 115–122
collective, the 4
collective Unconscious 12, 16, 90; Unconscious projection of 34–35
complex, complexes 21, 50; Jewish 49; Jung's 55; *Scapegoat Complex* (Perera) 118; *see also* Oedipal complex
concentration camps 97, 131; guards 103; survivors of 97, 105, 125, 131
Cousins, Norman 132
Crusades 89
Crystal, Billy 135

Daedalus 40
Dalai Lama 106
Daniel 12, 18, 96, 97
David (King) 27; Abner and 101–102; Absalom and 101; Bathsheba and 90; city of David (Jerusalem/Zion) 80–82; on deathbed instructions by 101; *Ir David* ("City of David") 82, 90;

"Jerusalem Madness" and believing oneself to be 89; hills of Gilboa cursed by 69; M'shiah ben David 109; Ruth and Esther and 66–67, 70; Star of David Nazi badges 128; Temple of 86; as wanderer 25

David, Larry 135

Delilah 18

Der Stürmer (a Nazi propaganda newspaper) 133–134

Dickens, Charles: *Oliver Twist* 70

depression 17, 93, 132, 137, 142, 143, 149, 152

Deuteronomy 96, 126

dietary law, Jewish 117, 119, 129

Dinah, rape of 101

Dome of the Rock 86; *see also* Golden Dome

Doré, Gustave 24; *Jacob Wrestling with the Angel 139*; *Legend of the Wandering Jew* 24

dreams: author of present work's dream 5–7, 15–17; author of present work's grandfather's dream 7; biblical 18; divine instruction via 37; dreams of the old versus the young 83; interpretation of 5, 7–19; Joseph's two dreams 111, 14; Jung's autobiographical work on 57, 59, 62, 130; patient M's dreams 16–18; Pharaoh's dreams 113; Rabbi Loew's dream 36; symbols and myths in 3; Talmud and Jung and 5–19; Wiesel on 74; *see also* Freud, Sigmund

dream work 125

Ego 12, 112; psychosis and 89; Self and 73, 83

Ego gratification 55

Ego ideal 118

Eichmann, Adolf 104

Einstein, Albert 136

Eitingon, Max 53

Eliade, Mircea: *Dayan* 24

Eliezer (Rabbi) 9–10, 126

Elijah the prophet 84, 126

Eliot, T. S. 44

Elisha 11

Eranos conferences 30, 39

Esau 26, 96, 100

Esther, Book of 24, 68, 70, 72–73, 75n2

Esther (queen) 38, 66–74, 75n2

Esther, Scroll of 66

Fastnacht 71, 75n12

Fastnacht Ball *63*

Ferdinand of Spain (King) 44

Ferenczi, Sándor 53, 150

Fiddler on the Roof (musical; film) 130

Ford, Henry 44

forgiveness 92–106; Judaism and 95–97, 99, 104, 114

"foundation stone" of the world 85–86

Fox, Matthew 106

Frankenstein (Shelley) 35, 40, 41

Frankl, Viktor 125, 130

Franz, Marie Louise von 133

Freeman, John 83

Freudians 4, 7, 8, 18, 53, 58

Freudian Society, Israel 45

Freudian therapy: author of present works' experiences with 3, 145, 146, 147

Freud, Sigmund 7, 9, 130; analysis of the unconscious by 133; on dreams 19; *History of the Psychoanalytic Movement* 57; interest in laughter 132–133; *Interpretation of Dreams* 52; *Jokes and Their Relation to the Unconscious* 133; Jung and 44, 52–53, 150; Jung's break with 57, 88, 144–145; Jung's issues with 59; Jung's rivalry with 56; medium (psychic) visited by 150; Nazi Germany's condemnation of 55; Oedipal theory of 12; on power of the unconscious 148; "secret society" protecting 53–54; "soulless materialism" of 57; Vienna followers of 57

Gabirol, Solomon Ibn 30

Galut (exile) 22, 25, 29, 31, 32, 33n11

Galut mitzrayim ("exile to Egypt") 26, 33n11

General Medical Society for Psychotherapy 54

Genesis, Book of: Abram/Abraham in 25, 103; Adam and Eve in 28; Cain and Abel in 28–29; concept of laughter in 133; God's creation of Abraham in 103; God's separation of Heaven and Earth in 85; Ishmael and Isaac in 100; Jacob and Esau in 96, 100; Jacob and Judah in 36; Jerusalem alluded to in 81; Joseph and his brothers in 101, 109, 111; Noah in *124*; tensions and task of forgiveness in 100–101; wrongs done in 100

German Jews 54

Gershon, Levi ben 69
gold: accumulation of 120; head of 59; house of silver and 32; worshippers of 119
Goldbergs, The (radio show) 135, 136
Golden Age 129
Golden Calf 96, 119
Golden Dome 85–86
golden donkey 119
gold envy, Jew 120
gold from lead 113, 125, 137
Goldhagen, Daniel Jonah 104
gold lending 121
gold within 4
Golem of Prague 34–43
Golgotha 86
Gordon, Moses *20*
Göring, Hermann 54
Göring, Matthias 54
Gregory IX (Pope) 122
Guggenbühl-Craig, Adolf *x*, 51, 142, 145
guilt 109; admission of 105; no admission of 104; public admission of 100; repentance and 105; sin and 95
guilty of treason 101

Hadas 70, 73
Hadassah 73
Haggadah 35, 37, 131
Haḥasid, Shmuel (Rabbi) 39
Hakotel 88
Hale, Edward Everett: *The Man Without a Country* 24
Halevi, Judah 30, 77
Halévy, Fromental: *Le Juif errant* 24
Haman 68–72
Ha'mapil prayer 10
Ḥanina (Rabbi)
Hasidic: culture 149; Jews 128; literature 67; Rabbi 127, 151; story 127
Hasidism 31, 149, 150; rabbis opposed to 150
Hebrews: Abraham as the first 24; Egyptians dining with 116; Spanish 131
Hebrew Bible 18, 29, 36, 67; *see also* Torah
Hebrew calendar 72
Hebrew language 2, 6, 16–17, 78–79; alphabet 39; "body" and "soul" as *nefesh* in 142; Bradford's self-teaching of 81; "forget," meaning in 82; "Galut" root as g-l-h in 26; Golem as word in 34; "mercy" in 103; "scapegoat" in 110

Hebrew-speaking Zionist schools, Poland 21
Hebrew University of Jerusalem 2, 45, 78, 140, 147
Heliopolis 115
Hephaestus 40
Herzl, Theodor 132
Heschel, Abraham Joshua 98, 106
Hezekiah (king) 11
High Holy Days 30, 97, 136
High Priest 86; Egyptian 115
Hillel (Rabbi) 129
Hinshaw, Robert *x*, 47, 59
Hivites 101
Ḥiya (Rabbi)
Hollis, James 125
Holocaust, the 57–58, 103–106, 125, 131; betrayal during 97; Eichmann's trial for crimes of 107n34; *see also* Auschwitz; concentration camps
Holocaust studies 115
Holocaust survivors 42, 77, 97; *see also* Frankl, Viktor; Wiesel, Eli; Wiesenthal, Simon
homunculus 40, 41
Honorius IV (Pope) 122
hope and resilience 131–132
Humman (god) 72; *see also* Haman
humor and resilience 133–137; *see also* trickster
Huna (Rabbi) 9, 13
Hurwitz, Siegmund 51, 56–57, 59, *62*

IAAP *see* International Association of Analytical Psychology
Imber, Naftali Herz 132
Inanna (goddess) 66, 112
Individuation 4, 100, 102, 145
Individuation process 84, 88, 90, 95; author of present work's engagement with 6, 59, 94, 102, 106, 140; as being lifelong 113; as search for spirit 151–152; sometimes irrationality of 150
Innocent IV (Pope) 122
International Association of Analytical Psychology (IAAP) 46, 48, 51
International General Medical Society for Psychotherapy 54
invidia auri Judaici ("Jew gold envy") 120
Ir David ("City of David") 82, 90
Isaac 24, 27, 109, 152; Abraham's near-sacrifice of 79, 84–85; Ishmael

and 100; Sarah's giving birth to 133; wandering of 25
Isaac ben Samuel of Acre (Rabbi) 39
Isabella of Spain (queen) 44
Ishmael 100
Ishmael (Rabbi) 129
Ishtar 66, 72
Isis 11

Jacob 27, 32, 109, 111; Esau and 26, 96; exile of 26, 100; dreams of 18; *El Sueño de Jacob* (Jacob and the Ladder) 5; renaming as Israel 113; soul connection to Benjamin 114; wandering by 25; wrestling with the angel 113, *139*; *see also* Joseph
Jacobson, Howard 136
Jacoby, Mario 49
Jaffe, Aniela 30, 47, 57, 59, *62*, 130, 144
Jefferson, Thomas 33n15
Jericho 11
Jerusalem: as Archetype and living symbol 76–90; legends of 84–86; pilgrimage archetype linked to 88–89; as symbol 83–84
"Jerusalem Madness" 89
Jerusalem Talmud 12
Jesus: exile of 86–88; Talmudic explanation for miracles of 86–88; *see also* Second Coming of Christ
Jether 101
Jethro 69
Jewish experience: hope and resilience and humor and 124–137
Jewish quota 47, 48, 50, 51, 56, 57, *62*, 130
Jews: as "chosen people" 130; as chosen by God to receive the *Torah* 28, 130; pattern of persecution of 130; tolerance and diversity among 98; *see also* anti-Semitism; Nobel Prizes won by Jews
Jewish survival 125, 127–128, 130; persecution and forced separation 130; in Christian or Muslim host countries 130
Joab 101
John XII (Pope) 122
jokes 126, 134, 137; *Jokes and Their Relation to the Unconscious* (Freud) 133
Jonathan 69
Jonathan (Rabbi) 7
Jones, Ernest 53, 54
Joseph: dream interpretations by 12; dreams of 11; *see also* Joseph and his brothers; Joseph's coat of many colors
Joseph and his brothers 109–114
Joseph's coat of many colors 111, 113–114
Judah 36, 101, 114: three transgressions of 96; tribe of 27, 36, 82
Judaism: anti-Judaism 115–119, 122; author of present work's valuing and appreciation of positive aspects of 78–79, 145; bad dreams in 13; biblical dreams in 18; collective memory and 130; dream interpretation in 19; essence of 140; forefathers of 110, 113; forgiveness in 95–97, 99, 104, 114; *Galut* in 25; Golem in 38; Hasidim's validation of 150; hope in 131; importance of dreams in 10–11; individuation in 102; Jerusalem (heavenly Jerusalem) in 82, 83, 90; Jews and 46, 48, 52, 55; Judah Halevi's defense of 30; Jungian approach to 1, 2, 3–4, 45, 141; Jung's attitude to 52, 55; Jung's lack of appreciation for 58; Jung's knowledge/lack of knowledge of 31, 148, 152; Kabbalah in 143–144; liberal 28; men forbidden to wear women's clothing 69; Orthodox 97, 103, 149; Orthodox vs. Reform 134; prayers to ask a dream for guidance 8; Purim a "minor holiday" in 66; rabbinic 7, 26; resilience and hope and humor in 125; responsibility and restitution in 101; stereotypical view of 29; stories and myths of 35; survival of 125, 127; three major holidays/festivals of 75n1, 86, 109; traditional 6; as tribe of Judah 27; two conflicting strains of 41; wandering and forced expulsions in 32; wandering response in 25; *see also* Esther; Halevi, Judah; Rashi
Judas, betrayal of 23
Judeans 27
Judith's slaying of Holofernes 38
Jung, Carl *63*; *Answer to Job* 99; antisemitism accusations against 3, 44–64, 149; *Collected Works* 130, 144; Freud and Jung as Moses and Joshua 53; *Memories, Dreams, Reflections* 57, 59, 62, 130; on power of the unconscious 148; "Seven Sermons of the Dead" 88; "The State of Psychotherapy Today" 55–56; *see also* Freud, Sigmund; Judaism; Nazi sympathizer

Jung, Emma *63*
Jung Foundation, New York *see* C. G. Jung Foundation, New York
Jungian: analysis 4, 6, 78, 143, 146; analysts 1, 6, 7, 15, 16, 21, 22, 45, 47, 48, 49, 50, 51, 59, *62*, 93, 125, 140, 142, 149; approach 3, 7, 8, 16, 17; communities 103; ideas 55; lens 2, 6, 89, 90, 101, 110, 150; perspective 9, 14, 21, 24, 26, 27, 34, 35, 41, 43, 47, 69, 72, 73, 88, 89, 90, 93, 95, 99, 100, 101, 113, 115, 116, 122, 125, 137, 152; stance 142; terms 79, 96, 98, 99, 109, 118; training 17, 19, 21; world 39, 45; writings 130
Jungian Club 51
Jungian psychology 30, 66; Clinic and Research Center for Jungian Psychology in Zurichberg *61*; search for spirit in 139–152; study of 148; *see also* Neumann, Erich
Jungians 4, 7, 8, 47, 102; dreams and dream interpretation by 12–19; community 58; confronting accusations of Jung's anti-Semitism 54; forgiveness and 105; Jewish 56, 130, 141; National Conference of Jungian Analysts, Los Angeles 52; Zurich 22
Jungian societies 57
Jungian studies 4, 6; New York Center for Jungian Studies 15, 45
Jungian therapy 3, 5
Jung Institute, Los Angeles 130
Jung Institute, Zurich *see* C. G. Jung Institute, Zurich

kabah (black stone) 85
kabbalah: dabblers in 41; field of 30; origins in France and Spain of 129; study of 143, 144; use of 37
Kabbalah, Book of the 21, 28, 38
kabbalistic: literature 67; tradition 83
kabbalists 10, 28, 39, 41; Jewish French and Spanish 129
Kahn, Madeline 135
Kali (goddess) 69
Kamtza 87
kehillah (community) 29, 127
Kings II, Book of 19
Kirsch, James 30, 59, 130
Kluger, Rivkah Scharf *x*, 3, 22, 45, 47, 59, *63*, 78, 140, 147

Kluger, Yehezkel or Yechezkel *x*, 3, 22, *63*
kosher 119, 126, 135; keeping kosher 146; non-kosher 145, 147

lamed 29
laughter 132–133, 137
League of Nations 132, 134
lehorot 29
Leib 36, 127
Leibovitz, Maury 47
León, Moses de 38
Levi 101
Lincoln, Abraham 70
Lingering Shadows conference and book 47, 64n1, 149
Lipstadt, Deborah 115
Louis IX 122
Luther, Martin 44, 117–118
Lysimachus 115

Magnus, Albertus 40
Mahanaim 21
Maharal, the (*Moreinu Harav Loew*), (Rabbi Judah Loew) 35–37, 42; *Gur Aryeh al Hatorah* 35; *Niflaot Maharal* 38
Maimonides (Rabbi Moshe ben Maimon) 30, 35, 94, 97–100, 102, 129; *Hilkhot teshuvah* (Laws of Repentance) 98–99
Malamud, René 49
Manetho (priest) 115
Marah, waters of 11
Marduk 72
Martin, Stephen 47, *60*, 64; *Lingering Shadows* 48
Marx, Groucho 135
Maslow, [Abraham] 132
Massachusetts Bay Colony 81
Mattathias 24
matzo: blood libel and 36–37, 119–120; the Golem's ability to smell poison in 37, 42; Passover 69
May, Rollo 132
Meier, C. A. 22, 46, 47, 50–51, 54–55, 57–58, *61*; on ancient Greek approaches to dreams 12; *Healing Dream and Ritual* 8
Meir (Rabbi) 7
Mengele, Joseph 104
meshuga 135
Messiah ben David 109
Messiah ben Joseph 109

Meyer, Michael 58
Meyers Briggs Type Indicator test 15
Miriam, leprosy of 11
Mishnah, the 95, 129
mishteh 68
Mitnagdim 150
mitzvah 68
monk: Albertus Magnus 40; Theobald 119
Mordechai 68, 70–74
Moses 11, 27, 97–98, 109; as biblical hero 73; in Egypt 38, 114; Exodus of 114; Freud and Jung as Moses and Joshua 53; Golden Calf and 96; month of death of 73; "Moses to Moses" 98; rod (or staff) of 75n6; speaking at birth 69; speaking to God directly 70; Ten Commandments received by 84; as wanderer 25; Zipporah and 69
Moses Maimonides *see* Maimonides
Moses, son of Rabbi Nachman *see* Ramban
Mount Ararat 84
Mount Carmel 84
Mount Hira 84
Mount Moriah 79–80, 84–86, 87, 91n22
Mount Olympus 43, 69
Mount Sinai 84, 96
Mount Zion 80
M'siah ben David 109
M'shiah ben Yosef 109
Muhammad (the Prophet) 28, 79, 90n2
Muslim countries: Jews practicing medicine in 128; Jews residing in 130
Muslims 30, 79; legends and myths of 85; in prayer 90n2; *see also* Dome of the Rock
mystical: answer 90; connections 78; experience 39; quality of the Unconscious 148; text 143; tradition 149
mysticism 30, 41, 59; Jewish 30
mystics 4, 126
myth: anti-Jewish 115; anti-Semitic 21, 128; Archetypes and 7; Assyrian 72; Biblical 69, 96; Christian 86; collective Unconscious and 16; Creation 42, 72; cultural 34; defining and questioning 34; Delilah in myth of Samson 18; dreams and 3, 12; Greek 24, 41, 43; history and 116; Jerusalem 84; Jewish 2, 29, 35, 66, 79, 85, 86, 96, 109, 111, 112; legends and 4; Muslim 85; power of 29; Purim 67, 75; Seleucid King and 119;
Sumerian 112; *see also* Esther; Golem; Wandering Jew
myth of the hero 37, 70

Nachman (Rabbi) 39
Nachmanides 39, 129
Nathan (Rabbi) 126
National Anthem of Israel 132
Nazi concentration camps *see* concentration camps
Nazi Germany 54–55, 103; blood libels and 122; book burnings in 122
Nazi party members 103
Nazis: anti-Semitism of 115; extermination of Jews by 120; fear of Switzerland being invaded by 51, 56; Holocaust and 104–106; Wandering Jew resurrected by 22
Nazi sympathizer: Jung as Nazi or 45–46, 54, 58, 59; ordinary Germans as 103–104
Nebuchadnezzar 19
Neumann, Erich: *Depth Psychology and a New Ethic* 130; *Great Mother, The* 130; Jung and 22, 30–31, 45, 55–56, 59; *Origins and History of Consciousness, The* 130
Neumann, Micah 45
New Testament 18
Nirenberg, David: *Anti-Judaism* 57
Noah, 97; Ark of 84; *Noah Receives the Dove* (Foster) *124*; son Shem 86
Nobel Prizes won by Jews 30, 105, 130, 136, 137n14, 150
Northern Ireland 92
Numbers, Book of 96
numinous, the 110

occultism 150
Oedipal complex 12
Oedipus 24, 60
Offenbach, *Tales of Hoffman* 41
Old Testament 18
Onoskelis the witch 69
Oppenheimer, Robert 150
orphan, motif or archetype of 66, 69, 70
Orthodox Jewish: community 2, 97, 98, 102, 151; environment 45, 102, 145; home 29, 140; life 78, 140; schools 93; synagogues 11, 99; world 78, 145, 147
Orthodox Jews 8, 80, 102, 145, 146; Rabbis 148, 150; Reform vs. 134; ultra- 98, 128

Orthodox Judaism 97, 103, 149
Ostow, Mortimer 58
Ottoman Empire 129
Ovid 40
Ozick, Cynthia 130

Paderewski, Ignace 134
Palestine 89, 132
Paracelsus 40–41
Passover 35–37, 66, 69; as celebration of month of Nisan 72; Esther and 68; as marking the first month of the Jewish year 72; as one of three major Jewish holidays/festivals 75n1, 88, 130–131; *seder* 35, 37, 131; *see also* matzo
Pentateuch, the 81, 130
Perera, Sylvia: on Ego ideal of Christianity 122; *Scapegoat Complex* 118
Philo of Alexandria 30
Pinocchio 40
Poland 21, 24, 38, 134, 136
Pope, Mathilde 49
Pope, Richard 50
Popes (Catholic) 36, 44, 104, 122
Postgraduate Center for Mental Health 47
Post, Laurens van der 9
Potiphar's wife 110, 112, 126
Pound, Ezra 44
Prometheus 40
Propedeuticum 16
psyche 3, 8, 14, 16; author of present work's 66, 79, 93–94; collective and individual 69; compensatory function of 132; Germanic 56; humor as healing for 133; humor as nonrational coping mechanism of 137; Jewish 35, 58, 59, 80; Jungian understanding of 95, 132, 133, 137; Jung's 57; Jung's approach to 141; objective 7; place of Jerusalem in 83, 90; "soul" as synonym for 142; Western 22, 77, 79, 82
psychoanalytical schools 45
psychic: elements 79; energy 12; equilibrium 132; pain 132
Purim 65; Jewish Saturnalia of 65–75; *Yom K'Purim* 67, 71; as word 72
Purim Spiels 69, 71
Puritans 81
Pygmalion 40

Rabbi Ashi *see* Ashi (Rabbi) 129
Rabbi Bezalel of Worms *see* Bezalel of Worms (Rabbi)
Rabbi Ḥanina *see* Ḥanina (Rabbi)
Rabbi Ḥiya *see* Ḥiya (Rabbi)
Rabbi Ishmael *see* Ishmael (Rabbi)
Rabbi Isaac *see* Isaac ben Samuel of Acre (Rabbi)
Rabbi Loew *see* Maharal (*Moreinu Harav Loew*)
rabbinic or rabbinical: commentaries 82; commentators 73, 112; court 98, 127; Judaism 7, 26; seminaries 69; source 13
Rabbi Rav *see* Rav (Rabbi)
Rabbi *Shlomo Yitzḥaki see Rashi*
rabbis: as paid position 130; as physicians 129; as teachers 129; Torah given by God to 126
Rabbi Zusya *see* Zusya (Rabbi)
Rabi, I. I. 150
Radner, Gilda 135
Rahab 70
Ramban (acronym for Nachmanides, Moses, son of Rabbi Nachman) 39
Rambam (acronym for Moses, the son of Maimon) 98
Rank, Otto 53
Rashi (Rabbi Shlomo Yitzḥaki) 35, 111
Rashid (Caliph) *see* al-Rashid, Haroun (Caliph)
"rat line" 104
Rauff, Walter 104
Rav (Rabbi) 100
Reik, Theodor 133
repentance 79, 97–99, 102; forgiveness and 105; *Hilkhot teshuvah* (Laws of Repentance) (Maimonides) 98
resilience: collective memory and 130; fostering 125; hope and humor and 124–137; *see also* hope and resilience; humor and resilience
Ribera, Jusepe de: *El Sueño de Jacob* (Jacob and the Ladder) 5
Ribi, Alfred 48–50
Roberts, David: *Jerusalem* 76
Robinson, Edward Arlington: *The Wandering Jew* 24
robots 35, 40, 42
Roger of Wendover 23
Rosenberg, Judel (Rabbi) 38
Rosh Hashanah 72, 97, 103
Roth, Philip 130; *Portnoy's Complaint* 136

Sacaea, festival of the 71, 62
Sacks, Jonathan (Lord Rabbi of the UK) 95, 102, 113

sadism 94
Samson 18
Samuel of Acre, Isaac ben (Rabbi) ("Rabbi Isaac") 39
Samuel (biblical) 69, 97
Samuel, Book of 81, 82, 96
Samuel the Righteous 39
Sanhedrin 38
Sarah 70, 133
Saturnalia 71, 75; *see also* Purim
Saul (King): Amalekites ordered by God to be killed by 96; as biblical hero 73; David and 25; death of 69; descendants of 70; depression of 149, 152; Esther's lineage traced to 67
scapegoating 72; shadow and 108–122
scapegoating rituals 110
scapegoats: ceremonial sacrifice of 71; Jews as 23, 36, 118–122; Leviticus's description of 95; symbolic 72
Scholem, Gershon 30, 39
search for spirit: Jungian psychology and 139–152
Second Coming of Christ 23, 24
Second Temple 26, 88
seder see Passover
Sefer habakbuk (Book of the bottle) 69
Sefer Yetzirah 36, 39
Seinfeld, Jerry 135
Seleucid Empire 119
Self: Archetype of 90; Ego and 73; incompleteness of 83; spirituality and 84
self-help 13
self-reflection 17, 112, 125
self-regulation 132
Sephardic tradition 128, 137n8
sex of a fetus, determining 42
sex, goddesses of love and 66
sexual freedom 71
sexual life 129
sexual overtures *see* Potiphar's wife
Shadow: anti-Semitism' 44; Archetype's 42; collective 70; collective's 58; confrontation with 70; David's 90; denial of 115; Frankenstein's 41; ghosts' non-casting of 70; God as light and 99; Jewish 58; Jung's 59; Jung's understanding of 70–71; light and 1, 72, 73, 84, 89, 98, 99; owning up to one's own 95, 100; projection onto Jews of 23, 29; projection onto the Other of 116; Joseph's claiming of 112; Purim and 67, 69, 71; scapegoating and 108–122; scapegoating as projection or manifestation of 109, 110; *see also Lingering Shadow* conference
"Shadow side" of nations and peoples 55
shame 93, 94, 151; bringing of 101
Shammai the Elder 129
Shavuot: as one of three major Jewish holidays/festivals 75n1, 88, 130–131
Sheba, Queen of 69
Shelly, Mary: *Frankenstein* 35, 40, 41
Shem 86
Shemer, Naomi 88
Sh'ma prayer 10
shoshana (rose) 66
Silverman, Sarah 135
Simeon 101
sinat ḥinam 86
Singer, Isaac Bashevis 130: Nobel Prize awarded to 136; Yiddish writing by 136
Singer, June: Boundaries of the Soul 111
Smith, Alfred 43n4
Socrates 30
Solomon 27, 57; as biblical hero 73; David and 101; dreams of 18
Solomon's Temple 86
Sophocles: *Oedipus at Colonus* 24
spirit *see* search for spirit
Spring, Janis Abrahms: *How Can I Forgive You?* 101
Stewart, Jon 135
sukkah 109, 110
Sukkot 8, 109; as one of three major Jewish holidays/festivals 75n1, 88, 130–131
synchronicity 46–47

Talmud: *Aggadah* section of 126; Babylonian 5, 12, 38; burning of 122; Creation of the Golem by the Rabbis of 41; Creation story of 38; dreams and 5–19; Jerusalem 12; Jerusalem as mentioned in 80, 84; Maharal's writings on 35; parodies of 69; put on trial 122; on repentance 98; represention of God in 99; sow (pig)'s reading of 117; study of 29–30; Talmudic explanation for miracles of Jesus 86–88; two elements of 4
Talmudic: commentator 35; scholars 36, 127; legends 69–70, 74, 126; tradition 39, 83
Ten Days of Awe 103
Tibet 106
Tishrei 103

Tobor the Great (film) 40
Tolchinsky, Shmuel 135
Tolkin, Mel 135–136
Torah 3; "Aryeh" in 36; on dreams and prophets 13; no "earlier" or "later" in 6; no extra words in 111; God's giving to rabbis of 126; Jerusalem and Zion in 81; Jews chosen by God to receive 28, 130; Rashi's commentary on 36; study of 29–30
transference 9, 30, 45, 46
transformation 26; of curse into blessing 32; humor as instrument of 137; inner 122; of negative into positive 26, 31, 125; pilgrimage and 88; wandering and 25, 28, 31
trickster, the 7, 132, 133, 137
Troubles, the (Ireland) 93
Twain, Mark 70, 89

Unconscious: anger 94; aspect of personality projected onto another 110; attitude of cultural anti-Semitism 31; confronting and coming to terms with one's Shadow 112; projects of collective Unconscious 34
Unconscious, the 4, 7; Archetype and 79; 'Aryan' 55; Auschwitz survivors' dreams and 131; dreams and 14; Freud's work on 133; Jewish 55; *Jokes and Their Relation to the Unconscious* (Freud) 133; Jung's study of 13; personal 16; psyche and 132; Self and 84; Shadow and 58, 122; *see also* Collective Unconscious
Union of American Hebrew Congregations 47

van der Post, Laurens *see* Post, Laurens van der
Vashti (queen) 67–68, 71–74
Vatican 104–105
Via Dolorosa 23

Wagner, Richard 44; *Flying Dutchman* 24
Wandering Jew 20–32; *Moses Gordon or the Wandering Jew* 20

Waugh, Evelyn: *Helena* 24
Werblowsky, Zwi 30, 45
Western Wall 88
wheat 87, 111, 119
Wiesel, Elie 130; as concentration camp survivor 105; falling out with Wiesenthal 105; on Jewish suffering 127; Nobel Prize awarded to 105; *Sages and Dreamers* 74
Wiesenthal, Simon 104, 105; as concentration camp survivor 105; falling out with Wiesel 105; on forgiveness 105–106; Nobel Prize awarded to 105; *Sunflower, The* 105
William of Norwich, martyrdom of 119
Wilson, Woodrow 134
wish fulfillment 18
World War I 134
World War II *see* Nazi Germany

Xerxes I of Persia 66

yeshiva, yeshivot 2, 4, 34, 69, 140
Yeshiva University 145
Yitzḥaki, Shlomo (Rabbi) *see* Rashi
Yom Kippur 67, 71, 86; evening of 99; forgiveness and 100, 102; liturgy 102; prayers on 97; rituals of 99; sacrifice of two goats on 109–110; sealing of fate on 103; synagogue service 95; Ten Days of Awe and 103; *see also* Yom k'Purim
Yom k'Purim 67, 71
Yose, R. 84
Your Show of Shows (television show) 135

Zentralblatt 54
Zeruiah, Joab ben 101
Zion 31, 76, 81–82; Mount Zion 80; "New" 81; *Protocols of the Elders of Zion* 120
Zionism, Archetype of 22
Zionist Congress, Basel 132
Zionist movement 31
Zionists 21
Zionist settlers 77
Zipporah 69
Zohar, the 28, 38
Zusya (Rabbi) 151

9781032842509